BODIES AND LIVES IN ANCIENT AMERICA

Bodies and Lives in Ancient America offers a broad overview of what it was like to live and die throughout North America before European contact. Using a unique life history approach, the book moves from pregnancy and birth through to senescence. Drawing on biological data gathered from human remains, as well as cultural and environmental data derived from archaeological investigations, the authors provide students with a wealth of information on health and other aspects of life that leave changes on the skeletal system. Rich case studies throughout demonstrate the temporal, cultural, and environmental variability across the continent prior to colonial times. The authors also examine how different groups faced a variety of challenges in their lives, including climate change and violence, and the effects these had on their health. The book concludes by considering the relevance of what ancient bones reveal for people today. Written in an engaging style, with complex paleopathology data synthesized and clearly presented, *Bodies and Lives in Ancient America* is an accessible introduction to the state of health across prehistoric North America.

Debra L. Martin is Professor of Anthropology at the University of Nevada, Las Vegas, USA.

Anna J. Osterholtz is a visiting Assistant Professor in Anthropology at the University of Nevada, Las Vegas, USA.

BODIES AND LIVES IN ANCIENT AMERICA

Health Before Columbus

Debra L. Martin and Anna J. Osterholtz

Routledge
Taylor & Francis Group

LONDON AND NEW YORK

First published 2016
by Routledge
2 Park Square, Milton Park, Abingdon, Oxon OX14 4RN

and by Routledge
711 Third Avenue, New York, NY 10017

Routledge is an imprint of the Taylor & Francis Group, an informa business

British Library Cataloguing in Publication Data

A catalogue record for this book is available from the British Library

Library of Congress Cataloging-in-Publication Data
Martin, Debra L.
  Bodies and lives in ancient America : health before Columbus /
Debra L. Martin and Anna J. Osterholtz.
    pages cm
  Includes bibliographical references and index.
  1. Indians of North America—Anthropometry.   2. Indians of North America—Health and hygiene—History.   3. Paleopathology—North America.   4. Human remains (Archaeology)—North America.   I. Osterholtz, Anna J.   II. Title.
  E98.A55M37   2016
  970.004'97—dc23
  2015018405

ISBN: 978-1-138-90287-9 (hbk)
ISBN: 978-1-138-90428-6 (pbk)
ISBN: 978-1-315-69646-1 (ebk)

Typeset in Bembo
by Apex CoVantage, LLC

Printed and bound in the United States of America by
Edwards Brothers Malloy on sustainably sourced paper

CONTENTS

FIGURES AND TABLE

Figures

Table

ACKNOWLEDGMENTS

For the title of the book, we wanted to acknowledge two influential scholars who came before us and taught us well: Rosemary Joyce, for her groundbreaking book *Ancient Bodies, Ancient Lives: Sex, Gender and Archaeology* (New York, NY: Thames and Hudson, 2008), and Wenda Trevathan, for her trailblazing book *Ancient Bodies, Modern Lives: How Evolution Has Shaped Women's Health* (New York, NY: Oxford, 2010). We are also indebted to the bioarchaeologists who have been publishing on health in America for the last several decades, setting a high bar for data collection and analysis. Our gratitude goes out to George Armelagos, Clark Larsen, Phil Walker, Jane Buikstra, Della Cook, and their generations of students who continue their work in areas such as the California coast, the American Southwest, the Mississippian region, and the Georgia Bight. The idea for this book began in 1991 while one of us (Martin) was a resident scholar at the School of Advanced Research in Santa Fe. After percolating for 25 years, the book came to fruition with the support of the Lincy Foundation and Chris Hudgins in the dean's office at University of Nevada, Las Vegas.

Working on this book made us appreciate where we are in our own life histories and the people and animals around us that make our particular moment in time and space not unlike those of people who lived hundreds of years ago in the very places we live today. They lived, they loved, they worked, they suffered, and they experienced extraordinary, ordinary lives. We dedicate this book to those original people who made the U.S. their home long before Columbus arrived.

1

ANCIENT BODIES, ANCIENT LIVES

The people who lived within what is now referred to as the U.S. prior to the colonial invasion in the 1500s were numerous and culturally diverse, and they spoke many different languages. But they did not use traditional forms of writing, so they did not leave behind tablets or scrolls detailing their daily lives, their diets, their ailments, their social institutions, or their political structures. All of this must be inferred from the remains of their built environment and constructed cultural milieu that have survived the ravages of time. The physical traces left behind are what archaeologists focus their research on. Information about ancient people only becomes available when archaeologists excavate, retrieve, and analyze the remnants of these complex, dynamic, and multidimensional ancient villages and early cities.

Bioarchaeologists are specialists who have many years of training in human biology and anatomy with a special focus on osteology (bones and teeth). While muscle, organs and flesh degrade quickly over time when placed under soil, often bones and teeth preserve indefinitely. In some places, such as the American Southwest, dry desert conditions facilitate the preservation of hard tissues such as bone and teeth for hundreds or thousands of years. In places where abundant rain, seasonal temperature fluctuations, and thick vegetation are found, human remains are far less likely to survive for long periods. Dry and undisturbed locations such as caves or places where freezing and thawing do not occur are also good for preserving hard tissues of the human body. Natural mummification of soft tissue and hair is rare although not unknown for the U.S. Naturally skeletonized bodies from the past are much more common.

Bioarchaeologists are anthropologists, and they are most interested in understanding human behavior over the long arc of time. Specifically bioarchaeologists focus on bodies because they reveal tangible biological features of each individual human and because bodies are also influenced and shaped by cultural and environmental forces. Remnants of these *biocultural bodies* in the form of bones and teeth are the data sets that they work with. With bone and teeth, combined with the context that they are found in, bioarchaeologists can partially reconstruct the lives of individuals, groups of individuals, communities, and populations. This text provides some snapshots into how that is done.

Working with human remains (also sometimes referred to as burials) and the bony remnants of humans from the past is fraught with ethical issues. There is near-universal disapproval of the scientific study of ancient American human remains from tribal representatives whose job it is to keep their ancestors from being dishonored and disrupted. Tribal scholars have written extensively about the pain and suffering that excavation and analysis brings to their communities because they often see these scientific activities as disturbing the dead and as acts of desecration in spiritual and sacred places (for examples of this, refer to Fine-Dare 2002). This is discussed in more depth later in this chapter because working with human remains in the U.S. may be seen as unethical by some, so the moral dimensions of this kind of work must be parsed out at every step. Within the community of scholars who specialize in skeletal analysis, each researcher working with human remains ultimately crafts his or her own set of guidelines based on his or her particular approach and philosophy. Researchers are guided by a mix of legislative, scientific, theoretical, and ethical principles. There is no one right way to work as a bioarchaeologists because each setting within the U.S. where there has been excavation and the study of human remains is unique with its own set of challenges and constraints.

From bones to bodies using social theory

Bioarchaeology is an evidence-based and interdisciplinary field of study within anthropology that focuses on human remains (skeletonized or mummified) from ancient and historic archaeological contexts. The goal of bioarchaeology is to elucidate how people in the past lived within their societies, how populations change over time, and how societies interacted within and between regions. Combined with social theory, these understandings of our collective past can act as a guide for clarifying troublesome aspects of the times we currently live in and for understanding how these present realities came to be. Social theories are frameworks that focus attention on particular facets of human social interactions, organizations, and behaviors (Powers 2010: 5). Without social theories to aid bioarchaeological studies of ancient health data from human remains, it would be quite descriptive and lacking in broader meaning and interpretation.

This text explores health in America before Columbus. The time frame focused on is about AD 1000 to 1500, which is the 500 years or so prior to contact with colonists following 1492. The term *America* is used here as a shorthand reference to the U.S. portion of North America. This geographically reins in what is covered. As one could imagine, adding Canada, Mexico, Central America, and South America would be extraordinarily difficult to synthesize in a single volume. The goal of this text is to provide a better understanding of the people that were in the U.S. prior to colonization and what in broad brushstrokes their experiences were like. Data derived from burials and human bones are rarely mentioned in U.S. history books, and even those texts that deal with Native Americans often focus more on the colonial period than on the precolonial period.

For much of the ancient world in America, there are no written records to reveal details of social life. Other forms of visual representation of daily life are available in the form of iconography, pottery images or rock art (Figure 1.1 and Figure 1.2), but human biological remains provide a uniquely rich source of information on the lived experiences of individuals and populations. Bioarchaeology relies on a biocultural approach to facilitate the integration of data from human remains (biology) with other diverse data sets emanating from cultural and environmental spheres of influence. In this approach, social theory enhances and illuminates aspects of life. Also, theory helps flesh out the larger political and economic structures that

FIGURE 1.1 Pottery image depicting two human figures on a Mimbres pot circa AD 1000 from the Mogollon culture (New Mexico and Arizona). While these forms of communication likely depict important aspects of the culture, it is difficult to say what that might be. Image courtesy Dallas Museum of Art, published with permission.

FIGURE 1.2 Rock art (petroglyphs) from New Mexico depicting a hunchback figure playing a flute. These are replicated across the ancient Southwest landscape, and they deliver some very specific message or communication, but to date, it is not clear what that might have been. Modified from an image created by Einar Einarsson Kvaran, courtesy of Wikimedia Commons under Universal Public Domain.

shape daily experiences and impact general health and well-being over long periods. Social theory also facilitates the capacity to formulate causal relationships that explain when, how, and why certain events in human history occurred.

Bridging social theory with bioarchaeology provides an effective way of formulating and evaluating hypotheses about humans and social life to interpret both synchronic moments in time as well as diachronic sequences of cultural history reaching far back in time. Bioarchaeology can provide intimate portraits of life that span the life course of individuals, providing snapshots of daily, seasonal, annual, and generational aspects of human experience. Life-course theory provides bioarchaeologists with insight into diet, health, injury, growth, maintenance, and reproductive functions because skeletal assemblages often include individuals of both sexes who died at varying ages (Agarwal and Glencross 2011b: 6; Halcrow and Tayles 2011: 337). In addition, bioarchaeological data provides information at multiscalar levels so that groups can be examined at the individual, community, regional, and interregional levels (Geller 2012). As a subdiscipline within anthropology, bioarchaeology focuses on cross-cultural comparisons of humans in varied and distinctive settings focusing, for example, on different subsistence economies, different political structures, or contrasting environmental settings. Even when there are written documents, the human remains and associated archaeological contexts often reveal a more nuanced, detailed, and authentic account of what social life was really like for individuals and groups.

Thus, bioarchaeological data are universally important when thinking about the past because of its added value in substantiating biological, cultural, and environmental dynamics. The data derived from the bodies of people long gone *do not* speak for themselves. Interpretations of bioarchaeological data rely heavily on the judicious use of social theories, either tacitly or explicitly. Some of the most applicable social theories being used by bioarchaeologists today are drawn from cultural and medical anthropology in part because it is in those areas where the body has been theorized in ways that facilitate thinking in more complex and nuanced ways about the concomitant forces affecting and shaping things such as poor health or early death.

Integrating bioarchaeological data with social theory is important because the stakes are high. The world is full of troubles and problems for which there are no easy answers. Bioarchaeological data reveal ways that humans in the past have innovated and overcome problems in different places under varying circumstances. The work that bioarchaeologists do traverses time and space, as well as biology and culture, in unique ways. It also provides scientific and empirical information on ancient and historic groups that cannot be easily obtained from other kinds of studies. Thus, its contributions to the anthropological enterprise of explaining complex human behaviors are distinctive and necessary in explicating relationships among the multitude of factors affecting human well-being.

Conceptualizing the work that bioarchaeologists do

Bioarchaeological training is an area of expertise within biological anthropology, and biological anthropology is one of the major subdivisions within the field of anthropology. Unlike other areas within biological anthropology, bioarchaeology is also intimately aligned with archaeological theory and method, as well as theoretical approaches emanating from cultural and medical anthropology. Training in bioarchaeology focuses primarily on the excavation and analysis of ancient and historic human remains. These can include a diverse range of possibilities including primary and secondary burials; tombs; cemeteries; mummified and skeletonized remains; ossuaries; naturally or culturally disarticulated, commingled, or modified bones; and isolated elements (see Martin et al. 2013: 117–150).

Ancient human remains are generally those found in association with archaeological sites. Much of the research conducted by bioarchaeologists focuses on human remains going back as far as archaic gatherers and hunters from thousands of years ago. Human remains from these early periods in America are quite rare.

More commonly, bioarchaeologists work on periods during and after the adoption of agriculture, which in the U.S. was well established by AD 1000. It is from archaeological sites dated to before and after this general date for which there are often significant numbers of associated burials.

Historic human remains often come from cemeteries and burial sites associated with contact and colonization. Historic human remains may be associated with archaeological sites but sometimes they are not. Increasingly historic skeletal assemblages are coming from settings such as historic cemeteries, almshouses, prisons, mental institutions, and medical schools. This is a rapidly growing area of inquiry within bioarchaeology (Nystrom 2011). Human remains associated with more recent events are often analyzed by bioarchaeologists who have come to specialize in forensic anthropology and forensic archaeology. For example, the now-abandoned Arthur G. Dozier School for Boys in Marianna, Florida, was a place where juvenile boys were sent during the early 1900s. It was, by all accounts, a brutal place where boys were routinely beaten and possibly beaten to death by staff members. The recent excavation and analysis of the cemetery by local bioarchaeologists demonstrated that boys often died with virtually no accountability by the state and that deaths due to mistreatment were never accounted for in the school's records (Ilen 2012). This application of bioarchaeological practice to contemporary issues (often referred to as the bioarchaeology of yesterday) is increasing as the line between bioarchaeology and forensic anthropology becomes less distinct.

Bioarchaeological practice in the U.S. is similar to research approaches in Canada and Britain, although bioarchaeology in Britain does not sit within academic anthropology departments as it does in the U.S. (Roberts 2006: 438–439). The growth of bioarchaeology worldwide (or osteoarchaeology, as it is sometimes referred to in other countries) can be measured by the increasing number of bioarchaeology books written by non-U.S. authors and editors. Other western European countries, as well as China, Australia, Mexico, and South America are currently practicing what is fairly close to bioarchaeology in the U.S. as witnessed by readers of the *International Journal of Osteoarchaeology* and the *International Journal of Paleopathology*. Shared methods, terminology, standards, and analytical techniques have become the norm. International conferences organized around paleopathology and other aspects of skeletal analysis have been ongoing for many years.

The flavor and richness of bioarchaeological studies are captured in an edited volume that covers analysis of skeletal remains for pathology in a global context (Buikstra and Roberts 2012). The volume tracks key historical figures and important historical moments in bioarchaeology and paleopathology across many different countries. Regions covered include Africa, the Americas, Eurasia, and Oceania. This volume reifies that bioarchaeologists who focus on disease speak to common theory, method, and data in their approaches. Another example of the similarities in approaches is the handbook edited by Blau (from Australia) and Ubelaker (from the U.S.), both having expertise in bioarchaeology and forensic anthropology. The *Handbook of Forensic Anthropology and Archaeology* (2009) contains more than 40 chapters written by bioarchaeologists and experts in osteology from every major country. Again, this illustrates the increasingly shared vision, techniques, and research strategies across international borders (Blau and Ubelaker 2009: 22).

Bioarchaeology in the U.S. today

There were three major intellectual shifts that are relevant to situating modern bioarchaeology in the U.S. The first was the movement toward integrating human remains with archaeological context in the 1970s and the adoption of the term *bio-archaeological research* describing this new approach (Buikstra 1977: 69). Another watershed moment came in 1990 with the passage of legislation in the U.S. referred to as NAGPRA (the Native American Graves Protection and Repatriation Act) mandating that bioarchaeologists integrate human remains with ethical consider-ations (Rose et al. 1996: 81–82). NAGPRA-like legislation was soon to follow in many other parts of the world. The third shift was the movement toward integrating human remains with social theory, resulting in what is called "social bioarchaeology" (Agarwal and Glencross 2011a: 3). Agarwal and Glencross characterize these three shifts as "waves of engagement" (2011a: 2), and they focus on the movement away from typological classification and description towards the use of ever-expanding new technologies to ask increasingly complex questions. They suggest that we are now in a third wave of engagement, stating that "contemporary bioarchaeology is now clearly a discipline poised to engage with social theory . . . in building a social bioarchaeology, scientists are engaged in the construction of the biological and social essence of individuals" (2011a: 3).

Similar to these developments in the U.S., bioarchaeologists in Canada, Mexico, South America, Australia, and Europe have also been moving more toward research that utilizes social theory and that aims to grapple with larger questions of human adaptability. Cutting-edge theoretical work has come out of bioarchaeological stud-ies from these countries, making clear that there is a larger international community of scholars whose methods, theories, and data are shared. For example, Sofaer's work in England on theorizing the body in bioarchaeology was one of the first dedicated to reshaping how human remains are viewed (2006: 11) and calling for remains to be interrogated and theorized in ways similar to other forms of material culture. Bodies in Sofaer's approach are seen as being not only as biological but also as symbolic and representational. This necessitates the inclusion of social theory in making meaning at that level of analysis. Sofaer's framework for theorizing ancient bodies is used widely by bioarchaeologists in the U.S.

Skeletons and their descendants

In the 1980s, Native Americans in the U.S. began an organized campaign against the excavation, removal, and analysis of ancient burials. Criticisms were leveled by indigenous communities regarding the racist and problematic act of storing their ancestor's remains and of conducting scientific experimentation on them with-out their consent. What unfolded for bioarchaeologists working in the U.S. at this time was an awakening to both the epistemological aspects of bioarchaeology as well the ethical issues involved in conducting research on ancient human remains. Also what became clear was that bioarchaeologists needed to articulate the precise ways that this kind of research mattered and was important, relevant, and necessary to do. Over and over at international meetings, such as the international World Archaeology Conference (WAC), and at the national American Association of Physical Anthropology (AAPA) meetings, tribal and indigenous representatives would come to bioarchaeological presentations and want to know why bioarchaeologists were doing research on their ancestors without their permission. That the research questions were of anthropological significance was true, but the reasons of anthropological significance sounded hollow and fell flat when explained to the living descendants of those being studied. Bioarchaeological research at that time was not articulated in a way that provided relevance to the descendants of the people being studied, or to a broader audience.

In the U.S. the passage of NAGPRA in 1990 was a watershed moment for the new generation of bioarchaeologists. This legislation made certain that Native American representatives would be part of all future decisions surrounding the excavation, curation, and analysis of human remains from precolonial periods in the U.S. (i.e., burials associated with archaeological sites dated to before the early 1500s). In most cases, if their work on human remains was to continue, it would have to be with the permission of the living descendants (Figure 1.3). And federal and state repositories across the U.S. were legally mandated to present an inventory of bodies in their custody to those tribes who were most likely to be descendants. Tribes then can request that the burials and associated items of cultural patrimony be returned to them.

As chronicled in "Owning the Sins of the Past," the passage of NAGPRA legislation was a huge event in the field, marking a shift in the ways that scientific studies in bioarchaeology should be done (Martin 1998: 185). More important, it signaled soul-searching and self-reflection within the scientific community and bioarchaeologists began asking themselves if this was the right career for them. Some bioarchaeologists moved into forensic anthropology and some refocused their research to other archaeological sites in Europe and Mexico where these kinds of issues were not yet being raised.

Larsen and Walker (2005) provide an extensive overview of the range of ethical issues raised by NAGPRA not only in response to Native American concerns but also to the concerns of bioarchaeologists who believe in the value of what the human remains can reveal. They raise the counter-issue that it can be considered unethical to *not* document the past because it is such a crucial part of the science of understanding human problems. Larsen and Walker present the ethical complexities that NAGPRA raises, but they emphasize that bioarchaeological research is relevant and important to continue doing.

As more bioarchaeologists consider the ethics of their work in paleopathology the world over and as more descendant communities demand having the final say over the handling of their ancestors' remains, ideas about what it means to do

FIGURE 1.3 Cindi Alvitre (Tongva) speaks to students of the 2012 Pimu Catalina Island Archaeological Field School regarding the respectful and culturally appropriate treatment of Tongva ancestors during a reburial ceremony held on Catalina Island. Photo taken by Desiree Martinez.

ethical bioarchaeology is evolving. Alfonso and Powell (2008) review the conflicts raised within bioarchaeology when the goal is to study ancestral bodies but the descendants assert that they do not want them studied. Human remains and human bodies are unlike other artifacts in that they take on special meaning in a number of different realms. Consider this: "Human bodies hold a special place because they are inscribed with symbolism as well as cultural and political significance. Bodies challenge both the practice of biological anthropology and its purported value-free objectivity" (Alfonso and Powell 2008: 6). Constructing a code of ethics that would cover all situations encountered from the field to the lab to the museum and to the classroom has proved challenging, but there has been progress. Márquez-Grant and Fibiger (2011) have published the *Routledge Handbook on Archaeological Human Remains and Legislation,* and with 60 chapters from bioarchaeologists from all over the world, it presents recent legislation, best practices for carrying out ethical studies, ways of collaborating with descendant communities, and ideas for carrying bioarchaeological work into the future with more reflexivity and sensitivity to the living whose ancestors they hope to study.

Two things continue to facilitate bioarchaeological work in the U.S. since the passage of NAGPRA and in the absence of new excavations and retrieval of new burials. One is that the ethics of working with human remains became the focus of seminars and sessions at national meetings. This self-reflection played a role in reorienting how bioarchaeology could be done and under what kinds of circumstances. The second thing is that these focused roundtables discussions facilitated talking more broadly about the value of collecting data from ancient remains and for thinking about issues such as diet, health, and demography today. Understanding fundamental aspects of social life in the past became a bridge for thinking of ways that these data were applicable to people today (see Martin et al. [2013] for numerous examples).

At the same time, biological anthropologists working with living populations were also questioning the effects of their studies on indigenous and tribal groups. Goodman and Leatherman (1998) brought together a diverse group of biological anthropologists to reimagine how using the biocultural paradigm combined with social theories about the formation, maintenance, and effects of inequality could invigorate the field. This edited volume, titled *Building a New Biocultural Synthesis: Political-Economic Perspectives on Human Biology*, is still relevant today and is replete with cross-cultural case studies on the ways that political-economic and gender theory brings nuance and richness to interpretations of patterns of morbidity and mortality. The volume is a testament to the ways that social theory brings scientific findings to bear on the present and future in more meaningful ways and is relevant to a much broader audience. Thus, the call for relevancy and bridging social theory with biological anthropology ran parallel in the 2000s to the call for doing so with bioarchaeology.

No one could have predicted the continued popularity and growth of bioarchaeology back in 1990 when NAGPRA was instituted in the U.S. and when NAGPRA-like legislation was adopted in many other countries such as Australia and Israel. Relatively rapid growth of bioarchaeology has occurred in the last ten years and bioarchaeology is today a fully acknowledged practice unto itself (i.e., not a hybrid) within biological anthropology (Martin et al. 2013: 1–6). As bioarchaeology matures in the U.S. and internationally, the increasing number of books and studies being published, the uptick in the number of symposia and sessions organized at AAPA and the Society for American Archaeology (SAA) meetings, and the expanding number of blogs and websites dedicated to bioarchaeology, make clear that it is an expanding, thriving, and robust subdiscipline within anthropology (Martin et al. 2013: 248–250). Graduate programs in bioarchaeology are well established in many of the major universities and in the last several years (2010–2015), there has been an annual uptick in the number of tenure-track academic positions posted on the American Anthropological Association website's Career Center (www.aaanet.org/profdev).

For bioarchaeologists in the U.S. there is an ethical imperative that has been created by the kinds of pushback from tribal and indigenous peoples the world over in reaction to the excavation and analysis of their ancestral remains. In the U.S., this culminated in not only NAGPRA but in other related kinds of legislation that dictate the inclusion of descendants in decisions made about the excavation, storage, and analysis of human remains. Specific criticisms aimed at skeletal analyses suggested that the research was of limited value to anyone but a small group of scientists. In countering these kinds of accusations, many bioarchaeologists now strive to make clear the ways that their research is relevant, and many bioarchaeologists obtain permission from living descendants to conduct research and often to collaborate with tribal representatives on what kind of research is done.

Bioarchaeology as engaged and relevant

The motivations for moving from more strictly descriptive or typological approaches to more interpretive and relevant analyses are coming from a number of different places. NAGPRA and legislation similar to it across the globe have increasingly given voice to descendant communities, who want to know why studies are being conducted on their ancestors. However, there are other motivations for relevancy. For example, the mission statement of the American Anthropological Association states:

> Anthropology is the study of humans, past and present. To understand the full sweep and complexity of cultures across all of human history, anthropology draws and builds upon knowledge from the social and biological sciences as well as the humanities and physical sciences. A central concern of anthropologists is the application of knowledge to the solution of human problems.

The American Anthropological Association website also makes a clear statement about ethics, engagement, and doing research that is relevant to today's world. The mission statement goes on to state:

> An engaged anthropology is committed to supporting social change efforts that arise from the interaction between community goals and anthropological research. Because the study of people, past and present, requires respect for the diversity of individuals, cultures, societies, and knowledge systems, anthropologists are expected to adhere to a strong code of professional ethics.
> (www.aaanet.org)

Without tapping into the relevance of bioarchaeology to the world we live in today, studies based on human remains continue to be limited as interesting and exotic narratives of how "other" people do things, not explicit examples of humans as a species on broader levels. If bioarchaeology is to be on the same level as other disciplinary approaches in the sciences (i.e., to obtain funding, to appeal to a broader audience of politicians and policy makers, to be of value to K–12 teaching, etc.) it must include the basic elements of the scientific process that explicitly includes the application of hypothesis testing and theory.

Another push for articulating the ways that bioarchaeological studies are relevant to today and engaged in problem solving are the agencies that fund bioarchaeological research. The National Science Foundation, one of the major sources of federal funding for bioarchaeological research, has made clear in their guidelines that successful proposals will be able to articulate the benefits to society of the proposed research (see nsf.gov). Likewise, the Wenner-Gren Foundation for Anthropological Research also asks that proposals for funding address the contribution that the research makes to both anthropological understanding and society at large.

Additional motivating factors for bioarchaeologists to be able to articulate the ways that their research is relevant to the present day are in teaching and generating interest in undergraduates. Departments of anthropology are increasingly under the gun to show that they are generating majors and that their courses are able to fill with the required number of students. Courses on the anthropology of popular culture and the archaeology of gender are attempts at luring students into anthropology via contemporary phenomenon. University funding is often provided under the guise of helping the local and national economy grow or of helping to solve problems such as lack of health care or homelessness.

Popularizing anthropological data has been increasingly done by nonanthropologists. Authors such as Pinker (2011), who has used anthropological data on violence, and Diamond and Ordunio (2005), who have used archaeological data to promote ideas about the collapse of civilizations, are often criticized for appropriating information that they do not fully understand or of misusing it to make their own points. Bioarchaeologists should feel some compulsion to be able to articulate their ideas and to engage with a popular audience regarding making their ideas relevant beyond their discipline.

Social bodies and lives, then and now

This text focuses on providing selected case studies that provide a snapshot of health and disease for ancient communities. These vignettes of community life are not necessarily representative of every bioarchaeological report on health ever published; rather, they are introductions to the kind of information that is available. Much like today, some individuals within some age defined, sex defined, or socially defined groups are more vulnerable to ill health and early death than are others. One thing that is known is that disease is rarely a random event. Disease is almost always patterned and linked causally to conditions of life within specific places at specific times. This permits utilizing the techniques from paleoepidemiology to population-level data. Epidemiology is the study of disease to understand its patterning and causes with an eye toward prevention and elimination in modern populations. Paleoepidemiology utilizes similar approaches with the goal of clarifying the patterns and underlying biocultural factors in the expression of disease.

Providing scenarios based on scientific data derived from the archaeological context and the human remains reveals insight and new information on how humans responded to and survived (or died in response to) environmental, economic, demographic, dietary, or political changes. Using theoretical frameworks, ideas about the relationship between power and social structure, age, class, gender, ethnic identity, and health are presented using a life history approach. In this way, connections between the past and the present, and lessons that can be learned from studying the past, are focused on (see Chapter 7).

Without social theory, bioarchaeological data may be inherently interesting but difficult to bridge to contemporary problems. Descriptive data derived from ancient human remains and archaeological settings form the building blocks for more integrated approaches. Armelagos (2003: 34) provides a compelling yet cautious exploration of the ways that modern bioarchaeology has the potential for broad understandings of human life when he states,

> Bioarchaeology as anthropology will not provide solutions to all the miseries that human face. However, it can provide insights that are essential for understanding our relationship to our environment, how we interacted with it throughout history, and how we are interacting with it now. Bioarchaeology is at the forefront in documenting the evolution and adaptation of human populations . . . [it] should search for relevance to contemporary life.

The current redirection of bioarchaeological research to questions about inequality, identity, gender, status, social control, and other areas of social life demonstrate the broader impacts of bioarchaeological research, and it is reshaping what bioarchaeology is. As stated before, bioarchaeology itself is a relatively new configuration

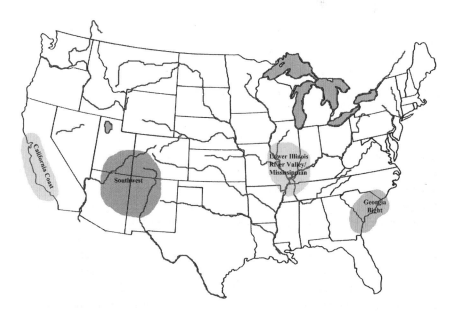

FIGURE 1.4 Map depicting the location of the archaeological sites discussed in the text.

within biological anthropology regarding having a set of guiding goals and established methods for the analysis of ancient and historic skeletal remains.

Taking all of this into consideration, four core areas of the U.S. are focused on in this text because they provide a broad overview along with some depth regarding the challenges faced by ancient people to survive and be healthy (Figure 1.4). They represent a variety of different environmental settings, subsistence practices, social organization, cultural contexts, and biocultural features. These also represent areas where there have been focused archaeological and bioarchaeological work over the last several decades and so there is a larger body of data to draw from. These areas are highlighted simply as a way to channel the discussions about ancient bodies and lives and what is known about everyday experiences, especially with respect to health.

Cultural sketches of core areas in the U.S.

California coast

Human habitation has existed as far as can be discerned based on the current coastline for at least the last 13,000 years (Figure 1.5). Islands off the coast, such as the Channel Islands, tend to lack many animals and plants located on the mainland. The largest endemic land mammals on the Channel Islands are the island fox and a species of spotted skunk. During the Pleistocene, pygmy mammoth lived on the Northern Channel Islands. Europeans brought with them herbivores, carnivores, and rodents that are now found there (Rick et al. 2005: 171–173).

This region is distinct from the Southwest and Midwest portions of this volume in that the groups inhabiting the California coast never relied on agriculture as a form of subsistence. Tracing the arrival of groups to the coastal region can be difficult, as sea levels have risen substantially over the last 13,000 years (Inman 1983). It is possible that earlier settlements and campsites have been lost. Despite this challenge, sites have been identified dating to between 12,000 and 13,000 years ago on the Northern Channel Islands. The earliest securely dated Channel Island site dates to approximately 10,400 ± 200 years (approximately 12,340 years BP) (Orr 1962). Diet is believed to be primarily based on marine resources at this time.

Numerous early sites have been identified, and these include large habitation sites and shell middens consistent with this mode of subsistence (see table 2 in Rick et al. [2005] for a thorough listing of these sites and associated dates). Many of these early sites are identified through shell middens, but numerous other sites have been found in caves near freshwater springs. These cave sites appear to be related to intermittent use, likely during dry seasons. Technology was expedient and tied to shellfish harvesting. Stone tools were made from local materials. Bifaces are relatively rare at early island sites. Arena points have been found at numerous sites. Erlandson (1994: 264) argues that these may have been used as dart points in the hunting of sea mammals while crescents were used in hunting waterfowl or seabirds.

During the Middle Holocene (7,000–3,500 years ago), the populations were subjected to both cultural and environmental changes. On the Channel Islands,

FIGURE 1.5 The coast of Southern California in the Santa Barbara region. Photo by downtowngal, courtesy of Wikimedia Commons, Creative Commons Attribution-Share Alike.

there is increased evidence of permanent settlement, technological innovation, artistic elaboration, and subsistence intensification. It is also during this period that the participation within a larger regional exchange system begins. In terms of site distribution, they tend to focus on the most productive portions of the islands including coastlines, marine terraces, caves, rock shelters, and interior hilltops (see table 3 in Rick et al. [2005] for a thorough list of sites and associated dates). By this time, sea levels were relatively stable, and intertidal and subtidal shellfish communities were a productive source of food for the inhabitants of the sites.

During the Middle Holocene, habitation on the islands was year-round and permanent. Inhabitants likely transported animals across, including island foxes. Middle Holocene inhabitants began to experience ecological circumscription, particularly after the establishment of permanent year-round settlements. This, in turn, spurred innovation in technology, change in settlement patterns, and changes in subsistence strategies. Intensification of subsistence methods led to an increase in population size. It is during this period that the composite bone fishhook may have been introduced (King 1990: 80). Tools were made from stone but also from marine mammal bone, abalone, and clamshells. Fiber-based technologies were also employed in the creation of nets, bags, baskets, twine, and rope; these have rarely survived in the archaeological record and are usually inferred based on indirect evidence in the form of basketry impressions and tarring pebbles used in the water-proofing of baskets.

Shell middens from this period vary from small, single-component sites (likely seasonally occupied) to large, dense concentrations likely related to large settlements such as villages. Environmental variation on the different islands and different parts of the various islands had a significant impact on both the degree of resource intensification and the degree of involvement with other islands or the mainland.

Interaction between the islands and the mainland was common during this period. As noted by Rick and colleagues (2005: 194), "Trade networks strengthened cooperative relationships, group cohesion, marriage alliance, and economic stability." Interaction between groups would have been very important for the creation of group identity, and because it is generally believed that the groups were ethnically distinct from each other, these interactions would have been mediated by complex social, political, and economic factors. Both utilitarian and exotic goods were exchanged between the island and the mainland. The Channel Islands were a center of production in shell artifacts, beads, and ornaments. Obsidian from the mainland was traded to the islands.

This summary only includes a portion of this period because the focus of this volume is in precontact social patterns. The "discovery" of California by Europeans, however, can be seen as a continuation of the cultural changes that are emblematic of this period. Recent research (e.g., Arnold 1992; 1996; 2001; Arnold and Green 2002) has shown that most people during this period were living in large, multi-family villages in defensible areas on the Channel Islands. There was a focus on production of beads and microblades (see table 4 in Rick et al. [2005] for a thorough list of sites from this period). Sites from this period, in some cases, extend into the historic period. By this time, cultural affinity with the historic Chumash can be firmly established. They were located in areas rich in resources (either marine or terrestrial), although there may have been an increased use of coastal resources over interior resources. Population size increases at numerous sites as well.

By the late Holocene, boat technology can at least be inferred. This type of boat known as a *tomol*, or *tiat*, is a plank-type seaworthy boat; these have been documented historically. They would have been used both to traverse the distance between the islands and the mainland and to access larger marine resources such as swordfish. Arnold (1995) argues that these would have been available for at least the last 1,500 years. The earliest plank canoes that have preserved date to around 1,300 years before present (Gamble 2002), but boat-making parts have been identified from earlier assemblages.

Technologically, the single-piece fishhook, harpoon, and a variety of arrow points become prevalent in assemblages. The bow and arrow appear on the Channel Islands around 1500 BC; this would have changed hunting patterns. Microblade technology is prevalent at this time; these were likely used as drills in the production of shell beads that would have been valuable trade items. These types of goods become more prevalent in the Late Holocene, with some ornaments increasing exponentially (Rick et al. 2005).

Economically, there is an increase in the importance of marine resources, particularly in fishing for deepwater fishes such as tuna, swordfish, and mako sharks (likely related to the use of plank canoe). Shellfish are still an important part of the economy; with increasing population sizes, it would have been important to make intensive use of all available resources. This also explains the increased exploitation of birds during this time as well. Both shellfish and birds made up a portion of the diet, but the overall diet decreased in diversity. While more of each of these types of food was included in the diet, the greater increase was coming from deepwater fishes.

Social complexity increases tremendously during this period. Using Kennett's model (Kennett 2005; Kennett and Conlee 2002; Kennett and Kennett 2000), Chumash cultural complexity increases between 1,500 and 650 years ago because of long-term population growth, resource intensification, and climatic instability. It is also during this period that changes in interpersonal violence become evident. Analysis of trauma and interpersonal violence has been extensively explored by various researchers (e.g., Hollimon 1990; Lambert 1993; 1994; 1997; 2007; Walker 1989). The cultural changes visible in the archaeological and bioarchaeological record are likely reflective of ecological changes and population increases. In general, with intensification in conjunction with population increases, health tends to suffer.

Archaeological research on the Channel Islands has a long history, extending back over 100 years. Beginning in the 1940s, this research gained new momentum through the introduction and heavy use of radiocarbon dating. This focus was renewed in the 1970s and 1980s and continues to this day.

Pueblo Southwest

This region of the U.S. is largely a desert landscape (Figure 1.6). The earliest habitations within the southwest are associated with the Clovis culture, largely defined through stone tool technology. The type of site for the Clovis is located in northeastern New Mexico, but these points have been found throughout the Southwest. As early as 9500 BC, there is evidence for human occupation and land usage; it is likely nomadic groups following game. Clovis groups are consistently associated with large now-extinct Pleistocene animals. Later, during the Holocene, a second type of point is typically found in association with smaller animals and bison. These Folsom points likely indicate the increasing scarcity of large game and the shift in subsistence base to smaller game. These two culture types and the change in focus from large to small game are indicative of climatic change to a warmer, more arid environment (Plog 1997).

Around 7000 BC, the Archaic period begins. At this time, groups were still nomadic, and so archaeological evidence of their habitation tends to be focused on technology and campsites. Archaic peoples were focused on hunting and gathering of resources. They inhabited the entirety of the Southwest, from northern Mexico to northwestern New Mexico. There is more evidence for gathering of foods and

FIGURE 1.6 Desert landscape typical of the American Southwest. Modified from an image created by Alanthebox, courtesy of Wikimedia Commons, under Universal Public Domain.

nuts as well as grasses and small game. Subsistence usage was dependent upon locally available resources. Game hunted included sheep, antelope, deer, bison, carnivores, and small game such as squirrel, rabbit, and gopher. Despite zooarchaeological findings at campsites, it is believed that this period marks a social change with a larger emphasis on the gathering of plants. Grinding stones begin to be common in assemblages. This change in subsistence is likely tied to climate change. Two transitions appear to have occurred. The first (5500–5000 BC) was a change in weather related to the retreat of the glaciers covering the northeastern U.S. Generally, this was associated with dryer weather, particularly in the summers. This would have brought with it more soil erosion, which may have led to the migration of larger game out of the area. A second shift (2500–2000 BC) is essentially the opposite of the first one and would have been associated with the formation of floodplains and created environmental conditions favorable for cultivation and irrigation of crops (Plog 1997: 48–49). It is not surprising, then, that this second shift sees the first experimentations with agriculture in the region.

Changes in vegetation patterns had an impact on movement because groups were highly mobile and would have rotated between established areas to take advantage of plant and animal resources throughout the year. Maize cultivation begins as early as around 3000 BC, but is firmly established by 1000 BC. It has been suggested that the adoption of agriculture was a response to improved environmental conditions (e.g., Guilday 1984), but this shift has also been interpreted as a way to increase efficiency of food collection at a time when population was increasing and access to some resources may have been restricted (Haynes 1984).

It is important to remember that at this time groups were still relatively mobile, likely shifting between cultivated crops at various times of the year and continuing to exploit game and wild vegetable resources. Dry caves may have been used as places for seasonal shortage based on the assemblages found in many caves in New Mexico. The use of these caves as both storage places and burial places has allowed for the reconstruction of behaviors based on perishable items that would likely not have survived open-air sites. These include basketry, fur cloth, cradleboards, and sandals, to name a few that have been found (Plog 1997).

Around AD 200, groups begin to settle down into permanent villages. This sedentism implies a reliance on a stable and nonmoving food source (i.e., cultivated crops). This shift is a show one, and it is not until around AD 600 through 800 that residential villages show signs of occupation year-round. It is likely that until this time, groups rotated between different semipermanent villages based on crops and available wild resources. One running theme throughout the vignettes in this book is that the transition to agriculture led to not only large social changes but also changes (usually negative) in the health of those practicing it. One reason for this is that the breadth of the diet narrows with the introduction of agriculture. Another is a decrease in the amount of protein eaten overall; without large-game hunting, protein would have been gained from the consumption of hunted meat. Even in modern agricultural groups, hunting still forms an important element of the diet.

A shift to agriculture may have been important for the creation of larger permanent settlements, with individuals coming together to share the benefits and the hard work of tilling and harvesting fields. This creation of larger settlements with more people would have introduced groups to new disease vectors. Crowd diseases such as tuberculosis and parasitic infections are far more common in large aggregated communities than small agricultural or nomadic groups. The introduction of crops from Mexico, such as beans, would have provided more protein than could be gained from wild plants and likely became an important part of the diet along with the maize that was already present. The introduction of these plants indicates cultural contact between groups, likely in a down-the-line exchange pattern (see chapters in Hegmon 2000).

People lived in semisubterranean structures known as pit structures, with areas for work outside the structure. These structures would have been grouped together around communal plazas and held numerous storage pits for grain and other goods. After around AD 200, ceramic vessels are created. These become an important element of society in that they allow for longer term and tighter storage than could be accomplished with basketry. Large grinding stones are also more common after this period. These would have been very cumbersome to move and tend to be incorporated into the architecture of the village.

It is also between AD 200 and 700 that regional differences become evident. For the Southwest, these groups include the Hohokam, Mogollon, and Anasazi groups. The focus of this book is to primarily examine Anasazi and some Mogollon groups. It should be noted that there is significant blurring at the edges of all culture areas, based on artifact styles (Plog 1997). It is therefore likely that social boundaries were also malleable and constantly negotiated.

The time from AD 700 to 1150 is marked by increasing aggregation and the creation of large communities tied to farming. These communities began to have communal ritual rooms, usually subterranean, called Kivas. This also marks the beginning of the Pueblo I period around AD 800. For the ancestral Pueblo people, inhabiting the Four Corners region, large settlements can be found in a variety of environments, from high desert to mountainous environments. The cliff dwellings at Mesa Verde, Navajo National Monument, Chaco Canyon, Mancos, and Ridges Basin are all examples of these settlements. They likely held important social and political roles in addition to serving as a focal point for agriculture. For example, Sacred Ridge – an early Pueblo I site near Durango, Colorado – appears to have held ritual significance based on the presence of large quantities of ground stone as well as large quantities of turkey bone (Potter and Chuipka 2007).

Exchange becomes a very important part of life during the Pueblo period, with the construction of large roads into and out of Chaco Canyon.

Around AD 1150 to 1200, several developments in the Southwest signaled major changes in both political structuring and population aggregation (Martin 1994: 100). Environmental reconstruction indicates major climatic fluctuations that necessitated a more creative use of cultural innovations to buffer the people from lower agricultural productivity. During this period, the large ceremonial center at Chaco Canyon ceases to be utilized, and there was widespread population movement with some clustering of communities in the more northern regions of the Southwest. This is a period of increasing droughts and population movements.

By AD 1350, many of the groups leave the northern areas of the Southwest and migrate and create large, dense settlements along the Rio Grande in New Mexico. The Hopi and Zuni Pueblos stay on the western side of the Southwest in the areas of Arizona, where their ancestors were for hundreds of years. Many of the other Pueblo groups migrated and reorganized into communities along the Rio Grande, which is where the Spanish conquistadores found them in the 1500s. Human remains from the hundreds of sites that have been excavated are very challenging to summarize, but there are some very good syntheses beginning to emerge (see for an excellent examples, Stodder 2008; 2015).

Mississippian/Lower Illinois River Valley

The Mississippi River bottom is unique in these culture areas for two reasons. First, it has abundant water resources. It also has a long history of exchange with other regions, including the Georgia Bight (through the Southeastern Ceremonial Complex). It may be difficult to look at archaic settlements, because these may have been wiped out by shifts in the course of the Mississippi River, but a long pattern of land usage can be documented throughout this region.

In truly massive excavations in the 1960s and 1970s, Struever and others excavated a site known as Koster (Struever and Carlson 1977). Excavations here removed more than 10 meters (around 30 feet) of earth, tracing land usage from archaic hunter-gatherer campsites to established settlements. This provided evidence of continued usage of the area dating to at least 9,000 years BP. It is from Horizon 11 that early domesticated dog burials, dating to around 8,500 years BP, were found (Morey and Wiant 1992). The dogs were found buried on their sides, suggesting deliberate burial. This same layer held the remains of numerous humans as well, suggesting a return to the land again and again and an understanding of ties to a specific locality.

Farther south, the area around modern St. Louis has numerous important settlements. The most recognizable to us today is Cahokia, but numerous other sites are found along the American Bottom. Late archaic remains can be found at Labras Lake and the Falling Springs sites. The Falling Springs site provides the earliest evidence of habitation, beginning at around 3500 BC and extending to 2300 BC. This site is identified through a side-notched projectile point complex. Similar tool types are found in nearby sites. Changes in tool morphology are typically used to identify culture change and interaction between sites. Yerkes (1987) interprets these sites as limited use sites. They tend to be located on the margin of the floodplain, and Yerkes suggests that they may have been located on the banks of the Mississippi River and that other contemporaneous sites may have been destroyed when the river shifted in its course through time. The "base camps" at Labras Lake provide an idea of life during the archaic in this area. These consist of hearths, storage pits, artifact concentrations, domestic areas, and postholes (Yerkes 1987: 58). An understanding of diet comes from recovered botanical remains; carbonized hazelnut, acorn, and black walnut shell were all recovered (1987: 61). Deep roasting pits were found as well, suggesting processing for nut oils or the processing of other food with the shells used as fuel.

Milner (1990: table 1) provides a framework for the examination of periods beginning with the Late Woodland. He defines the Late Woodland as extending from AD 300 to 800. The Late Woodland in the American Bottom is also present in assemblages from Labras Lake, near Cahokia. These are identified through the ceramic assemblages. By the Late Woodland, maize can be found (although it is rare). Much more common are local domesticated plants, such as marsh elder, and nonnative cultigens, such as chenopodium, knotweed, and maygrass. Exotic cultigens, such as squash and tobacco, have also been found (Yerkes 1987: 80). Groups also took advantage of aquatic resources such as fish and turtle, as well as hunting local game such as white-tailed deer and muskrat.

Keyhole structures are found at numerous Late Woodland sites; these consisted of rectangular rooms with narrow ramps extending east. These may have also had ceremonial functions, but their exact role is unclear (Yerkes 1987). Rectangular pit houses have been interpreted as habitation structures; these have a good degree of variation in terms of size and number of postholes, but all have hearths and numerous pits, including areas for storage and refuse disposal. Some shallow pits were likely used for human burials. Milner (1990) argues that population estimates in the thousands for the region is likely because of the expanse of territory available to the inhabitants, as well as the farming techniques being used.

The Emergent Mississippian period dates to between AD 800 and 1000. This period is defined based on significant cultural changes from the Late Woodland through a combination of changes in artifacts, features, settlement, and subsistence characteristics as well as the changing political structure (Milner 1990: 4). Among these changes are new ceramic types that demonstrate significant differences to what came before and after. This is a time of increasing social complexity, the creation of multiple mound sites, and the foundations of the social complexity that will become a hallmark of the Mississippian period. Emergent Mississippian communities tend to be smaller and occur along bottomland ridges or clustered around an open central area. Milner describes these as "nucleated" settlements (1990: 15).

The Mississippian period dates to between AD 1000 and 1400. This period is marked by the solidification of social strata (Milner 1990). Elites were segregated from the majority of the population; this is especially visible in the mortuary customs. Elites had access to exotic materials. Mound 72 at Cahokia is one such elite mortuary area. Elites buried here were accompanied in death by dozens of human sacrificial victims (Fowler et al. 1999; Koziol 2010; Rose 1999) (Figure 1.7). Elite burials can also be found at other sites in the American Bottom as well. These, however, tend to be smaller and simpler than those found at Mound 72. This suggests that local elites (at secondary sites) were still ranked lower than those at Cahokia (Milner 1990).

Mississippian period houses consisted of rectangular houses with wall trenches, numerous storage and refuse pits, hearths, and postholes. Also present at Mississippian period village sites are special use areas, including nut-processing areas and possible ritual areas. Norris (1978) notes that there are numerous types of houses present during this period and suggests that different houses may have been

FIGURE 1.7 Mound 72 at Cahokia outside of St. Louis, Missouri. Modified from an image created by Carptrash, courtesy of Wikimedia Commons, Creative Commons Attribution- Share Alike.

occupied by the same group during different seasons of the year. In effect, summer and winter houses may have been utilized.

When examining the larger regional polity of Cahokia, smaller sites in the area, such as Labras Lake and Lily Lake may have formed the production units that fed into the larger political unit of Cahokia, allowing it to grow as a regional political and trade center (Fowler 1978). They tended to have few or no mounds associated with the habitation structures. These large ceremonial mounds immediately come to mind when one considers Cahokia, but it is important to remember that this type of political hierarchy had a large foundation of smaller sites providing labor and agricultural goods for the maintenance of a small elite. Outlying settlements in the Mississippian period tend to be low-density communities, consisting of dispersed farmsteads with associated features. They may be located near main river valleys on the floodplain (Milner 1990). Some of these outlying sites were abandoned in the Mississippian period, while others existed longer. This may be reflective of fluctuating power relations within the larger regional sphere, but it is unclear as to why some would continue and others would fade away.

Georgia Bight

The Midatlantic Coastal Plain has been occupied by various groups since at least 10,000 BC, based on the presence of Paleoindian stone tools. Based on changes in the coastline (the general rise in ocean levels), it is unlikely that these groups were coastal (Figure 1.8). Because of the rise in ocean levels, it is likely that any evidence

FIGURE 1.8 A view from St. Catherine's Island in the Georgia Bight region. Modified from an image created by William D. Bone, courtesy of Wikimedia Commons, Creative Commons Attribution- Share Alike.

of coastal occupation is now submerged (Reitz 1988). During the Pleistocene, it is possible that the estuaries along the tidal zone were used, although their exact location is unknown. Estuaries are not stable environments, and so their use in deep time is unclear.

By the time of the Early and Middle Archaic periods (between 8500 and 2500 BC), climate and coastlines were relatively stable. Early Archaic tools and sites have been found in association with the upper coast plain and major rivers. Middle Archaic sites are also found in association with minor river systems. There are minimal indications of the use of the nearby islands during this period.

Late Archaic sites (2500–1000 BC) sites are often found in the lower estuaries. These also include ceramics and are found on both the mainland and the barrier islands. Late Archaic sites are also found associated with rivers. The common denominator in the site locations is some type of access (either direct or nearby) to marine resources. Typical Late Archaic tidewater zone sites are circular rings of shell and linear shell middens, but some nonshell midden sites have also been found. Subsistence, measured by archaeological remains, seems to have been based on marine fishes with terrestrial animals making up only a very small portion of the assemblages. Plants identified include pine, red cedar, hickory oak, hackberry, blackberry, buckthorn, grape, and mustards (Marrinan 1975; Trinkley 1976). Altogether, this indicates multiseason usage of the sites (Reitz 1988).

The peoples inhabiting the Georgia coast region went through a great amount of social and economic changes throughout time. Until around 2200 BC, groups were foraging, relying on both marine and terrestrial resources. A transition to preagrarian lifeways occurred between 2200 BC and AD 1150. This was followed by a mixed economy consisting of both hunting and gathering and agricultural adaptations until contact at around AD 1550 (Larsen 1981: 422).

The Early Woodland occupations (1000–500 BC) are found on the coastal plain as well as the tidewater areas of the mainland. In South Carolina, there are a high number of coastal sites associated with this period as well. Other sites are located in the lower reaches of the estuaries and tidewater mainland of Georgia and South Carolina. Reitz (1988) suggests that the site locations in this period suggest that ocean levels may have dropped significantly. In some locations during this period, deer make up a significant proportion of the faunal assemblage with marine resources making up a much smaller portion. Those that are present, however, indicate multiseason usage of the site.

The Middle Woodland dates to between 500 BC and AD 700. These sites are found along creeks as well as along the coastal plain and tidewater zone based on ceramics found at the sites. In some cases, mainland stone was transported to the barrier islands, and island shells are often found on the mainland. Faunal assemblages dating to this period tend to have more marine resources, with deer composing smaller percentages (Reitz 1988).

The Late Woodland period (AD 700–1000) is typified by both small and large sites along the rivers and tidal zones. Late Woodland ceramics have also been found on river bluffs as well. The barrier islands were also utilized during this period.

Deer were found in the faunal assemblages at some sites but are completely absent from others. Maize has been found in the form of cob fragments in the Mattassee Lake project area, but this feature contained ceramics that may have been deposited during the Mississippian period and so may represent an intrusive element from a later time.

Beginning in the Mississippian period, we see evidence of domesticated crops and construction of large mounds. There is a general site hierarchy during this period, with a large primary center, small secondary centers, and tertiary sites. This may be similar to the political structure visible during the Mississippian period in the American Bottom, with the secondary and tertiary centers providing labor and economic support to the main center. Reitz (1988) notes that there may be two political regions: the Savannah region (from St. Helena to St. Catherine's Island) and the Altamaha region (from St. Catherine's Sound to the Satilla River) (Crook 1978).

This is a period of large-scale social change with the introduction of agriculture. Larsen and others (e.g., Hutchinson and Larsen 1988; Hutchinson et al. 1998; Larsen 1981; 1983; Ruff et al. 1983) have been instrumental in the use of human remains from this region as social indicators of subsistence change.

In general, this area shows increasing social complexity through time. Some of the residence patterns may be indicative of social restriction: there may have been social or political structures in place with some individuals able to move more freely into some subsistence zones than others (Reitz 1988: 152). Multiseasonal occupation is evident at many sites. The influence of agriculture in increasing social complexity is a difficult analytical package to unwrap. As Reitz notes, there is no evidence that population pressure was a factor in the expansion away from the coastal plain. There is also no evidence that estuarine resources were not used after cultivation began. Mississippian sites are larger, and the presence of a site hierarchy is suggestive of increased social stratification. Based on biological evidence, maize was a part of the diet (Larsen et al. 1992), but the role it played is unclear.

Plan of the book

To give both depth and breadth on health in ancient America, the chapters that follow provide a general arc of lives and bodies from pregnancy and birth, through early and late childhood, to adolescence, and into the young, full, and mature adult years followed by the elderly (Roksandic and Armstrong 2011: 341). We emphatically stress that this book is not a synthesis of all available data on health and disease from all archaeological sites in the U.S.; rather it is a sampling of core areas within the U.S. that provide particularly rich and detailed evidence for allowing interpretive meaning and broader implications about that evidence. Ancient cultures in the U.S. have complex, rich, and long histories that predate the written records of the colonial invaders in the 1500s. American history texts often start at this point as if there were no history for Native Americans prior to the 1500s. As Lambert writes, "assumptions of the preeminence of Western contact in the formulation of New

World social process minimizes the importance of its unique landscapes, events, trajectories, and solutions" (2002: 208). This text works against that minimization of indigenous history by providing snapshots of life prior to contact.

There is extensive variability across the U.S. in terms of environments, cultures, languages, customs, subsistence activities, and political-economic structures. Thus, it is safe to say that one narrative could not capture what life was life for the hundreds of different Native American groups living in the U.S. prior to contact. This book draws heavily from data produced over many years of study by numerous bioarchaeologists from four core regions (discussed earlier) to demonstrate some of that variability and cultural complexity. These core areas provide highlights of what is known about health and disease but are not by any means representative of the whole of the U.S. bioarchaeological findings. The period focused on is generally from around AD 900 to 1400. These four core areas are complemented and expanded on by presenting data from earlier periods and other regions when necessary to show what is similar or unique about the patterns within the core areas.

As emphasized already, disease is hardly ever a random occurrence. That is why in the U.S. so much faith is placed in the Centers for Disease Control in Atlanta, Georgia. Every major endemic and epidemic disease to have been studied is *patterned*. People become vulnerable to particular diseases or trauma and injury at particular times in their life because a suite of factors such as biology, behavior, location, overall health status, age, and sex place them in harm's way. Tracking these patterns in the ancient world is challenging but it can be done as Chapters 3 through 6 demonstrate.

A life-history approach is utilized to examine more closely the important stages within a human lifetime including birth, infancy, childhood, adolescence, adulthood, and the elderly years. This approach aided in organizing the information about important biocultural factors that come into play for different groups during these stages, such as diet, nutrition, living conditions, and things that could harm people at different stages of life. Life-history theory is used to help explain the traits for each group that govern these life events and highlights various adaptations that are made with each stage. Providing only information on disease is not as useful as providing information on the rich context within which disease is buffered or experienced due to various behaviors. Hill summarizes this well when she states that "[i]dentifying health hazards alone, without studying the priorities that govern human decisions, will not affect the mortality rate of individuals who willingly and knowingly incur such risks" (1993: 78).

Before starting in on the core area studies, Chapter 2 focuses on how bioarchaeologists make sense and meaning out of "reading" the changes and abnormalities they see on the bones. A selective overview of the most common skeletal and dental diseases and trauma are provided.

Basic techniques for the analysis of human remains are provided and act as a backdrop to the chapters that follow. Specific diseases and injuries are introduced in this chapter and how to scientifically quantify and analyze them are reviewed.

Although not every disease or medical event that threatens health can be gleaned from the bones, many of the more common diseases and ailments do, such as staph and strep infections, nutritional inadequacies and anemia, and degenerative diseases and osteoarthritis. This chapter emphasizes that disease is rarely static, and often people do recover or they adjust and adapt to living with a disease. In some cases they die. Health over the course of a lifetime can improve or stabilize or deteriorate. Common ailments such as a staph infection can run their course in predictable ways. Chapter 2 provides the way these kinds of dynamic events around disease may have played out for ancient people based on the kinds of evidence obtained from bones and teeth.

Chapter 3 provides a broad overview of pregnancy, maternal health, and infant mortality for the core areas to understand the kinds of things that may have made some pregnant women and some mothers more at risk for dying young than others. Maternal morbidity and mortality have been assumed to be related to the stresses of pregnancy during the peak reproductive years. More recent evidence, however, points more to other kinds of factors that can place women at risk for illness and death that are not solely about pregnancy and birth but that have to do with cultural practices such as sexual division of labor, gender inequality, and lack of access to adequate resources (Stone In Press). Maternal health and neonates/infants (aged from birth to about 2 years) are the focus of this chapter.

Children and adolescents are examined in Chapter 4 to clarify trends in disease and trauma during the years preceding adulthood, generally divided into early and late childhood and adolescence (Roksandic and Armstrong 2011: 341). Many studies focused on children have shown that the process of weaning makes children more vulnerable to a host of pathologies. In general, ancient children who survive the peak weaning years during early childhood (ages 2–6) tend to do quite well and survive the late childhood (ages 6–10) and adolescent years (ages 10–18) and move into young adulthood. Data from the core regions explored in this chapter show that childhood health is also linked to subsistence activities, diet, environment, resources, and cultural practices that sometimes protect children and at other times link them to illness.

Chapter 5 takes an extended look at adult health profiles for the core areas. Patterns in disease and early death are strongly linked with a range of cultural factors such as religion, diet, culturally sanctioned violence, warfare, and political-economic processes that make resources differentially available to community members. Immigrant status, ethnicity, and gender all are connected in causal ways with either better or worse health, depending on the power structure and the nature of resource distribution. For adults both disease and violence within the cultures and periods tend to overshadow their lives, and for this reason these two categories are focused on.

The elderly adults, which in ancient America would be persons older than 50, are examined in Chapter 6. While some archaeological sites produce an abundance of individuals in the older age categories, others have hardly any. Growing old in ancient America was a risky business, and in general, the elderly represent a small proportion of the overall cemetery or burial collections. It must be remembered that the average age at death in the 1800s was around 40 years and that it was not until the early 1900s that life expectancy doubled to about 80 years where it has stayed up until the present (with some variations in the U.S. by region, ethnicity, socioeconomic status, age, and other factors) (Finch 2010).

Chapter 7 starts with a series of questions about the importance and relevance of knowing more about health in the ancient new world. The past can be used as a guide to the future and in terms of human health, longevity, and the ability to adapt to dynamic changes, it is of interest to know how to best avoid diseases that kill and injuries that maim. The big questions of our time can actually be partially answered by some of the data presented in this text. Will increasing climate change and hotter temperatures make people more violent? (Not necessarily.) Do diverse diets lead to better health? (Yes, if accessible.) Are there ways to prevent maternal mortality and infant mortality? (Yes.) These and other timely questions are juxtaposed with information from the text as a way to invite broader engagement with finding the solutions to many of the problems plaguing the U.S. today.

Note to students and instructors

This text is written for an audience of students and laypeople who have had no exposure to bioarchaeology except through the media reports and specialty telecasts. The information about health in ancient America is presented in a way that invites further inquiry and research by going to the references that are cited. Often these references are old and date to the 1970s and 1980s, but this is because these are the original references and because they are the best references for various points made in the text. Careful decisions have been made as to what to include in this text, and any information not covered was made in alignment with the goal to keep the narrative accessible and engaging for readers with little or no background in the areas of paleopathology and bioarchaeology.

To sum up

This text provides case studies on health conditions and quality of life in the U.S. prior to colonization in the early 1500s relying on four core areas from which there is a great deal of excellent data on human health. The general health and lifestyle of people living hundreds of years in the past capture our imagination, in part, because it is so difficult to consider a world without modern medical advances, at least here in the U.S. There are no historic or modern analogs to look to in reconstructing the past. As L.P. Hartley (1988), the British novelist, famously said, "[t]he past is a foreign country: they do things differently there," and we take this to mean that it is very difficult to understand the lifestyles of our friends and neighbors let alone those living deep in the past. Yet, information about the health status of the earliest inhabitants gleaned from their tangible bony remains is available and provides a glimpse at how the people who came before us dealt with newborn babies, climate change, food shortages, repressive political regimes, violence, and inequality.

References

Agarwal SC, and Glencross BA. 2011a. Building a Social Bioarchaeology. In: Agarwal S, and Glencross BA, editors. Social Bioarchaeology. Chichester: John Wiley & Sons. p 1–11.

Agarwal SC, and Glencross BA. 2011b. Social Bioarchaeology. Chicester: John Wiley & Sons.

Alfonso MP, and Powell J. 2008. Ethics of Flesh and Bone, or Ethics in the Pracrice of Paleopathology, Osteology, and Bioarchaeology. In: Alfonso MP, Arriaza B, Brooks M, Cash P, Drew N, Eklund J, and Gustafsson M, editors. Human Remains: Guide for Museums and Academic Institutions. Lanham, MD: Altamira. p 5–20.

Armelagos GJ. 2003. Bioarchaeology as Anthropology. In: Gillespie SD, and Nichols DL, editors. Archaeology Is Anthropology. Washington, DC: Archaeological Papers of the American Anthropological Association, No. 13. p 27–41.

Arnold JE. 1992. Complex Hunter-Gatherer-Fishers of Prehistoric California: Chiefs, Specialists, and Maritime Adaptations of the Channel Islands. American Antiquity 57(1):60–84.

Arnold JE. 1995. Transportation Innovation and Social Complexity among Maritime Hunter-Gatherer Societies. American Anthropologist 97:733–747.

Arnold JE. 1996. The Archaeology of Complex Hunter-Gatherers. Journal of Archaeological Method and Theory 3(2):77–126.

Arnold JE. 2001. The Chumash in the World and Regional Perspectives. In: Arnold JE, editor. The Origins of a Pacific Coast Chiefdom: The Chumash of the Channel Islands. Salt Lake City: The University of Utah Press. p 7–8.

Arnold JE, and Green TM. 2002. Mortuary Ambiguity: The Ventureno Chumash Case. American Antiquity 67(4):760–771.

Blau S, and Ubelaker DH. 2009. Handbook of Forensic Anthropology and Archaeology. Walnut Creek, CA: Left Coast Press.

Buikstra J, and Roberts C. 2012. The Global History of Paleopathology: Pioneers and Prospects. Oxford: Oxford University Press.

Buikstra JE. 1977. Biocultural Dimensions of Archeological Study: A Regional Perspective. In Blakely RL, editor. Adaptation in Prehistoric America. Athens: Southern Anthropological Society Proceedings, No. 11, Univeristy of Georgia. p. 67–84.

Crook MRJ. 1978. Mississippian Period Community Organizations on the Georgia Coast [Dissertation]. Gainesville: University of Florida.

Diamond JM, and Ordunio D. 2005. Guns, Germs, and Steel: The Fates of Human Societies. London: W. W. Norton.

Erlandson JM. 1994. Early Hunter-Gatherers of the California Coast. New York: Plenum.

Finch CE. 2010. Evolution of Human Lifespan and Disease of Aging: Roles of Infection, Inflammation and Nutrition. PNAS 107(1):1718–1724.

Fine-Dare KS. 2002. Grave Injustice: The American Indian Repatriation Movement and NAGPRA. Lincoln: Univerity of Nebraska Press.

Fowler M, Rose JC, Vander Leest B, and Ahler SR, editors. 1999. The Mound 72 Area: Dedicated and Sacred Space in Early Cahokia. Springfield: Illinois State Museum.

Fowler ML. 1978. Cahokia and the American Bottom: Settlement Archaeology. In: Smith BD, editor. Mississippian Settlement Patterns. New York: Academic Press. p 455–478.

Gamble LH. 2002. Archaeological Evidence for the Origin of the Plank Canoe in North America. American Antiquity 67:301–315.

Geller PL. 2012. From Cradle to Grave and Beyond: A Maya Life and Death. In: Stodder ALW, and Palkovich AM, editors. The Bioarchaeology of Individuals. Gainesville: University Press of Florida. p 255–270.

Goodman AH, and Leatherman TL. 1998. Building a New Biocultural Synthesis: Political-Economic Perspectives on Human Biology. Ann Arbor: University of Michigan Press.

Guilday JC. 1984. Pleistocene Extinctions and Environmental Change: Case Study of the Appalachians. In: Martin PS, and Klein RG, editors. Quaternary Extinctions: A Prehistoric Revolution. Tucson: University of Arizona Press. p 250–258.

Halcrow SE, and Tayles N. 2011. The Bioarchaeological Investigation of Children and Childhood. Social Bioarchaeology. Malden, MA: Wiley-Blackwell. p 333–360.

Hartley LP. 1988. The Go-Between. 1953. London: Penguin.

Haynes CV. 1984. Stratigraphy and Late Pleistocene Extinctions. In: Martin PS, and Klein RG, editors. Quaternary Extinctions: A Prehistoric Revolution. Tucson: University of Arizona Press. p 345–353.

Hegmon M, editor. 2000. The Archaeology of Regional Interaction: Religion, Warfare, and Exchange across the American Southwest and Beyond. Boulder: University Press of Colorado.

Hill K. 1993. Life History Theory and Evolutionary Anthropology. Evolutionary Anthropology: Issues, News and Reviews 2(3):78–88.

Hollimon SE. 1990. Division of Labor and Gender Roles in Santa Barbara Channel Area Prehistory [Unpublished PhD disseration]. Santa Barbara: University of California.

Hutchinson DL, and Larsen CS. 1988. Determination of Stress Episode Duration from Linear Enamel Hypoplasias: A Case Study from St. Catherines Island, Georgia. Human Biology 60(1):93–110.

Hutchinson DL, Larsen CS, Schoeninger MJ, and Norr L. 1998. Regional Variation in the Pattern of Maize Adoption and Use in Florida and Georgia. American Antiquity 63(3):397–416.

Ilen G. 2012. Florida's Dozier School for Boys: A True Horror Story. NPR. http://www.npr.org/2012/10/15/162941770/floridas-dozier-school-for-boys-a-true-horror-story.

Inman D. 1983. Application of Coastal Dynamics to the Reconstruction of Paleocoastlines in the Vicinity of La Jolla, California. In: Masters P, and Flemming N, editors. Quaternary Coastlines and Marine Archaeology. New York: Academic Press. p 1–49.

Kennett DJ. 2005. The Island Chumash: Behavioral Ecology of a Maritime Society. Berkeley: University of California Press.

Kennett DJ, and Conlee CA. 2002. Emergence of Late Holocene Sociopolitical Complexity on Santa Rosa and San Miguel Islands. In: Erlandson JM, and Jones T, editors. Catalysts to Complexity: Late Holocene Societies of the California Coast. Los Angeles: Cotsen Institute of Archaeology, University of California. p 147–155.

Kennett DJ, and Kennett JP. 2000. Competitive and Cooperative Responses to Climatic Instability in Coastal Southern California. American Antiquity 65:379–396.

King CD. 1990. Evolution of Chumash Society: A Comparative Study of Artifacts Used for Social System Maintenance in the Santa Barbara Channel Region Before A.D. 1804. New York: Garland Publishing.

Koziol KM. 2010. Violence, Symbols, and the Archaeological Record: A Case Study of Cahokia's Mound 72 [Dissertation]. Little Rock: University of Arkansas.

Lambert PM. 1993. Health in Prehistoric Populations of the Santa Barbara Channel Islands. American Antiquity 58(3):509–521.

Lambert PM. 1994. War and Peace on the Western Front: A Study of Violent Conflict and its Correlates in Prehistoric Hunter-Gatherer Societies of Coastal California [Unpublished PhD dissertation]. Santa Barbara: University of California.

Lambert PM. 1997. Patterns of Violence in Prehistoric Hunter-Gatherer Societies of Coastal Southern California. In: Martin DL, editor. Troubled Times: Violence and Warfare in the Past. Amsterdam: Gordon and Breach. p 77–109.

Lambert PM. 2002. The Archaeology of War: A North American Perspective. Journal of Archaeological Research 10(3):207–241.

Lambert PM. 2007. The Osteological Evidence for Indigenous Warfare in North America. In: Chacon RJ, and Mendoza RG, editors. North American Indigenous Warfare and Ritual Violence. Tucson: University of Arizona Press. p 202–221.

Larsen CS. 1981. Skeletal and Dental Adaptations to the Shift to Agriculture on the Georgia Coast. Current Anthropology 22(4):422–423.

Larsen CS. 1983. Deciduous Tooth Size and Subsistence Change in Prehistoric Georgia Coast Populations. Current Anthropology 24(2):225–226.

Larsen CS, Schoeninger MJ, van der Merwe NJ, Moore KM, and Lee-Thorp JA. 1992. Carbon and Nitrogen Stable Isotopic Signatures of Human Dietary Change in the Georgia Bight. American Journal of Physical Anthropology 89(2):197–214.

Larsen CS, and Walker PL. 2005. The Ethics of Bioarchaeology. In: Turner TR, editor. Biological Anthropology and Ethics: From Repatriation to Genetic Identity. Albany: State University of New York. p 111–119.

Márquez-Grant N, and Fibiger L. 2011. The Routledge Handbook of Archaeological Human Remains and Legislation: An International Guide to Laws and Practice in the Excavation and Treatment of Archaeological Human Remains. London: Taylor & Francis.

Marrinan RA. 1975. Ceramics, Mollosks, and Sedentism: The Late Archaic Period on the Georgia Coast [PhD dissertation]. Gainesville: Unversity of Florida.

Martin D. 1994. Patterns of Diet and Disease: Health Profiles for the Prehistoric Southwest. In: Gumerman, GJ, editor. Themes in Southwest Prehistory. Santa Fe, NM: School of American Research Press. p 87–108.

Martin D. 1998. Owning the Sins of the Past: Historical Trends in the Study of Southwestern Human Remains. In: Goodman AH, and Leatherman TL, editors. Building a New Biocultural Synthesis: Political-Economic Perspectives in Biological Anthropology. Ann Arbor: University of Michigan. p 171–190.

Martin D, Harrod RP, and Pérez V. 2013. Bioarchaeology: An Integrated Approach to Working with Human Remains. New York: Springer.

Milner GR. 1990. The Late Prehistoric Cahokia Cultural System of the Mississippi River Valley: Foundations, Florescence, and Fragmentation. Journal of World Prehistory 4(1):1–43.

Morey DF, and Wiant MD. 1992. Early Holocene Domestic Dog Burials from the North American Midwest. Current Anthropology 33(2):224–229.

Norris T. 1978. Excavations at the Lily Lake Site: 1975 Season. Reports in Contract Archaeology No 4. Edwardsville: Southern Illinois University.

Nystrom KC. 2011. Postmortem Examinations and the Embodiment of Inequality in 19th Century United States. International Journal of Paleopathology 1(3–4):164–172.

Orr PC. 1962. The Arlington Springs Site, Santa Rosa Island, California. American Antiquity 27:417–419.

Pinker S. 2011. The Better Angels of Our Nature: The Decline of Violence in History and its Causes. London: Penguin UK.

Plog S. 1997. Ancient Peoples of the American Southwest. London: Thames and Hudson.

Potter J, and Chuipka JP. 2007. Early Pueblo Communities and Cultural Diversity in the Durango Area: Preliminary Results from the Animas-La Plata Project. Kiva 72(4):407–430.

Powers CH. 2010. Making Sense of Social Theory. New York: Rowman and Littlefield.

Reitz EJ. 1988. Evidence for Coastal Adaptations in Georgia and South Carolina. Archaeology of Eastern North America 16:137–158.

Rick TC, Erlandson JM, Vellanoweth RL, and Braje TJ. 2005. From Pleistocene Mariners to Complex Hunter-Gatherers: The Archaeology of the California Channel Islands. Journal of World Prehistory 19:169–228.

Roberts CA. 2006. A View from Afar: Bioarchaeology in Britain. In: Buikstra JE, and Beck LA, editors. Bioarchaeology: The Contextual Analysis of Human Remains. London: Academic Press. p 417–439.

Roksandic M, and Armstrong SD. 2011. Using the Life History Model to Set the Stage(s) of Growth and Senescence in Bioarchaeology and Paleodemography. American Journal of Physical Anthropology 145(3):337–347.

Rose JC. 1999. Mortuary Data and Analysis. In: Fowler M, Rose JC, Vander Leest B, and Ashler S, editors. The Mound 72 Area: Dedicated and Sacred Space in Early Cahokia. Springfield: Illinois State Museum. p 63–82.

Rose JC, Green TJ, and Green VD. 1996. NAGPRA Is Forever: Osteology and the Repatriation of Skeletons. Annual Review of Anthropology 25:81–103.

Ruff CB, Hayes WC, and Larsen CS. 1983. Changes in Femoral Structure with the Transition to Agriculture on the Georgia Coast. American Journal of Physical Anthropology 60:247–248.

Sofaer J. 2006. The Body of Material Culture: A Theoretical Osteoarchaeology. Cambridge: Cambridge University Press.

Stodder ALW, editor. 2008. Reanalysis and Reinterpretation in Southwestern Bioarcaheology. Arizona State University Anthropological Research Papers No. 59. Tempe: The Arizona Board of Regents.

Stodder ALW. 2015. Quantifying Morbidity in Prehispanic Southwestern Villages. In: Herhahn, C, and Ramenofsky, AF, editors. Causation and Explanation: Demography, Movement, and Historical Ecology in the Prehistoric Southwest. Boulder: University of Colorado Press. p 250–286.

Stone PK. In Press. Biocultural Perspectives on Maternal Mortality and Obstetrical Deaths from Past to Present. Yearbook of Physical Anthropology.

Struever S, and Carlson J. 1977. Koster Site: The New Archaeology in Action. Archaeology 30(2):93–101.

Trinkley M. 1976. Paleoethnobotanical Remains from Archaic-Woodland Transitional Shell Middens along the South Carolina Coast. Southeastern Archaeology Conference Bulletin 19:65–67.

Walker PL. 1989. Cranial Injuries as Evidence of Violence in Prehistoric Southern California. American Journal of Physical Anthropology 80(3):313–323.

Yerkes RW. 1987. Prehistoric Life on the Mississippi Floodplain: Stone Tool Use, Settlement Organization and Subsistence Practices at the Labras Lake Site, Illinois. Chicago: The University of Chicago Press.

2

BIOCULTURAL PERSPECTIVES ON HEALTH AND DISEASE

Knowledge about the health of ancient indigenous peoples in America is limited both by geographic regions and by culturally significant periods leading up to contact. It is not surprising that no clear picture of trends in health for the many different groups has emerged. One of the best attempts to compile a database on what is known about ancient and historic health can be found in Steckel and Rose's (2002) *The Backbone of History: Health and Nutrition in the Western Hemisphere.* Some regions in the U.S. are very well documented for changes over time relating to diet, health, and trauma (e.g., violence and warfare), and these are drawn on in the rest of the text to highlight the very unique and specific ways that ecology, demography, diet, and social organization underlie patterns and trends in health.

Disease has long been used by scholars from many disciplines as one measure of human adaptability particularly during stressful periods of rapid change or instability. Disease states compromise individual responses but also can have an impact on activities at the household and community levels. Thus, the analysis of health and disease can serve to link biological and social consequences of change in human groups. *Paleopathology* is the term used by bioarchaeologists to refer to diseases in ancient groups. The focus on paleopathology (ancient disease) and paleodemography (ancient age, sex, and population structure) are at the heart of what bioarchaeologists do when they carry out their analysis of human remains.

Paleopathology and the biocultural nature of disease

Bioarchaeologists have been on the forefront of contributions to method and theory in the understanding of ancient health. For several regions in the U.S., there are health chronologies spanning hundreds of years. For example, Walker (1996) documented health and dietary reconstruction for the ancient inhabitants living in Southern California; these data highlight the diversity of adaptations to coastal environments. Using a multimethodological approach involving analysis of a number of skeletal lesions and detailed reconstruction of the environment, Walker demonstrated that ancient people living in marginal island environments (ca. 800 BC to AD 1150) show greater evidence of health problems than those who lived on the mainland where food was more abundant and diverse. The islanders were shorter in stature (160 versus 162 cm) and had more lesions indicative of anemia (75% vs. 25%). In addition to clarifying the relationship between resources and health conditions, Walker also showed that there were changes over time with health conditions worsening (increases in infectious disease from 20% to 30%) because of contaminated drinking sources and diarrheal disease.

Other regions of the U.S. have also provided scientific data from the human remains on important questions concerning social hierarchy and colonization. For example, Larsen (2015) has focused on health patterns for inhabitants of the Georgia Bight, and Buikstra and Cook (1980), Milner and colleagues (1991), and Spencer (2013) have provided detailed pathology data for groups living in the ancient Illinois River Valley. Lovejoy (1985) provided analyses of health conditions for the large and well-preserved Libben site in Ohio, and Goodman and co-workers (1984) revealed health changes over time for Dickson Mounds in Illinois. The southeastern regions of the U.S. have yielded abundant skeletal material that has been analyzed by Powell and colleagues (1991). The American Southwest has likewise provided relatively large skeletal collections from numerous sites and health conditions from these have been summarized by Stodder and colleagues (2002) and Martin and colleagues (2001).

In thinking about these kinds of population level studies, it is important to keep in mind that those events that are regarded as demographic or pathological on the aggregate scale are *life-history events* on the individual level and are important to members of the extended social grouping (Swedlund 1994). Birth, weaning, puberty, sicknesses, marriages, and death are biological and cultural transitional periods that find expression through ritual and other cultural behaviors in virtually all societies. These life-history events also provide the underpinning for generational histories, and they are also points of focus for kin and group identities. Taken in their cumulative context, life histories provide the data for the estimation of larger population processes that effect growth and regulation, dispersal and density, structure and composition, migration and immigration, and health and injury. Finally, life-history events provide a tangible and graphic reminder of how a society is doing because when these events are disrupted, it tears at the social fabric of societies. The loss of an infant to a family, when warfare takes young males, or when a disease ravages through a group—all present tangible experiences requiring ideological and adaptive responses on individual and population levels.

Hrdlička, one of the founders of the American Association of Physical Anthropology (AAPA), was one of the first scholars to systematically collect data on diseases from ancient skeletal remains from a variety of archaeological sites in the U.S. and Mexico. Trained as a physician and an anthropologist, he viewed human biology within an evolutionary and comparative framework. His monograph, titled

Physiological and Medical Observations among the Indians of the Southwestern United States and Northern Mexico (1908), was the first examination of skeletal remains to document pathology (Buikstra et al., 2012). He noted with some surprise the absence of vitamin deficiencies and presented an overall listing of degenerative and traumatic pathologies. He looked at bones from a variety of sites, but he did not interpret the findings within an archaeological context, limiting his ability to interpret the meaning of those diseases within a broader context.

In the 1930s, there was a major methodological breakthrough in skeletal biology with Hooton conducting the first large-scale systematic analysis of human remains from Pecos Pueblo in New Mexico (1930). What is important about the study is that Hooton conducted a population-level analysis using both quantitative and qualitative assessments of genetics, stature, disease status, and biological characteristics. One chapter is devoted to paleopathology, and in it Hooton provides physical anthropologists with a new way of interpreting the findings using epidemiological methods (Hooten 1930: 306–330). *Epidemiology* is the branch of medicine that deals specifically with understanding the patterns and frequencies of various diseases by variables such as age, sex, ethnicity, class, and geographic area. Hooton was the first to analyze pathologies by age and sex and was able to provide a demographic orientation that to this day is one of the founding principles of paleopathology.

Using biocultural data to disrupt stereotypes

Historically, human remains were often analyzed without reference to their cultural context. Context in this sense refers to both the specific site and the artifactual associations of a burial at the time of discovery, and it refers to the specifics of the particular culture from which the burial comes. Human remains and burials are often used for dramatic effect in popular science magazines such as *National Geographic* and *Discovery*. Individuals lacking interest or experience in archaeological context who attempt to draw inferences from burials are frequently unaware of the necessity of such context and make interpretations. The biological facts of the burial seldom tell the whole story. One such error in the literature on southwestern paleopathology, written by medical physicians, erroneously identified the bark hood of ancient cradleboards (pallet to which infants are bound for ease in transportation) as therapeutic corsets (Carlson and Armelagos 1965). The implication of that faulty interpretation was that advanced medical knowledge existed and prophylactics were utilized. In a review of the archaeological context within which the bark hoods were found, Carlson and Armelagos were able to show a strong association of the hoods with infant burials and with cradleboard practices that persisted from ancient to historic times (Figure 2.1).

During the 1950s, reports began to surface that suggested that modern Indian rates of infant mortality (death) and adult morbidity (illness) were very high and disproportionate to the rates for the general U.S. population (Moore et al. 1972). For one group, the Navajo, preventable or controllable diseases, such as infections, tuberculosis, diabetes, and alcoholism, were carefully documented. The patterns of

FIGURE 2.1 Example of a cradleboard. "Apache babe in carrier" by Edward S. Curtis, circa 1903. Public Domain, Library of Congress, Digital ID cph.3b43191, courtesy of Wikimedia Commons.

illness and death attributed to those and other diseases were shown to be alarmingly high when compared to non-Indian rates and were similar to those for less developed and poorer nations (Kunitz 1983). Many stereotypes emerged about Native Americans and their vulnerability to poverty and disease that persist even today.

In the absence of empirical data, it has been common to visualize the ancient past as a scaled-down version of the modern counterpart. For example, Colton uses these images of the ancient Southwest inhabitants garnered from his experience of living with Hopi Indians in the 1920s. He wrote that "families live close together, and the excreta are deposited in the narrow plazas, streets, middens and passages near the houses . . . water is contaminated from excreta . . . infant mortality . . . is very great" (1936: 342) (Figure 2.2). Colton goes on to paint a picture of life in the village fraught with unsanitary practices and rampant disease. Using the present to imagine the past, Colton suggested that ancient village life must have also been

FIGURE 2.2 Historic Hopi village. Archaeologists working in the Southwest in the 1930s often visited these villages to imagine what the past must have been like because there is cultural continuity from ancient to modern times. Adapted from the original "Indian Pueblo Housetop" by Edward S. Curtis, circa 1906. Public Domain, courtesy of Wikimedia Commons.

fraught with disease and sickness. Again, in the absence of empirical data, stereotypic notions about ancient, historic, and modern people are created in a vacuum.

Titiev (1972), a cultural anthropologist living in a Hopi village in 1933, repeatedly mentions the unsanitary conditions and poor general health of many of the inhabitants as well, but he related contemporary attitudes about health and sickness to earlier ancestral conditioning to such a lifestyle. Colton felt that because people living within Indian reservations in the U.S. were suffering at higher levels than the general U.S. population, that they must have been sick in the past as well. In contrast to this, Titiev thought that it was because they were sick in the past and, colonized in the present, they were sick today. Titiev saw health more as a consequence of the past. Colton's and Titiev's observations are relevant for our understanding of both the contemporary experience, as well as for ancient peoples, but they had no empirical data with which to test these hypotheses. Ultimately they both were wrong about how disease works, and both contributed to the formulation of various stereotypes about Native Americans. Bioarchaeology offers a solution to this problem by providing scientific data from the biological remains that can be used to test hypotheses about what the past was like.

Without understanding disease within a broadly chronological, ecological, cultural, and historical perspective, it is problematic to rely solely on ethnographic analogies or analogues of the present to explain the past. Generalizations about ancient people are seen everywhere from commercials for the paleodiet (www.youtube.com/watch?v=rfbkUT0Qx2Q) to websites extolling the virtues of living as our ancestors did in balanced harmony with nature (www.mindbodygreen.com/0-14051/10-reasons-you-should-eat-move-live-like-your-ancestors.html). These are largely based on stereotypes of what people think the ancestors' lives were like. These stereotypes are difficult to dismantle, even when there is evidence to disprove them or to suggest that there was more complexity and nuance involved in living and surviving in ancient times.

One of the major goals of this text is to present a wealth of empirical data so that ancestral lifestyles can be envisioned in a way that is more in line with the complex and varied interpretations derived from bioarchaeological data on what life was like. Bioarchaeological data support that while there were some groups that experienced good health, there were also groups for which illness, disease, trauma, injury, and early death were the defining features during some parts of their long histories.

Paleopathology data from ancient societies permit a reevaluation of another entrenched idea regarding indigenous people and their knowledge and understanding of complex ecological systems. For example, an American archaeologist working in the southwestern regions in the 1915 stated that "originally there existed a delicate natural balance which, as long as it remained undisturbed, permitted the land to be vastly more productive than it is today" (Morris 1939: 6). These sentiments are still around. Embedded even deeper in these ideas rests the assumptions that politics, economics, and ideology were de-emphasized or nonoperational in ancient times. Krech (1999) explored what he called the myth of the ecological Indian, and later Harkin and Lewis (2007) provided case studies that demonstrated that there was variability in different tribal groups in terms of their use and manipulation of natural resources and that no singular idea fits every ancient group.

Without data about the effects of environmental change and cultural processes on morbidity and mortality, it is easy to have simplistic and stereotypic scenarios presented that become part of what people think when the precolonial history of indigenous people is discussed. Without data, it is difficult to test hypotheses regarding a range of relevant factors such as the availability of food and resources, the ability to respond and adapt to environmental changes, or the relationship between disease and social structure.

Beyond the stereotypes about ancient people, Native American scholars have also criticized the treatment of human remains by bioarchaeologists (Deloria 1989). With the passage of NAGPRA legislation and better ethical treatment of human remains, there are now collaborative projects between bioarchaeologists and Native Americans. As pointed out by West (1993), the former director of the National Museum of the American Indian, biological remains represent a database with the potential to bring important information *to* Native Americans. In an attempt to rectify certain misunderstandings (on all sides) of what the potential of biological data are, bioarchaeology as a field of study now strives to integrate human remains into research programs in ways that are responsive to Native American concerns and useful in overturning myths and dismantling stereotypes.

Human remains represent a uniquely rich data set for a wide range of investigations emanating from subdisciplines such as archaeology, biological anthropology, forensic medicine, disease ecology, and public health. As seen earlier, human remains are also highly contested by descendant groups. It begs the questions, Why bother to study human remains? Why is it important to use ancient skeletal remains to document patterns of health and disease for indigenous groups, especially when conditions for people living today in marginalized areas is arguably more pressing? and Why not concentrate efforts on people living today because the need there is so great? The reply is that often the ultimate cause of poor health and maladaptation is not proximally located; rather, it is an "upstream" manifestation of a situation displaced temporally and/or spatially (McKinlay and McKinlay 1974). Furthermore, bioarchaeologists have the methods to extract information about the past that encompass environmental, cultural, and biological factors. Disease can be located in time and space, and an examination of the interrelatedness of ecological, behavioral, and biological variables can be made (Goodman et al. 1984; Larsen 1987). Studying the long and deep human history of disease provides unique and valuable perspectives on disease today, and therein may lie ways to prevent disease (Tishkoff and Verrelli 2003).

Disease has certainly affected the course of human history (Zuckerman et al. 2012). It has only been through the bioarchaeological record that researchers have come to understand how changes over time in environment, political and economic structure, subsistence and diet, and settlement patterns can and do have profound effects on population structure and rates of morbidity and mortality. A particularly commanding set of examples for this can be found in the volume *Paleopathology at the Origins of Agriculture* (Cohen and Armelagos 1984), which focuses on the changes in health related to shifts in subsistence economy in many different locales around the world.

In summary, bioarchaeology offers a dimensional, nuanced, and complex way of thinking about ancient people and their well-being and helps to make connections between the past and the present. In this way, simplistic or stereotypic understandings about the groups living long ago can be disrupted and replaced with a more nuanced way of thinking about the people who came before us. The linking of demographic, biological, and cultural processes within an ecological context is essential for dealing with the kinds of questions that interest archaeologists and biological anthropologists today. These include understanding the relationship between political centralization and illness, the impact of population reorganization or collapse on mortality, and the relationship between social stratification, differential access to resources, and health. These kinds of problems demand a multidimensional approach because they cross over numerous disciplinary boundaries.

Components of bioarchaeological research projects

There is a variety of ways to conceptualize the tasks and objectives of bioarchaeologists, but at the heart of bioarchaeology is the analysis of the bodies and biological remnants of people who died. These remnants can be soft tissue in a variety of naturally or culturally altered states, but the great majority of bioarchaeology is focused on skeletonized remains. Bioarchaeologists are experts in human osteology and in the study of the evolution, structure, and function of skeletons and bone tissue. Bioarchaeologists are also often referred to as skeletal biologists with skeletal biology encompassing every facet of how bone and related tissues evolved from the earliest vertebrate fishes (phylogeny), as well as how bone growth and development are shaped by biomechanics, nutrition, hormones, culture, and other variables (ontogeny) and how bone changes or is altered when affected by disease (pathology).

Bioarchaeologists working today in a variety of biocultural contexts (ancient, historic, and forensic) need to have had many years of advanced training in osteology that includes exposure to different kinds of skeletal collections, that is, skeletons from a variety of time periods and cultures. For those in graduate school, bioarchaeology demands a serious commitment to a range of advanced course work in osteology combined with course work in related areas such as anatomy, nutrition, growth and development, pathology, and archaeology. Two particularly useful texts for bioarchaeologists are one by White and his colleagues (2012) that focus on human osteology and an edited volume by DiGangi and Moore (2012) that provides detail on analytical techniques.

Bioarchaeologists are experts in osteology and paleopathology

Certainly there are some key fundamental features of what constitutes almost all studies in bioarchaeology, and at its core are the analytical tools to glean information from skeletonized human remains. Every study of human remains begins with an estimation of age at death, sex, and stature when possible. Every skeletal collection represents different kinds of biases that affect the numbers of infants, children, and adults in any given assemblage, and these biases must be addressed. In some cases, the identification of the demographic profile within an assemblage can itself be meaningful. Marklein and Fox (In Press), for example, examined the distribution of children within mass burials as a mechanism for the identification of epidemic disease.

The detailed analysis of pathologies (referred to as paleopathology) is one of the primary aspects of data produced from the analysis of human remains. Pathologies reflect a multitude of lifestyle and dietary habits that provide important insights into what life was like for ancient and historic people in terms of diet, health, lifestyle, and age at death.

Paleopathology is one of the primary methodological approaches to the study of skeletonized human remains. As mentioned earlier, it has a long history within physical anthropology on an international scale, and this has been thoroughly documented in an edited volume by Buikstra and Roberts (2012) that chronicles the early and continued growth of this aspect of skeletal analysis not only in the U.S. and England but also on a global scale. Paleopathology is so central to bioarchaeological research that the terms are often used interchangeably. Brickley and Ives (2008: 1) state that understanding human diseases in antiquity, "is a fundamental goal of the study of bioarchaeology." They go on to refer to "the understanding of bone biology and its relevance within many disciplines of bioarchaeology," suggesting that it is a large and encompassing set of approaches (2008: 40). This view continues to expand, however, as new methods relying on data derived from a wide range of bone tissues at different levels now offer insights into individual identity and life history that go well beyond the diagnosis of disease (e.g., Knudson and Stojanowski [2009] present case studies in bioarchaeology that are based on a variety of new biochemical methods applied to skeletal analyses).

Thus, paleopathology is a prolific place where bioarchaeologists have focused much of their attention. Scholars who have expertise in this collaborate with colleagues and utilize published literature from clinical medicine, orthopedics, and human biology, to name just a few. In the recently published edited volume titled *A Companion to Paleopathology* (Grauer 2012), there are 30 chapters, each detailing the state-of-the-art and best practices for the analysis of pathology from human remains. An important aspect of analysis is combining a detailed explication of how a diagnosis for any given disease is being made. This necessitates drawing on medical and clinical literature, as well as integrating multiple levels of analysis including histological and morphological approaches when possible.

Trained experts in human osteology and paleopathology, bioarchaeologists provide a wealth of information about human biology, diseases, and behavior, as well as social systems and long-term trajectories under different kinds of stressors. This breadth raises the question, What are the intellectual ties that bind bioarchaeology across the diverse approaches and variety of data sets? The answer lies in the integration of scientific, largely quantitative, data derived from human skeletal remains with other kinds of information. How this is done can take many forms, as the hundreds of case studies mentioned in this book reveal, but what crosscuts almost all studies is the integration of data sets with the express purpose of answering specific kinds of research questions related to human behavior and social life.

Bioarchaeology emphasizes a range of methodological approaches

For some, bioarchaeology is first and foremost and archaeological endeavor. Oxenham and Tayles (2006), bioarchaeologists from New Zealand and Australia working in Southeast Asia, suggest that bioarchaeology emphasizes the uniquely human biology component of the archaeological record. They feel that it is an emphasis on one of the more important pieces of the archaeological record that many archaeologists fail to appreciate. While most archaeological focus is often on pottery and tools, they point out that "human remains *are* the people who created the pots, the tools, the houses, the middens and the modified landscapes" and are therefore "central to any research of past society that uses archaeology as the means of data recovery" (Oxenham and Tayles 2006).

Bioarchaeologists with a strong history of scholarly research and publications tend to utilize words such as *context* and *integration* in their opening statements on what bioarchaeology is vis-à-vis their current project. In an edited volume titled *The Bioarchaeology of the Human Head*, Bonogofsky (2011: 1) writes that bioarchaeology "integrates biological data and archaeological context, stressing the interaction between biology and behavior" and that "researchers are increasingly recognizing the advantages of such an integrated approach and putting it into practice in a variety of temporal and spatial contexts." This captures the intent and direction of bioarchaeology by emphasizing the cross-cultural and diverse periods from which the studies are derived.

Tung's (2012: xv) book titled *Violence, Ritual, and the Wari Empire* offers that "[b]ioarchaeological inquiry can tell us about the lived experiences of people . . . it provides a direct means of analysis by focusing on the human body itself . . . [it] show[s] how social structures and the environment may have profoundly affected . . . behavior and health." Perry and Buikstra (2012: 1) refer to bioarchaeology in their introduction to an edited volume on *Bioarchaeology and Behavior: The People of the Ancient Near East*, as simply "contextualized skeletal biology." These texts both frame research questions that can be answered with the empirical data using not only the skeletal remains at hand but also using additional lines of evidence drawn from the reconstruction of social organization and social structures.

Baadsgaard, Boutin, and Buikstra (2012) edited a volume titled *Breathing New Life into the Evidence of Death: Contemporary Approaches to Bioarchaeology*. In the introductory chapter the authors define bioarchaeology as "the contextual interpretation of human remains," and they go on to suggest that there is no *one* way to accomplish this because bioarchaeology "encompasses myriad strategies for the study of mortuary remains from archaeological sites" (Buikstra et al. 2012: 3). In their view, what bioarchaeology is and what bioarchaeologists do incorporates many different approaches and strategies. In differentiating their notion of bioarchaeology from some others, they state that "Buikstra's bioarchaeology has increasingly focused upon social theory across a broad range of situations, including archaeological, historical, and ethnohistorical contexts" (2012: 9). This illustrates the move toward having social theory be an integral part of the research strategy.

Perhaps in response to these variations in defining precisely what bioarchaeology aims to be, Buikstra introduced the notion of "the bioarchaeologies" to denote the different approaches that bioarchaeologists appear to take (see Buikstra 2006: 348; Buikstra et al. 2012: 9). However, DiGangi and Moore (2012: 13–14) dismiss that these approaches warrant being known as separate bioarchaeologies, stating that "[r]egardless of the approach taken towards bioarchaeological inquiry, the questions being asked are the same."

What seems clear from these characterizations of bioarchaeology is that it has generally replaced the areas of studies and expertise formerly called osteology and skeletal biology. Yet all bioarchaeologists have deep and broad training, experience with, and commitment to the fields of osteology including bone morphology, biology, physiology, and pathology as detailed in the previous section. These are core fundamental aspects of any analysis of human remains. Whether bioarchaeologists go on to emphasize the archaeological context, dietary questions, sex ratios within burial populations, or mitochondrial DNA depends on their particular interests. Most important, all bioarchaeologists share common notions about osteology, cultural context, and integration.

Thus, bioarchaeology is methodologically and analytically united across many approaches, diverse strategies, and different kinds of question asking and hypothesis testing. A favorite definition of ours was penned by Ortner (2006: xiv) who offered that "bioarchaeology is an interpretive framework for the diverse data obtained today . . . integration of cultural and biological data is central . . . [t]his linkage brings a far richer understanding of biological data." If one defines bioarchaeology as an interpretive framework, as suggested by Ortner, it maintains a central core feature of what distinguishes bioarchaeology from osteology and skeletal biology and yet unites all researchers within this field. It also implies that interpretation can only come from an integration of biology with culture, that is, the whole of the context within which these humans whose remains are being queried lived within. It also recognizes that within this interpretive framework, some studies will take more descriptive approaches and others will be more integrative and broad.

The diversity in approaches is further supported by the kinds of studies any scholar decides to carry out. Bioarchaeological studies are pieces of a puzzle that help explain *why* there are such things as disease and early death in some populations but not others. Bioarchaeology has the capacity to address long-standing human problems associated with social behaviors underlying violence and warfare, hierarchy and inequality, subsistence activities and sustainability, and pain and suffering. Additionally, bioarchaeologists have begun to grapple with notions of identity of the individual within society and ethnic identity at more aggregate levels. A growing number of bioarchaeologists are exploring the similarities and differences within the sexes by analyzing the underlying cultural processes that produce and reproduce social behaviors such as patriarchy and the sexual division of labor or the problems that underlie differential patterns in mortality and morbidity and age-related health problems. Additionally, bioarchaeological studies often shine a light on infants and children in terms of the risks they may face. Thus, there is a wide range of approaches to how studies are undertaken and presented, but they are all attempts at explicating human behavior in particular settings and periods.

Bioarchaeology integrates osteology within a biocultural context

In most bioarchaeological studies, remnants of skeletons and bones are used as a proxy to reconstruct bodies within their cultural setting. Precisely because bioarchaeology is anthropology (Armelagos 2003), it places some of the focus on the actions (behaviors, habits, and occupations) and beliefs (ideology, social structures, subsistence, and economics) of humans and what these reveal about their life histories. Bioarchaeologists often focus on how humans adapt to diverse environments and the ways that biological and cultural processes work together to shape individual life histories and group survival. Thus, processes that can cause early death such as poor diet, disease, or violence are of central importance.

As anthropologists, bioarchaeologists are highly specialized within their area, yet they must remain generalists in the ways that observations of the human condition are interpreted. Addressing these kinds of complex topical areas requires researchers to use and synthesize information from many different areas within anthropology (including archaeology and biological anthropology) along with an impressive array of methods and data from other fields. Models and frameworks have been developed over the years to be used as heuristic devices. These are important for helping to organize and systematize the ways that data are collected and analyzed.

One of the earliest attempts to model complex factors having to do with archaeological bodies and the social processes that affect bodies was by Buikstra, who together with a group of biological anthropologists with osteological and archaeological training, had a vision of working with human remains that departed from prior approaches by directing research into more contextualized and integrative areas. Buikstra describes this history as a major conceptual and theoretical breakthrough with the incorporation of archaeological and mortuary context, and the application of an interdisciplinary perspective. The model she presented (Figure 2.3) became the basis for shifting the study of ancient burials from descriptive to a more integrated scientific approach (Buikstra 1977: 71). In this new approach, human remains were placed within a larger context that included the mortuary component, grave goods, and the relationship of the burials to the larger archaeological site reconstructions. In this way, studies of the dead were seen as being linked to studies of the living in terms of social behaviors and biological well-being.

Goodman and colleagues (1984: 14) provided a more focused and detailed framework that emphasized modeling physiological disruption (or, stress) within a larger context of environmental and cultural factors that prevent or manufacture

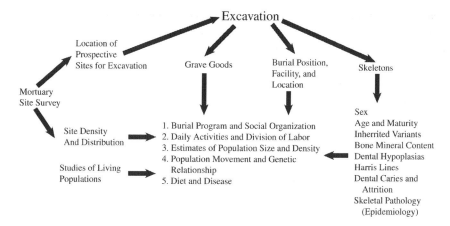

FIGURE 2.3 A model demonstrating all of the important variables that need to be considered beyond the analysis of the human remains. Adapted from Buikstra (1977: 82), with permission from author.

stress. This model was designed for population-level analysis of disease and thus incorporates ideas about the physiologically stressed body from the fields of epidemiology and stress research (Figure 2.4). This model is general enough so that it can be modified for particular populations to address specific problems, and it provides a systematic framework for integrating information regarding human adaptability and health with the larger biocultural and ecological context. In this model the physical environment is viewed as the source of resources essential for survival. If there are constraints on the resources, then the ability of the population to survive may be limited accordingly (Figure 2.4, box 1).

Cultural systems and beliefs are important to our understanding of overall health and sensitivity to stress. In most cases, these systems and beliefs act as buffering mechanisms, protecting individuals during physiologically dangerous times such as weaning or changes in environmental conditions. Sometimes, however, cultural

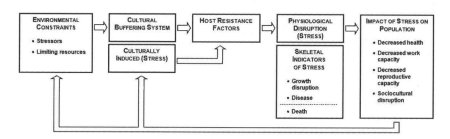

FIGURE 2.4 A model demonstrating the systemic stress perspective and the kinds of variables that can be brought to bear on the analysis of the human remains.

systems can act to introduce stress or dietary deficiency. This is particularly true in the case of some food taboos that may limit nutritional intake based on life stages. For example, food taboos existing during pregnancy may make some foods off-limits to pregnant women (e.g., Osterholtz et al. 2014). In some cases, marriage patterns may also increase the prevalence of genetic anomalies or expose adolescent girls to pregnancies at very young ages (e.g., Baustian 2010).

The adaptation of human populations is more often enhanced by a cultural system that buffers the population from environmental stressors (Figure 2.4, box 2). The technology, social organization, and even the ideology of a group provide a filter through which environmental stressors pass.

Although cultural and behavioral responses may effectively buffer inhabitants during some environmental perturbations, stressors in some places at some times may be so significant that cultural responses are not successful buffers. For example, if cultigens were relied on increasingly through time, it would make it difficult to meet dietary requirements should there be crop failure several years in a row. This problem would be compounded if the group size was growing and if there was an investment in a rigid set of adaptive strategies. On the other hand, increased sharing, storage capacity, trading, and redistribution of limited resources along with flexibility in resource type and procurement could offset the stress produced by crop production. Thus, reliance on cultigens is perceived as both a buffer during ecologically favorable times and a stressor during periods of drought.

The inability of an individual to resist a stressor results in physiological disruptions (Figure 2.4, box 4). The severity of the disruption depends on many factors. Age, sex, health status, genetic composition, and nutritional constitution are especially critical factors. For example, a nutritional deficiency that occurs during a critical phase of growth may affect several biological systems. Decreased activity, increased use of fat stores, and decreased skeletal growth are a few of the possible responses. A similar deficiency that occurs after growth ceases may have little lasting effect on the biological system.

Target organs must be considered in studying the impact of stressors. For example, the adult human skeletal system is relatively immune to mild and short-term nutritional deficiencies. However, the skeletal system is in constant communication and cooperation with other systems. The primary functions of the skeleton are support and locomotion; storage and regulation of minerals (especially calcium and phosphorus); protection of the brain, spinal cord, and other organs; and the production of red blood cells (White et al. 2012). The diversity of functions in this one system indicates the degree to which the entire body dependents on the skeleton. Thus, a careful "reading" of subtle morphological changes can be very revealing of physiological disruptions.

Although the record is far from complete, many stressors leave markers on bones and teeth. These markers can be used to reconstruct the history of morbidity and mortality experienced during infancy and childhood. From this record of the type, severity, frequency, and distribution of ill health, we can begin to draw inferences about the presence of stress and its functional and adaptive effects on the individual and on the group. The adult skeleton may not show effects of mild stressors, but the growing bones and teeth of children often are altered in measurable ways. Specifically, chronic or episodic physiological stress can disrupt growth, and these disruptions often leave permanent markers on bone and teeth that persist into adulthood. These retrospective indicators of previous physiological insults are among the most useful indicators of diet and disease for ancient skeletal remains.

Multiple stress indicators are used to determine the degree and patterning of the stress by looking for patterns of acute and chronic stress, for patterns of stress among different subgroups by age and sex, and for patterns of severity of and response to pathogens in the environment. Understanding physiological disruption and the impact of stress on the population feeds directly back into the understanding of cultural buffering and environmental constraints, and is presented in the model as a feedback mechanism (Figure 2.4, box 5). It is extremely important to understand how disease and death have important functional and adaptive consequences for the community. Poor health can reduce work capacity of adults without necessarily causing death. Decreased reproductive capacity may occur if maternal morbidity and mortality are high in the youngest adult females. Individuals experiencing debilitating or chronic health problems may disrupt the patterning of social interactions and social unity and may strain the system of social support.

The documentation of patterns of ancient disease should ultimately be channeled back into the discussion of human behavior and culture change. In modern society, health of infants and children is delicately linked to the function of mothers, families, and communities. Similar dynamics exist for all human groups, and these interrelated issues must be explored for ancient communities. The archaeologist is in a unique position to monitor the dynamics between changes in the ecological and cultural environment and changes in human response.

To address these hypotheses, the demographic and biological impact of stress must be measured by skeletal indicators of growth disruption, disease, and death. Pathological alterations on bone are assessed primarily through the systematic description of lesions. Patterns of growth and development also provide information on stress. Demographically, a majority of the human remains recovered are under the age of 18, and we are able to document growth and development of both dental and skeletal tissue during critical stages and compare this to known values for well-nourished and healthy groups, as well as modern groups living in similarly marginal areas. Identifiable, age-specific disruptions in growth yield important information on patterns of childhood developmental disturbances and physiological disruption. The distribution and frequency of specific diseases (nutritional, metabolic, infectious, and degenerative) are also an essential part of the osteological analysis. The patterning and frequencies of nutritional diseases, such as iron-deficiency anemia, are documented for many precontact populations and has obvious implications for understanding adequacy of diet. Infectious diseases, likewise well documented for many skeletal series, provide an indicator of demographic patterning, population density, and degree of sedentism.

Others have added new dimensions and enhanced the biocultural model by factoring in things such as mortuary context and funerary goods, as well as archival and historical documents. Sheridan (1999, 2002) created an expanded version of the biocultural model that emphasized historical information (Figure 2.5). This is just one example of how bioarchaeologists organize complex data sets from a diverse range of topics. This has led to more sophisticated ideas about the ways that human biology and culture are embedded in a matrix of contexts that can be reconstructed using multiple lines of evidence. For her research, this biocultural model helps to integrate a wide range of data from the archaeological record, historical documents, and the human remains. Her research questions include understanding the patterns of social stratification and differential access to limited resources as well as poor childhood health and occupationally related stress on the bodies of the adults. Without using a model such as this as a purely heuristic device, it would be difficult to maintain integration across the various data sets.

Thus, to factor in all the complexity of factors that affect demography and health for ancient groups there are many different approaches. Bioarchaeologists have to decide what is most useful for weighing the importance among a number of

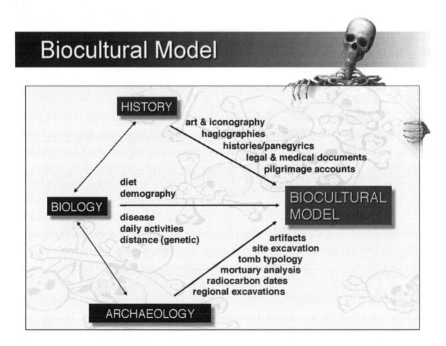

FIGURE 2.5 A model demonstrating variables that may be utilized if there is access to ethnohistoric documents and other kinds of evidence. Adapted from Sheridan (1999, 2002) with permission from author.

factors. To focus more clearly on major spheres of interaction, the preceding models (Figures 2.3–2.5) have advanced how bioarchaeology and paleopathology studies are conducted. The cultural and noncultural stressors that cause observed bone changes can often be inferred. Occurrence of stress markers at different stages in the life cycle can be examined and compared to the mortality rates of the group as a whole. Life history events end up structuring many of the biocultural approaches to understanding disease and early death. For example, sick mothers can give birth to sick children. Weaning places many biological stresses on infants. Thus, life history is crucial in thinking about the more important places where disease and trauma may prove crucial in overall survival.

In summary, our interest in the inhabitants of the ancient past is not to learn about specific health problems so much as it is to learn about humans in general and their unique ways of coping with change over time. When are humans able to be resilient and flexible in the face of change, and when are they forced to migrate or die trying to adapt to new life-threatening situations such as drought or warfare? What has been the process of sedentism, and what is the relationship of sedentism to health? What has been the impact of sedentism on population growth? What has been the process of aggregation and how has it affected the pattern of disease? If there has been an increase in disease, how have the populations responded to the increase in disease load? Biocultural perspectives and bioarchaeological modeling can answer these kinds of questions. Bioarchaeological studies take advantage of dietary and health data to provide time depth and geographic variability to the understanding of short- and long-term consequences and mechanisms of adaptation to change.

Indicators of disease and trauma on bone and teeth

Methods for the analysis of skeletal remains have advanced tremendously in the last 10 years, and this has increased the capacity of researchers to obtain biological information on diet, health, and trauma that was previously unavailable. As shown earlier, paleopathology necessitates the understanding of skeletal responses to stress and change within the context of all potential variables that have an effect on the skeletal system's ability to respond. Quantifiable changes in skeletal and dental materials reflect disturbances in growth and development, as well as in bone maintenance and repair (Scheuer and Black 2000). The cultural and biological stressors that cause observed bone changes can often be inferred. Occurrence of stress markers, lesions, or abnormalities at different stages in the life cycle can be examined and compared to the mortality rates of the group as a whole.

The impact of disease and trauma depends on their duration and virulence. An unusually strong stressor that is short in duration may have relatively little effect on bones and teeth. The unavailability of food for a few days can usually be tolerated by adults but may be dangerous for infants. A stressor that is relatively minor in the short run (such as a low-level toxin) may create a significant problem for survival if it persists. If stress is long lasting, severe, and uncontrolled, it may have devastating effects. It will be reflected in an increase in morbidity and mortality and a decrease in productivity and reproduction.

Life history, disease, and trauma

Critical to understanding disease and trauma on bone is what is generally referred to as "host resistance" (Goodman et al. 1984). Because of both biological and cultural differences in the availability of and access to resources and reserves, not all individuals are equally at risk. A host who is in good health can often meet the challenge of even a severe disease stressor. On the other hand, an individual who is not in good health may find it difficult to resist even a relatively minor one. For example, an infectious disease resulting in gastroenteritis will have a much greater impact on a poorly nourished individual than on one who is well nourished. Selye (1976) has demonstrated that an individual who is continually stressed may eventually exhaust the physiological capacity to resist any stressor.

Certain segments of the population may be at greater risk at certain ages because their biological requirements are not matched by biological resources. Newborns, for example, are born with very immature immune systems. They must rely on immunity conferred during their time in utero and transferred via breast milk from the mother. Because of their state of biological immaturity, infants are frequently unable to rally from stressors that have only mild effects on a more mature individual. Mortality is particularly high during the first year in many marginal communities.

Once weaning begins, a second peak in both morbidity and mortality is frequently seen. Infants and young children become dependent on their own natural defenses at a time when these defenses are just beginning to develop. If nutrition is inadequate, as it frequently is at this age in marginal communities, those defenses will be further hindered. Thus, it is not unusual to see weaning age infants and children undergoing repeated bouts of chronic diarrhea, upper respiratory disease, and malnutrition.

Sometimes infants and children rebound from illness and make it through these high-risk periods. Despite recovery, the repeated insults may have a lasting adaptive cost in terms of such functional abilities as growth, reproduction, activity patterns, cognition, behavior, and social performance. In documented cases from living populations, infants and children do continue to succumb to repeated exposures to stressors, and these negative effects can last for generations (Clarkin and Levy 2004).

In the discussion of host resistance, some clarification of the unit of analysis is necessary. In any study of stress, the first level of analysis is the individual. The study of disease in archaeological populations begins with the evaluation of an individual skeleton. However, it is critically important to move to a population level to understand the full impact of diseases on host resistance and fitness at the community level.

The inability of an individual to resist disease will result in physiological disruptions. The severity of the disruption depends on many factors. Age, sex, health status, genetic composition, and nutritional constitution are especially critical factors. For example, a nutritional deficiency that occurs during a critical phase of growth may affect several biological systems. Decreased activity, increased use of fat stores, and decreased skeletal growth are a few of the possible responses (see chapters in Lewis 2009; Thompson et al. 2014). A similar deficiency that occurs after growth ceases may have little lasting effect on the biological system.

Target organs must be considered in studying the impact of stressors. For example, the adult human skeletal system is relatively immune to mild and short-term nutritional stress. However, the skeletal system is in constant communication and cooperation with other systems. The primary functions of the skeleton are support and locomotion, storage and regulation of minerals (especially calcium and phosphorus), protection of the brain, spinal cord, and other organs, and production of red blood cells. The diverse set of functions in one system indicates the degree to which the entire body is actually dependent on the skeleton. Thus, a careful reading of a variety of subtle morphological changes can be very revealing of physiological disruptions.

Although the record is far from complete, many stressors leave markers on bones and teeth. These markers can be used to reconstruct the history of morbidity (disease) and mortality (death) experienced during infancy and childhood. From the record of type, severity, frequency, and distribution of ill health, we can begin to draw inferences about its functional and adaptive effects on the individual and on society.

The adult skeleton may not show effects of mild stressors, but the growing bones and teeth of children are often altered in measurable ways. Specifically, chronic or episodic physiological stress can disrupt growth, and the disruptions often leave permanent markers on bone and teeth that persist into adulthood. Retrospective indicators of previous physiological insults are among the most useful indicators of diet and disease for prehistoric skeletal remains.

Biocultural stressors: changes and lesions on bones and teeth

The response of the human skeleton to stressors is deceptively simple: at the microscopic level, osteons (the building blocks of bone) can be deposited or resorbed, or there can be a response that combines these processes. Although the patterns of response to stress are relatively simple, it must be kept in mind that the interpretation of the responses is more complex.

Many diseases leave their "signatures" on bone. Tuberculosis, syphilis, and leprosy cause skeletal changes specific to each pathogen. In leprosy there are resorptive changes in the base of the nasal cavity and the terminal digits of the hands and feet (Waldron 2009). Many pathogens, however, leave only generalized changes in the skeleton. One frequently observes a reaction on the bone periosteum (the fibrous sheath covering bone to which tendon sand ligaments attach) reflecting a pathogenic change of unknown origin. Periosteal reactions, inflammations that leave a roughened appearance on the outer layer of bone occur when the fibrous outer layer is stretched and subperiosteal hemorrhages occur (Aufderheide and Rodríguez-Martin 2011). Microorganisms such as *Staphylococcus* (staph) and *Streptococcus* (strep) can cause these changes in bone. Even though it is difficult to determine which pathogen is the cause of the lesion, the occurrence of the condition reveals that the individual was infected. Some pathogens such as viruses may not leave evidence on bone, and the paleopathologist must be careful not to overinterpret the finding (Ortner 2003).

Nutritional stressors need to be carefully diagnosed. In part, the difficulty centers on the attempts to find single cases of well-known deficiencies such as rickets and scurvy (Armelagos et al. 2014). Although a few mineral and vitamin deficiencies leave specific lesions that are easily diagnosed, a major breakthrough in analyzing nutritional disease resulted from a movement away from using attempts to isolate single nutritional deficiencies to focusing on generalized undernutrition. Because single nutritional deficiencies are quite rare, this refocusing not only better fits the available skeletal materials but has more biological significance as well.

Because of the interest in generalized nutritional stress, new methodologies that utilize multiple indicators, systematically analyzed, have become available to provide an understanding of nutritional inadequacies (Sutton et al. 2010). There are a number of lesions such as porotic hyperostosis, defects in enamel development, and premature bone loss that, when coupled with evidence of growth retardation, can provide clues to a pattern of generalized nutritional deficiency.

Porotic hyperostosis, one form taken by bony lesions, is found on the cranium and the orbital roof. It develops when the cranial bones expand in response to an anemia. As the bones expand, the outer layer of bone becomes thinner and may eventually disappear, thereby exposing the diploë (the space between the inner and outer tables of bone). There are a number of genetic conditions, such as sickle cell anemia and thalassemia, that cause anemic responses. In addition, iron deficiency will also cause a milder anemia that frequently results in porotic hyperostosis lesions. In iron-deficiency anemia, there is a relatively minor skeletal response with changes on the cranial bone surface noticeable but not severe. This pattern – and its high frequency in children between ages 1 and 3 and in young adult females – is the most diagnostic feature of nutritional anemia (Walker et al. 2009).

The pattern of growth in skeletal populations may also provide information about the population's physiological state. Because we are by necessity using cross-sectional data, comparison with growth studies that use longitudinal series is very difficult. Furthermore, growth curves need to be constructed relative to developmental rather than chronological age. As development may also be delayed under stressful conditions, the effect may decrease the power of this analysis. Nonetheless, skeletal biologists often see indication of growth retardation in archaeological populations.

Comparison of growth patterns of archaeological populations is often difficult to interpret because of lack of control of genetic factors, the cross-sectional nature of the sample, and age assignment. However, there are situations, such as when populations experience shifts in subsistence, in which growth data may be powerful tools of explanation (see the examples in Cohen and Armelagos 1984).

The analysis of defects in dental enamel provides another measure of growth disruption. Dental enamel hypoplasia is a deficiency in enamel thickness that results from a disruption in the formation of the matrix. Enamel defects can result from systemic disruption, hereditary conditions, and localized trauma. Unlike bone, once enamel matures, it cannot be remodeled. Enamel is secreted in a regular ringlike pattern, and the crown development provides a permanent chronological record of any physiological disruption. An understanding of rates of enamel formation allows one to define the time in development at which the metabolic disruption occurred.

There are two ways in which the chronological distribution can be used. First, the chronological pattern of hypoplasia in adults can be analyzed to see the age at which they, as children, were exposed to physiological disruption. Second, the impact of this disruption on other aspects of their morbidity and mortality can be evaluated. Hypotheses concerning the long-term effects on longevity of childhood stress can be tested using these kinds of data. For example, the age at death of an individual can be examined with respect to the number and timing of growth disruptions within the enamel; this may give an indication that individuals exposed to greater stress at a younger age are more prone to additional stress during their lives (Goodman and Armelagos 1988).

Bone and teeth yield a variety of indicators of stress that will be individually discussed in the following sections. In the preceding section we focused on signs that are most often related to infection and nutrition. Other bone lesions are associated with traumatic conditions and degenerative diseases. It can be generally concluded that bone alterations not only document the impact of disease and other stressors but also indicate something about the individual's ability to respond to stress. Multiple stress indicators are used to determine the degree and patterning of the stress by looking for patterns of acute and chronic stress, for patterns of stress among different subgroups by age and sex, and for patterns of severity of and response to pathogens in the environment. In a sense, then, studies of prehistoric populations are relatively rich in indicators of stress. Some of these signs point toward specific insults, while others are of a more general nature. It is only when all the indicators of stress are analyzed in relation to other variables that a clear picture of adaptation is obtained.

The documentation of patterns of disease in ancient populations should ultimately be channeled back into the discussion of human behavior and culture change. In modern society, the health of infants and children is delicately linked to the function of mothers, families, and communities. Similar dynamics for all human groups exist and these interrelated issues must be explored for ancient communities. Bioarchaeologists are in a unique position to monitor the dynamic between changes in the ecological and cultural environment and changes in human response.

Bringing this back to formulating a biocultural perspective on disease and trauma, Wells hinted at the concept 50 years ago when he wrote that

> the pattern of disease or injury that affects any group of people is never a matter of chance. It is invariably the expression of stresses and strains to which they are exposed, a response to everything in their environment and behavior.

It reflects their genetic inheritance (which is their internal environment), the climate in which they live, the soil that gave them sustenance and animals or plants that share their homeland. It is influenced by their daily occupations, their habits of diet, their choice of dwellings and clothes, their social structure, and even their folklore and mythology.

(1964: 87)

This quote captures perfectly the task of the bioarchaeologists interested in ancient disease and trauma and provides a way to imagine ancient bodies and lives as entangled in numerous interacting biocultural webs.

Techniques for the analysis of bone and teeth

The bioarchaeology community has long been concerned with the inconsistent and ultimately noncomparable ways that skeletal data are collected, analyzed, and reported. In an effort to encourage consistency and comparability, standards for data collection exist in the form of manuals (Buikstra and Ubelaker 1994b) and on institutional websites such as the Smithsonian Institution (http://osteoware.si.edu/) and Killgrove (https://github.com/killgrove/OsteologyDatabase). These standards simply list the most commonly used metrical and observational analyses used by most bioarchaeologists in the U.S. These standards include the collection of data from the skeleton, data on mortuary context, the condition and status of the skeletal remains themselves, the location, severity, and status of pathological and nonpathological lesions, metric and nonmetric observations, and demographics are systematically recorded for each discrete individual.

In general, for reconstructing diet, demography, disease, and trauma, it can be best accomplished with attention to 10 major categories (Table 2.1). These ten indicators provide maximum comparability with other published studies as well as conform to the standardization of skeletal and dental indicators of stress (Buikstra and Ubelaker 1994b). Additional information on collecting these data is briefly discussed later and is more fully addressed in Bass (1987). Buikstra and Ubelaker (1994b), White and colleagues (2012), and DiGangi and Moore (2012).

Because differential diagnosis is often difficult and requires multiple confirmations, the collection of data on pathological lesions was based on a thorough description of the condition. As detailed in Buikstra and Ubelaker (1994b), bone has a limited response to any kind of physiological disruption and it can be broken down into four basic categories: osteoclastic or resorptive lesions, osteoblastic or proliferative lesions, lesions related to trauma, and a miscellaneous category rarely used when the other three do not quite fit the observed condition. After scoring the bone lesion within these large descriptive categories, a further assessment can be made. For example, if there was an osteoclastic or resorptive lesion, it can be further described by choosing among the following: superficial cortex only, subcortical involvement, granular walled, stellate, porotic hyperostosis, osteoporosis or osteopenia, and a miscellaneous category for all other descriptors. If there was an osteoblastic or proliferative lesion, it can be further described in the following manner: cortical pitting/striations only, periostitis with subperiosteal apposition, osteomyelitis with destruction of the cortex, a combination of the preceding, osteitis and increase in bone density, osteoma/benign tumor, osteophytosis, and a miscellaneous category. Location and status of the lesion are likewise recorded using a series of prompted responses.

Estimation of age at death and sex

Estimation of age at death for all individuals and sex estimates for adult individuals is critical to any analysis that involves interpretations of demography, illness and death, and differential susceptibility of subgroups in the larger population. Age at death and sex form the basis for all subsequent analyses, and errors or biases at that level have an impact that multiplies as one begins to do more statistical manipulations of the data. Most analyses of death, diet, and disease involve the partitioning of individuals by age and sex according to a variety of observed conditions such as pathologies or metrics.

Skeletal populations are more readily diagnosed for age and sex than are individuals. Errors are minimized by use of multiple methodologies. Accuracy of age at death and sex estimates are also greatly improved by understanding the range of variability of a population. Whole skeletons within a given population can be used as references for partial skeletons. Differences in morbidity and mortality between males and females have important implications for the maintenance, longevity, and social organization of human groups. The correct determination of sex of skeletal remains is very important to the study of ancient behavior and population dynamics.

Because many human remains are often fragmented, partial skeletons or single bones such as the pelvis, cranium, or femur can be used. The measurements and observations from the pelvis generally include the angle of the sciatic notch, the presence or absence of the preauricular sulcus, the magnitude of the subpubic angle, the width of the medial aspect of the ischiopubic ramus, and the ischiopubic index (Figure 2.6). The cranium provides a number of sexually dimorphic indicators such as the length of the mastoid process, the degree of prominence of the muscular ridges (temporal line, nuchal crest, supraorbital ridges, and the posterior root of the zygomatic process), the bicondylar breadth (width) of the mandible, the breadth of the ascending ramus of the mandible, and the palatal index. For the femur, the vertical diameter of the head and the bicondylar width can be used in sex assignment.

Infants, children, and teenagers can be aged by dental eruption and calcification and secondarily by long bone growth and epiphyseal union. Dental development is based on comparing the degree of calcification and, when appropriate, the sequence of eruption. Subadult dentitions in the 6- to 18-year age range provide a functional rate of wear for each of the three molars. The rate of wear determined from these individuals can then be used to estimate age of adults by means of seriation and reference to those of "known" ages.

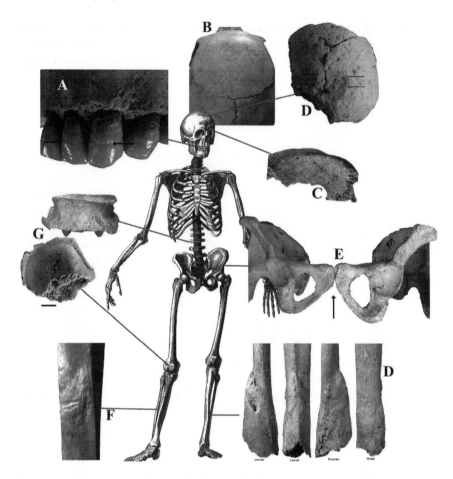

FIGURE 2.6 A composite showing the kinds of indicators of stress that can be seen on bone and teeth. (A) Linear enamel hypoplasias (dental defects), (B) porotic hyperostosis (healed), (C) cribra orbitalia (healed), (D) Trauma (top: cranial depression fracture, bottom: displaced tibial fracture), (E) comparison of sex differences in the pelvis (female on left, male on right), (F) periosteal reaction (healed), (G) osteoarthritic changes (top: vertebral osteophytes, bottom: patellar lipping and eburnation).

Age at death estimation for adults is based on several criteria. Techniques for aging using both the auricular surface and the pubic symphysis are very accurate but take a long time to practice and learn.

Porotic hyperostosis and cribra orbitalia

Porotic hyperostosis (found on the cranial vault) and cribra orbitalia (found in the eye orbits) are two manifestations of a nonspecific nutritional disorder resulting in anemia (Walker et al. 2009). Anemia can potentially affect any bone of the skeleton that is involved in the production of red blood cells. The extent of the involvement of postcranial, as well as cranial bones, usually indicate how severe an anemia is and whether it is associated with genetic abnormalities of hemoglobin or with nutritionally induced anemia (Stuart-Macadam 1987). These lesions are produced by bone marrow proliferation that is diagnostic of anemia. The lesion, as the name implies, has a very porous (coral-like) appearance that develops when diploë (the trabecular portion of the cranial bone that separates the inner and outer surfaces) expands outward (Figure 2.6). With the expansion of the diploë, the outer layer of bone becomes thinner and may eventually disappear, exposing the trabecular bone (diploë), which is quite porous.

The lesions of porotic hyperostosis typically involve thinning and destruction of the outer tables of the cranial vault, accompanied by thickening and exposure of the deeper diploic tissue. Porotic hyperostosis is usually symmetrically distributed and presents as a tight cluster of small porous openings that are visible to the naked eye.

The scoring system distinguishes lesions by severity in expression, location, and amount of remodeling that had occurred. Remodeling in this case means the amount of new bone that has formed in response to the lesion because almost all bone destruction triggers new bone formation. If the disease persists, the effect of remodeling will not be seen because bone will be destroyed as quickly as it is formed. If the disease ceases or lessens, however, there will be a visible replacement of formerly diseased bone with newly mineralized bone. Thus, the amount of healing is subject to the length of time that the disease has been acting on bone, the severity of the disease response, the speed of new bone formation, and the overall health status of the individual.

Nonspecific infection

Although it is true that only a limited number of disease conditions leave diagnostic markers on the skeletal system, it is fortunate for skeletal biologists that some common and highly prevalent microorganisms that cause illness do initiate changes in the morphology of bone tissue. Lesions that affect bone are primarily from chronic conditions. Acute or epidemic conditions do not usually affect the skeleton because microbial attack is swift and death occurs soon after (Ortner and Putschar 1985). The two types of infection (chronic and acute) provide different kinds of information concerning past populations (Figure 2.6). Epidemics reveal information on population responses to relatively short-term crises and high death rates. Chronic (and typically nonlethal) conditions are important to track at the community level because it may be these illnesses that shed the most light on everyday occurrences of nutritional adequacy, diet, the level of transmissible diseases, and the state of waste disposal and hygiene. In other words, low-level, lingering, but nonlethal bouts of infection can reveal something about lifestyle and group living that the more virulent and epidemic infections cannot.

Most examples of infectious disease found on skeletal remains are nonspecific in nature. That is, the lesions can be caused by a number of pathological conditions, and differential diagnosis concerning exact etiology is often difficult. The most common causes of infectious disease are microorganisms such as *Staphylococcus* and *Streptococcus*, making up nearly 90% of cases (Ortner and Putschar 1985: 106). The general inflammatory response always begins as a vascular phenomenon (Ortner and Putschar 1985: 104). Dilated capillary walls burst and cells normally retained in the circulatory system are released. These cells, which include albumins, globulins, and fibrinogen, along with leukocytes, travel to the bacteria. Leukocytes can engulf and destroy bacteria, or the bacteria, if numerous or virulent, can disintegrate the leukocytes and continue to increase in number. Pus is produced when leukocytes (along with proteins and fibrin) are at the site of the bacterial invasion. The severity of the inflammatory response is tempered by the number of microorganisms left to multiply in the system.

There is some disagreement among paleopathologists as to the use of descriptive terms and diagnostic criteria. For example, osteomyelitis results from the introduction of pyogenic infection (pus producing – not all infections are), usually via the bloodstream, and the skeletal response involves the periosteum, cortex, and medullary cavity of the bone. It results from a systemic bacterial invasion (usually from bacteria such as *Staphylococcus* or *Streptococcus*) of the body. Osteitis is another form of this phenomenon, but the reaction is primarily localized within the cortical bone. Osteitis can only be radiologically diagnosed. Periostitis occurs when the reaction is restricted to the outer shaft or periosteum. It can occur as a direct response to a skin infection, through trauma, through systemic bacterial invasions, or from other soft-tissue infections, such as muscle or tendon (Ortner and Putschar 1985).

Diagnosis and cause of the infection can be difficult. Some paleopathologists have advocated using general descriptive categories for classification of the skeletal changes (Larsen 1987; Martin et al. 1991; Palkovich 1980; Powell 1988). Referred to as nonspecific infectious lesions, the skeletal lesions are categorized as periosteal reactions because most of the skeletal response takes place on the outer periosteal surface of bone. For assignment of severity (trace/slight, moderate, or severe) the following kinds of categories are generally used, (a) the extent of the involvement, (b) the nature of the tissue destruction, and (c) the overall amount of destruction. Location of the lesion is specific to the bone; for flat cranial and pelvic bones, the location was recorded for quadrants such as upper left, and for long bones, the location was recorded with respect to proximal, distal, and mid-shaft locations. Additionally, cranial bones should be analyzed for periosteal reactions endocranially, when possible.

The amount of healing should be recorded as no healing (or active and unremodeled), some healing (remodeling in progress), and totally healed (with only remnant pitting or scars from the previous insult. Unremodeled lesions generally display a very fibrous and vascularized irregular new layer of bone. Remodeled lesions show resorption and redistribution of new bone as it becomes incorporated into the normal cortex. It appears as dense, smooth bone with some minor but patterned irregularities.

Periosteal reactions due to infectious diseases are usually systemic in nature, affecting multiple long bones, bilaterally in most cases. When scoring a femur for periosteal reactions, as an example, other long bones should be observed in concert to see if they were involved as well. If there were other bones involved, the femur should be scored as having a periosteal reaction. If it seemed to be an isolated event, it is considered to be a localized traumatic response and scored as a trauma. Ortner and Putschar (1985) point out that trauma-induced periosteal reactions tend to be small, localized, and nondestructive. Systemic infectious diseases tend to be generalized and destructive, and they often affect multiple bones. Thus, the label of periosteal reaction should be reserved to confer the status of systemic infectious disease response.

Enamel defects

Enamel hypoplasias, defined as developmental defects in enamel thickness, are easily studied and provide an indelible indicator of periods of stress during tooth crown development (prenatally to 12 months for deciduous teeth, and birth to 7 years for permanent teeth; Figure 2.6). They have been increasingly favored as indicators of stress in studies of precontact and historic skeletal populations. In the vast majority of cases, defects found in archaeological materials fit a chronologic pattern and appear to be the result of systemic metabolic stress (Rose et al. 1985). Thus, they are frequently referred to as chronologic or linear enamel hypoplasias (LEHs), reflecting the linear and chronologic nature of the defects caused by systemic stress at a specific point in time. Although enamel hypoplasias due to systemic stresses are common and easily discerned from defects due to nonsystemic factors, it is difficult to attribute a more exact cause to these defects.

Goodman and Rose (1990) have proposed a threshold model for considering the etiology of LEH development as the additive consequences of four factors: (1) unknown etiological factors, (2) underlying nutritional status, (3) disease, and (4) tooth susceptibility. Although the exact nature of the physiological stress cannot be deduced, the model illustrates how one or several factors can come together to place an individual at risk for developing dental defects. In general, the data suggest that many precontact populations are stressed to some degree, and when compared with contemporary populations from underdeveloped areas, they often have similar or higher frequencies of defects. The chronology of defects suggests that the postweaning period is particularly stressful. Variability in rates within and between populations provides evidence that this indicator is sensitive to stress differences across age, sex, and temporally divided subgroups and between populations.

The data are generally presented both as "chronologies" of defects and as overall frequencies of defects per tooth. Because most teeth exhibited some degree of attrition, one or more developmental periods were frequently recorded as missing. Therefore, to increase sample size, the tooth-specific rates are based on the frequency of defects per middle and cervical third.

LEH data can also be used to estimate the age of weaning in many populations. Because weaning is a traumatic process to the infant, LEHs can often form during this time because of disruptions in growth of the enamel. The age of weaning can be used to discuss issues of interbirth interval as well. Typically a woman will not begin to ovulate until breastfeeding of one infant ceases. If weaning occurs around the age of 1, for example, a woman would be able to become pregnant again around that time, giving an interbirth interval of approximately 2 years.

Subadult size

The ability to assess subadult growth and adult morphology from skeletal remains provides a powerful tool for the assessment of nutritional status and disease states in archaeological populations. Metric studies of skeletal populations have great potential for providing information concerning variation in adaptation to environments. Variation in size among contemporary groups, at least to the age of 10, is almost completely dependent on the environment. The problem of controlling for genetic differences among populations is reduced in studies where variation is examined in time-successive populations or among groups with known genetic relatedness. Thus, it is possible to discern environmental changes and differences based on their effect on skeletal morphology. Despite the potential for growth studies in ancient populations, a number of practical factors have limited their development. Archaeological series are frequently plagued by small sample size, particularly after 5 years of age. This is the primary reason for the paucity of comparative studies of growth of ancient subadults.

There is the technical problem of measuring long bones with and without epiphyses (the unattached growing ends of long bones), which are frequently lost in the very young. This irregularity has the potential of adding considerable measurement error. Likewise, the death assemblage entails a cross-sectional design (i.e., individuals are measured at a single point in time at death) and can be used to infer periods of peak stress only when conditions are relatively stable over time. Cemetery-based studies do not represent the healthy or "average" child but, rather, those who died. It is difficult to ascertain the degree to which the analysis of a "death assemblage" affects the obtained estimates of growth, though it clearly biases toward a more dampened curve. Also typical is poorer preservation of the ends of the long bones in the young; this bone is relatively fragile and may not preserve well during excavation and/or lab storage.

Adult size and stature

Although the measurement of long-bone lengths and stature and the interpretations based on these data are relatively simple, a great deal of recent controversy has surrounded the measurement and interpretation of robusticity and sexual dimorphism. This controversy involves the methods of measuring robusticity and sexual dimorphism as well as the meaning of these measures. Sexual dimorphism is most frequently computed as the simple ratio of mean male to mean female heights (Gray and Wolf 1980) or ratios of bone lengths to thickness (Bass 1971). In either case, it is possible to compare changes in robusticity through time or among groups and to compare the relative differences in robusticity between males and females (sexual dimorphism).

The key question here concerns the use and meaning of these measures. Kennedy (1998) presents an exhaustive account of the ways in which the human skeleton can provide information on division of labor, possible occupational specialization, and biological features representative of specific activities. Other researchers have suggested that robusticity indexes may provide a means of analyzing the physical demands placed on adults (Larsen 1987). The relative degree of robusticity between males and females can provide a means for assessing the degree and type of labor delegated to males and females.

Degenerative disease

Osteoarthritis is among the oldest and most commonly known diseases afflicting humans. Measuring the amount of arthritic involvement with skeletal remains is sometimes difficult because of the potentially large number of areas to be assessed (each vertebra and all joint systems) and the range of variation in bony response among individuals (Figure 2.6). While many factors may contribute to the breakdown of skeletal tissue, the primary cause of osteoarthritis is related to biomechanical wear and tear and functional stress (Ortner and Putschar 1985). Biomechanical stress is most apparent at the articular surfaces of long bone joint systems and is referred to as degenerative joint disease (DJD). The patterning of DJD has been linked to behavioral factors, and individuals who habitually engage in activities that put strain on the joint system are more likely to demonstrate a breakdown in bone (Merbs 1983). There also may be a relationship between DJD and other health problems.

DJD is generally defined by changes in the articular surface areas of joint systems. Following the exposure of subchondral bone, the articular surface regions become pitted, with marginal lipping and erosion; eventually eburnation takes place. Eburnation is the formation of a very hard callus on bone surfaces that are rubbing together without being cushioned by lubricating fluids. DJD is not an inflammatory disease but develops with age and the breakdown of the cartilage and lubricating system. The condition is slowly progressive but is not found to occur in all older adults in the same form. Thus, the condition probably is the accumulation of years of alterations of the articular cartilage and breakdown of the joint and occurs with extreme variability across individuals. Lifestyle and activity play an important role in either buffering an individual from arthritis or enhancing the chance that the condition will appear. For instance, a professional athlete may begin to exhibit DJD at a far younger age than an individual who does not engage in consistent rigorous exercise and activity. The weight-bearing joints such as the lower back, hip, and knees and those exposed to chronic trauma such as the shoulder and elbow are most frequently affected (Jurmain 1991). The pattern, distribution, severity, and onset by age class and sex in adults can be used to interpret the role of cultural activity, as well in the overall understanding of quality of life for individuals within the community.

Vertebral osteophytosis is a form of degeneration that is characterized by lipping (extra bony growths usually in long spikes) on the vertebral bodies. This has been associated with changes in the intervertebral discs. Commonly found in ancient and modern populations, this degeneration typically begins at 30 years of age and affects almost all individuals by the age of 60. The lipping may range from a slight sharpness to complete fusion of contiguous vertebral bodies.

For analysis of the bony response to biomechanical wear and tear on both joint systems and vertebral elements, we scored for two basic morphological characteristics. These include the bony growth of osteophytes (hypertrophic osteogenesis) and the destruction of the joint surface (macroporosity and bone breakdown; Mann and Murphy 1990). On both joint systems and vertebral elements, the degenerative changes occur on the joint surface (where two bones articulate), the areas that are contiguous with but peripheral to the joint, and on various parts of the bone that come indirectly into contact with other bones in the movement of joint systems (such as vertebral spines and processes and various fossae and landmarks on long bones).

The systematic assessment of DJD and vertebral osteophytosis can provide an indicator of lifestyle and work habits in ancient populations. However, clinicians working in the area of gerontology and arthritis today caution the direct correlation of osteoarthritic changes and pain and dysfunction (Jurmain 1999). Any morphological changes less than total fusion of vertebral bodies or joint systems cannot be directly linked to inability of individuals to function nor can severity of osteoarthritis be linked directly to habitual use of the body in certain occupations (Merbs 1983).

Trauma

Traumatic lesions encompass a broad range of clinical classifications that include fractures, crushing injuries, wounds caused by weapons and other devices, dislocations, and an assortment of degenerative problems such as exostoses, osteochondritis dissecans, and spondylolysis (Wedel and Galloway 2014). These types of injury are primarily caused by physical force or by contact with sharp or blunt objects. The cause of traumatic lesions can often be determined by analyzing the intensity and direction of the force. Interpretations concerning trauma are generally more direct than other kinds of pathologies, especially if the age, sex, and health status of the individuals are known. For example, if the traumatic lesion occurs with periosteal reaction and infectious inflammation, a severe condition that originally involved the soft tissue, as well as the bone, is implied. Simple fractures that do break through the soft tissue and skin rarely become infected. Also, the degree to which a trauma has healed provides a clue to the relationship between the event and the possible contribution of the trauma to morbidity and mortality.

Fractures in long bones, ribs, and vertebrae are the most frequently reported of the traumatic lesions in the paleopathology literature and the most easily assessed (Walker 2001). Fractures can be classified into a number of categories ranging from micro stress fractures to greenstick breaks to comminuted and complete breaks (Figure 2.6). However, the response of bone to any kind of fracture is the same. There is immediate vascularization and new bone forms within a few days after the break occurs. Calcium salts are released from dead bone fragments and from the living bone and are used in calcifying the callous matrix that forms a binding and connecting sheath around the two fractured ends. Within two weeks, calcification is underway, and the internal remodeling and reorganization of the bone callus begins. The healing process can last for months or years, depending on the age and health of the individual and the severity of the break (Ortner and Putschar 1985). Even a poorly aligned or unaligned bone will eventually mend itself if infection does not interfere with the healing process. The process occurs much more quickly in children than in adults. The union of two bone ends can be complete in four to six weeks in children, while in adults the process may take four or five months (Merbs 1989).

Depression fractures occur most frequently on crania and have been reported for many individuals in the archaeological record (Walker 2001). Merbs (1989) defines a depression fracture as one produced by a force applied to just one side of a bone whereas compression fractures are produced when there is force from two sides; however, these distinctions can be difficult to make in archaeological specimens and shallow holes in the cranium are often referred to as depression fractures. Depression fractures usually result from a blow to the head by a blunt object. On the cranium, this results in a depression in the outer bony table, and if the skin is broken, there will be some infectious response as well. The pathophysiological responses are similar in cranial fractures: there is a coagulation of blood at the site with resultant formation of new bone at the fracture site. After the site has completely remodeled and healed, usually a telltale depression in the cranium at the original site remains.

The location of the cranial depression fracture can be informative. Forensic research has been prolific on the role of differentiating between accidental and intentional interpersonal trauma with respect to cranial fractures. Wedel and Galloway (2014) have compiled forensic sources to give a thorough overview of the direction of force and how various cranial and facial fractures (such as LeFort and Tripod fractures) are caused. With respect to the cranial vault, fractures falling above the "hat brim line" are more likely to be the result of interpersonal violence, while those falling below are more likely the result of accident (Kremer et al. 2008; Maxeiner and Ehrlich 2000). This line is roughly horizontal, occurring just superior to the orbital margins and continuing around the skull, leaving the mastoid processes and inferior occipital and prime areas for accidental fracture. This research is based on numerous surveys of hospital intake forms using modern samples from various European countries (e.g., Erdmann et al. 2008; He et al. 2007; Johansen et al. 1997; Kremer et al. 2008; Lee et al. 2007; Lewis and Peruisea 1959).

In archaeological specimens, fractures and traumatic lesions in the process of healing or with complete healing are fairly straightforward in diagnosis. However, when traumatic events occur around the time of death, it can be difficult to distinguish the perimortem bone damage from postmortem changes. Although numerous researchers have attempted to isolate the differences between perimortem and postmortem breaks, without other information regarding the context of the burial and the nature of the death, it is almost impossible to make firm diagnostic interpretations (White 1992). For example, although bone crushed from the blow of a blunt object will shatter bone differently when it is fresh versus later when it is dry, recovery of all of the pieces of bone is necessary for distinguishing the timing of the breaks (Mann and Murphy 1990). This is because of the way that the term *perimortem* is used in bioarchaeology. We use this term to indicate that the bone has sufficient collagen to respond as though it were vital; that is, it will bend before it breaks. This process can take a significant amount of time, making the identification of peri- and postmortem fractures (if those occur relatively soon after death) very difficult. Dry bone, bone that has lost significant amounts of collagen from the bony matrix through either decomposition or possibly burning, will respond differently. The amount of bone beveling and the type of fracturing (spiral vs. straight) have been used important indicators of the timing of the traumatic event; however, in reality these are related to plasticity of the bone at the time of the event. Another example of problematic diagnosis is that the nonunion of a fractured end of a long bone could be interpreted upon recovery as an amputation if the distal end is not also recovered.

Bones that are in the process of healing need to be cautiously interpreted. The rate of repair and remodeling is modified by age, type of fracture, where the fracture occurs, degree of vascularization, amount of motion between the broken ends, and presence of infection. Infection at the site of the bone fracture can seriously hamper repair, and the determination of the timing of the fracture on archaeological specimens is rarely possible without determining the nature of the healing process in conjunction with a wide number of variables having to do with the individual. Careful observation of the entire skeleton of individuals with trauma can aid in the understanding of not only the timing of the event but also related health problems. For example, a healed fractured femoral neck may contribute significantly to osteoporosis and osteoarthritis in adjacent bones (Merbs 1989). Asymmetry in body proportions may occur when unaligned bones heal making compensatory biomechanical changes necessary. These kinds of secondary changes are important to note because they could contribute significantly to our understanding of the quality of life and changes in health that may accompany a traumatic lesion.

The extent to which fractures disable and deform individuals can sometimes be assessed, and this information can be very important in understanding community health dynamics. Adults crippled by unaligned fractures could be less productive in subsistence activities. Furthermore, lifelong accumulated adjustments in the form of limping and inefficient gait would also enhance osteoarthritic changes in joints and other health problems.

Specific types of trauma can provide a direct inference about behavioral patterns. Certain activities predispose individuals to certain types of accidental or intentional trauma. Moreover, various forms of interpersonal violence (warfare, scalping, mutilation, lacerations, cannibalism) and of surgical intervention (trephination, amputation) can sometimes be specifically identified (e.g., White 1992). Fractures of the forearm (radius and ulna) can reveal information about the activities of the group. A common fracture seen in many archaeological specimens is at the distal end where the wrist is located, and these are generally referred to a Colles fracture. They result from an individual who is falling extending the arms to break or soften the fall. Fractures that occur farther up along the forearm may result from the raising of the arm in front of the face to ward off a blow (parry fractures; Walker 2001).

The patterning of the trauma within a population can be very enlightening regarding environments conducive to accidents, as well as inter- and intragroup strife. The occurrence of multiple injuries, injuries from artifacts and weapons, and the demographic pattern by age and sex can provide insights into the use of force or violence in a society or the potential problems in lifestyle and subsistence activities that lead to accidents.

Dental wear, caries, and antemortem loss

Teeth can be categorized according to the following conditions: (1) present, (2) lost antemortem, (3) lost postmortem, (4) unerupted, (5) agenesized (congenital absence), and (6) unknown (due to missing alveolar bone; Hillson 1996). The distinction between antemortem and postmortem loss is made based on the presence of bone remodeling in the root socket. Although this is a standard technique, it may slightly under-enumerate the number of teeth lost before death. For our purposes here, the most important category involves the frequency of antemortem loss versus the frequency of combined present teeth and those lost after death.

Several dental pathologies are of interest in reconstructing past lived experience. These are dental wear (attrition), carious lesions (cavities), and antemortem tooth loss, in addition to LEHs (discussed earlier). *Dental wear* is a general term referring to the loss of the occlusal or chewing surface of teeth and to the interproximal surface between teeth. Wear may be divided into two components, dental attrition, due to direct tooth-on-tooth contact, and dental abrasion, due to the introduction of foreign matter.

Antemortem tooth loss is also of interest both because it reflects dental health and because it may entail functional impairment. Antemortem loss is frequently associated with the above noted dental conditions: dental abscessing, extreme alveolar resorption, excess attrition, and caries. Antemortem loss may, in fact, be due to any one or a combination of these factors. Antemortem tooth loss represents the ultimate diminution of functional, masticatory capacity. Rampant tooth loss may have a strong effect on the health and nutritional status of the individual. With endemic tooth loss, foods become increasingly more difficult to chew, thus limiting the range of dietary options. Based on the assumption that most dental pathologies increase with agriculture, one might hypothesize that tooth loss will also increase as a secondary effect of dietary shifts.

Identification of carious lesions (cavities) provides insight into both diet and individual oral health. Severe occlusal carious lesions are common and, in combination with fissure and cuspal caries, provide a measure of the total amount of occlusal surface caries. Like the other pathologies, data concerning carious lesions should be examined with respect to biological data such as age at death and sex.

Entheseal changes

Activity patterns and habitual physical stress can be observed in the attachment sites of muscles that are in specific places along the bone surfaces, and these roughened areas are called enthuses (Villotte and Knüsel 2013). The raised and roughened areas serve to anchor tendons and ligaments to the bone and to stabilize habitual or chronically stressful movement. Entheses can be observed in degrees (none to slight, moderate, and severe expressions) along the attachment sites of major long bones to assess how much mechanical loading was being done over the course of the lifetime prior to death.

There is increasingly an understanding of how these data can be interpreted. There is a general understanding of the importance of interpreting entheseal changes within a careful framework that takes into account the age and sex of the individual under study (Milella et al. 2011; 2012). With this developing understanding of how best to interpret this line of data, new methodologies have been published in a special issue of the *International Journal of Osteoarchaeology* by Henderson and Alves Cardosa (2013).

To sum up

The indicators of stress reviewed here are not an exhaustive survey of every available type of analysis. It is a selection that maximizes information on demography and disease and allows future researchers to rapidly evaluate what is presented here for comparative purposes (Table 2.1). Indeed, each indicator of stress could form the basis of a major comparative study, but that is not the purpose of this volume. We have been selective about what we focus on; these form a basis for understanding health and activity in the past. By no means, do these 7 characteristics represent the total that can be used to understand lived experience in the past.

The fundamental biological needs of humans have not changed in thousands (maybe even millions) of years. However, the means for expressing and satisfying those basic needs continue to vary greatly from culture to culture. As anthropologists, we are intrigued with the patterns of variability because they teach us something about the capacity of humans to change, modify, adapt, and alter their cultural and behavioral responses to meet their needs. Much of our future survival

TABLE 2.1 Summary of skeletal and dental indicators of stress

Data	How Data Is Used	Citation
Age at Death and Sex Estimation	Demography, sex differences, population structure	Buikstra and Ubelaker (1994a), Bass (1995), Scheuer and Black (2000, 2004), Ubelaker (1999)
Cribra Orbitalia Porotic Hyperostosis	Examination of anemia, nutritional deficiency	Stuart-Macadam and Kent (1992), Ortner (2003), Martin et al. (1985), and others
Periosteal Reaction	Infectious diseases, changes in activity patterns	Ortner (2003), Aufderheide and Rodriguez-Martin (1998), and others
Linear Enamel Hypoplasia	General childhood stress indicator, estimate age at weaning	Goodman and Rose (1990), Hillson (1996), and others.
Caries	Dietary shifts, general nutrition, age and sex differences	Cook and Buikstra (1979), Costa Jr. (1980), Lukacs (1996, 2008), Shollmeyer and Turner (2004), Walker and Erlandson (1986), and others
Degenerative Joint Disease Osteoarthritis	Changes in activity patterns, sexual division of labor	Aufderheide and Rodríguez-Martin (2011), Brown et al. (2008), Mann and Murphy (1990), Ortner (2003), and others
Trauma	Interpersonal violence, social/class distinctions	Walker (1989, 1997), Brink et al. (1998), Brink (2009), and others.

may depend on our ability to recognize the limits of human responses and coping mechanisms, especially in adverse and extreme conditions of environmental catastrophe, malnutrition and famine, and rapidly changing ecological, political, and economic conditions.

Several major points need to be emphasized for the analysis of demography and health. First, human biological remains are essential to an understanding of the adaptation of populations. Second, the biological remains can provide important insights into the adaptation of human groups for the last 5,000 years, but their full potential has yet to be realized. Third, with the development of good chronology, changes over time, and an understanding of environmental changes, regional analyses of the biocultural adjustments made by human groups can be understood and applied to solving today's problems.

Skeletal analysis used as anthropological inquiry takes advantage of dietary and health data to provide time depth and geographic variability to the understanding of short- and long-term consequences and mechanisms of adaptation to change. Studies on health and disease must incorporate skeletal remains to address health status over time and to provide indisputable data on aspects of diet, health, and death. It is difficult to assess how fully human groups perceive the deterioration of health, but the question of changes in human behavior to cope with disease and death is an intriguing one. Bioarchaeological data permit us to enter into these larger debates.

References

Armelagos GJ. 2003. Bioarchaeology as Anthropology. In: Gillespie SD, and Nichols DL, editors. Archaeology Is Anthropology. Washington, DC: Archaeological Papers of the American Anthropological Association, No. 13. p 27–41.

Armelagos GJ, Sirak K, Werkema T, and Turner BL. 2014. Analysis of Nutritional Disease in Prehistory: The Search for Scurvy in Antiquity and Today. International Journal of Paleopathology 5:9–17.

Aufderheide AC, and Rodriguez-Martin C. 1998. The Cambridge Encyclopedia of Human Paleopathology. Cambridge: Cambridge University Press.

Aufderheide AC, and Rodríguez-Martin C. 2011. The Cambridge Encyclopedia of Human Paleopathology, reprint edition. Cambridge: Cambridge University Press.

Baadsgaard A, Boutin AT, and Buikstra J, editors. 2012. Breathing New Life into the Evidence of Death: Contemporary Approaches to Bioarchaeology. Santa Fe, NM: School for Advanced Research Press.

Bass WM. 1971. Human Osteology: A Laboratory and Field Manual. Columbia: Missouri Archaeological Society.

Bass WM. 1987. Human Osteology: A Laboratory and Field Manual, third edition. Columbia: Missouri Archaeological Society.

Bass WM. 1995. Human Osteology: A Laboratory and Field Manual. Columbia: Missouri Archaeological Society.

Baustian KM. 2010. Health Status of Infants and Children from the Bronze Age Tomb at Tell Abraq, United Arab Emirates [Unpublished MA thesis]. Las Vegas: University of Nevada.

Bonogofsky M, editor. 2011. The Bioarchaeology of the Human Head: Decapitation, Decoration, and Deformation. Gainesville: University Press of Florida.

Brickley M, and Ives R. 2008. The Bioarchaeology of Metabolic Bone Disease. London: Academic Press.

Brink O. 2009. When Violence Strikes the Head, Neck, and Face. The Journal of TRAUMA: Injury, Infection, and Critical Care 67(1):147–151.

Brink O, Vesterby A, and Jensen J. 1998. Pattern of Injuries Due to Interpersonal Violence. Injury, International Journal of the Care of the Injured 29(9):705–709.

Brown KR, Pollintine P, and Adams MA. 2008. Biomechanical Implications of Degenerative Joint Disease in the Apophyseal Joints of Human Thoracic and Lumbar Vertebrae. American Journal of Physical Anthropology 136:318–326.

Buikstra J, Baadsgaard A, and Boutin AT. 2012. Introduction. In: Baadsgaard A, Boutin AT, and Buikstra J, editors. Breathing New Life into the Evidence of Death: Contemporary Approaches to Bioarchaeology. Santa Fe, NM: School for Advanced Research Press. p 3–29.

Buikstra JE. 1977. Biocultural Dimensions of Archaeological Study: A Regional Perspective. In: Blakely RL, editor. Biocultural Adaptation in Prehistoric America. Athens: Southern Anthropological Society Proceedings, No. 11, University of Georgia Press. p 67–84.

Buikstra JE. 2006. On to the 21st Century. In: Buikstra JE, and Beck LA, editors. Bioarchaeology: The Contextual Analysis of Human Remains. Burlington, VT: Academic Press.
p 347–358.

Buikstra JE, and Cook DC. 1980. Palaeopathology: An American Account. Annual Review
of Anthropology 9:433–470.

Buikstra JE, and Roberts CA, editors. 2012. The Global History of Paleopathology: Pioneers
and Prospects. Oxford: Oxford University Press.

Buikstra JE, and Ubelaker DH. 1994a. Standards for Data Collection from Human Skeletal
Remains. Fayetteville: Arkansas Archaeological Survey.

Buikstra JE, and Ubelaker DH, editors. 1994b. Standards for Data Collection from
Human Skeletal Remains: Proceedings of a Seminar at the Field Museum of Nat-
ural History, Organized by Jonathan Haas. Fayetteville: Arkansas Archaeological
Survey.

Carlson RL, and Armelagos GJ. 1965. Cradleboard Hoods, not Corsets. Science 149.3680
(1965):204–205.

Clarkin JF, and Levy KN. 2004. The Influence of Client Variables on Psychotherapy. In:
Lambert MJ, editor. Bergin and Garfield's Handbook of Psychotherapy and Behavior
Change, fifth edition. New York: John Wiley & Sons. p 194–226.

Cohen MN, and Armelagos GJ, editors. 1984. Paleopathology at the Origins of Agriculture.
New York: Academic Press.

Colton HS. 1936. The Rise and Fall of the Prehistoric Population of Northern Arizona.
Science 84(2181):337–343.

Cook DC, and Buikstra JE. 1979. Health and Differential Survival in Prehistoric Populations: Prenatal Dental Defects. American Journal of Physical Anthropology 51(4):
649–664.

Costa RL, Jr. 1980. Incidence of Caries and Abscesses in Archaeological Eskimo Skeletal
Samples from Point Hope and Kodiak Island, Alaska. American Journal of Physical
Anthropology 52:501–514.

Deloria V, Jr. 1989. A Simple Question of Humanity: The Moral Dimensions of the Reburial
Issue. Native American Rights Fund Legal Review 4.

DiGangi EA, and Moore MK, editors. 2012. Research Methods in Human Skeletal Biology.
Oxford: Academic Press.

Erdmann D, Follmar KE, DeBruijn M, Bruno AD, Jung SH, Edelman D, Mukundan S, and
Marcus JR. 2008. A Retrospective Analysis of Facial Fracture Etiologies. Annals of Plastic
Surgery 60(4):398–403.

Goodman AH, and Armelagos GJ. 1988. Childhood Stress and Decreased Longevity in
a Prehistoric Population. American Anthropologist 90:936–944.

Goodman AH, Martin D, Armelagos GJ, and Clark G. 1984. Indications of Stress from Bones
and Teeth. In: Cohen MN, and Armelagos GJ, editors. Paleopathology at the Origins of
Agriculture. New York: Academic Press. p 13–49.

Goodman AH, and Rose JC. 1990. Assessment of Systemic Physiological Pertubations from
Dental Enamel Hypoplasias and Associated Histological Structures. Yearbook of Physical
Anthropology 33:59–110.

Grauer AL. 2012. Introduction: The Scope of Paleopathology. In: Grauer AL, editor. A Companion to Paleopathology. Malden, MA: Blackwell Publishing. p 1–14.

Gray PJ, and Wolf LD. 1980. Height and Sexual Dimorphism of Stature among Human
Societies. American Journal of Physical Anthropology 53:441–456.

Harkin ME, and Lewis DR. 2007. Native Americans and the Environment: Perspectives on
the Ecological Indian. Lincoln: University of Nebraska Press.

He D, Zhang Y, and Ellis E, III. 2007. Panfacial Fractures: Analysis of 33 Cases Treated Late. Journal of Oral and Maxillofacial Surgery 65(12):2459–2465.

Henderson CY, and Alves Cardoso F. 2013. Special Issue Entheseal Changes and Occupation: Technical and Theoretical Advances and Their Applications. International Journal of Osteoarchaeology 23(2):127–134.

Hillson S. 1996. Dental Anthropology. Cambridge: Cambridge University Press.

Hooten EA. 1930. Indians of Pecos Pueblo: A Study of Their Skeletal Remains. New Haven, CT: Yale University Press.

Hrdlička A. 1908. Physiological and Medical Observations among the Indians of the Southwestern United States and Northern Mexico. Bulletin, No 37, Bureau of American Ethnology. Washington, DC: Smithsonian Institution Press. p 103–112.

Johansen A, Evans RJ, Stone MD, Richmond PW, Lo SV, and Woodhouse KW. 1997. Fracture Incidence in England and Wales: A Study Based on the Population of Cardiff. Injury, International Journal of the Care of the Injured 28:655–660.

Jurmain R. 1991. Paleoepidemiology of Trauma in a Prehistoric Central California Population. In: Ortner DJ, and Aufderheide AC, editors. Human Paleopathology: Current synthesis and Future Option. Washington, DC: Smithsonian Institution Press. p 241–248.

Jurmain R. 1999. Stories from the Skeleton: Behavioral Reconstruction in Osteoarchaeology. Amsterdam: Gordon and Breach Publishers.

Kennedy KAR. 1998. Markers of Occupational Stress: Conspectus and Prognosis of Research. International Journal of Osteoarchaeology 8:305–310.

Knudson KJ, and Stojanowski CM. 2009. Bioarchaeology and Identity in the Americas. Gainesville: University Press of Florida.

Krech S. 1999. The Ecological Indian. New York: Norton.

Kremer C, Racette S, Dionne C-A, and Sauvageau A. 2008. Discrimination of Falls and Blows in Blunt Head Trauma: Systematic Study of the Hat Brim Line Rule in Relation to Skull Fractures. Journal of Forensic Sciences 53(3):716–719.

Kunitz SJ. 1983. Disease Change and the Role of Medicine: The Navajo Experience. Berkeley: University of California Press.

Larsen CS. 1987. Bioarchaeological Interpretations of Subsistence Economy and Behavior from Human Skeletal Remains. In: Schiffer MB, editor. Advances in Archaeological Method and Theory, Volume 10. San Diego, CA: Academic Press. p 339–445.

Larsen CS. 2015. Bioarchaeology: Interpreting Behavior from the Human Skeleton. Cambridge: Cambridge University Press.

Lee KH, Snape L, Steenberg LJ, and Worthington J. 2007. Comparison between Interpersonal Violence and Motor Vehicle Accidents in the Aetiology of Maxillofacial Fractures. ANZ Journal of Surgery 77:695–698.

Lewis GK, and Peruisea SC. 1959. The Complex Mandibular Fracture. American Journal of Surgery 97(3):283–296.

Lewis ME. 2009. The Bioarchaeology of Children: Perspectives from Biological and Forensic Anthropology. Cambridge: Cambidge University Press.

Lovejoy C. 1985. Dental Wear in the Libben Population: Its Functional Pattern and Role in the Determination of Adult Skeletal Age at Death. American Journal of Physical Anthropology 68:47–56.

Lukacs JR. 1996. Sex Differences in Dental Caries Rates with the Origin of Agriculture in South Asia. Current Anthropology 37(1):147–153.

Lukacs JR. 2008. Fertility and Agriculture Accentuate Sex Differences in Dental Caries Rates. Current Anthropology 49(5):901–914.

Mann RW, and Murphy SP. 1990. Regional Atlas of Bone Disease: A Guide to Pathalogic and Normal Variation in the Human Skeleton. Springfield, IL: Charles C Thomas.

Marklein K, and Fox SC. In Press. In Morbo et in Morto: Transforming Age and Identity within the Mortuary Context of Oymaağaç Höyük, Northern Turkey. In: Osterholtz AJ, editor. Theoretical Approaches to Analysis and Interpretation of Commingled Human Remains. New York: Springer.

Martin D, Goodman AH, and Armelagos GJ. 1985. Skeletal Pathologies as Indicators of Quality and Quantity of Diet. In: Gilbert RI, Jr., and Mielke JH, editors. The Analysis of Prehistoric Diets. Orlando, FL: Academic Press. p 227–279.

Martin DL, Akins NJ, Goodman AH, and Swedlund AC. 2001. Harmony and Discord: Bioarchaeology of the La Plata Valley. Santa Fe: Museum of New Mexico, Office of Archaeological Studies.

Martin DL, Goodman AH, Armelagos GJ, and Magennis AL. 1991. Black Mesa Anasazi Health: Reconstructing Life from Patterns of Death and Disease. Carbondale: Southern Illinois University Press.

Maxeiner H, and Ehrlich E. 2000. Site, Number and Depth of Wounds of the Scalp in Falls and Blows – A Contribution to the Validity of the So-Called Hat Brim Rule [Original title in German]. Archiv für Kriminologie 205(3–4):82.

McKinlay JB, and McKinlay D. 1974. A Case for Refocusing Upstream: The Political Economy of Illness. In: American Heart Association, editor. Applying Behavioral Science to Cardiovascular Risk. Washington, DC: American Heart Association. p 7–17.

Merbs CF. 1983. Patterns of Activity-Induced Pathology in a Canadian Inuit Population. Archaeological Survey of Canada Mercury Series, No 119. Hull, Ottawa: Canadian Museum of Civilization.

Merbs CF. 1989. Trauma. In: Iscan MY, and Kennedy KAR, editors. Reconstruction of Life from the Skeleton. New York: Alan R. Liss. p 161–199.

Milella M, Giovanna Belcastro M, Zollikofer CPE, and Mariotti V. 2012. The Effect of Age, Sex, and Physical Activity on Entheseal Morphology in a Contemporary Italian Skeletal Collection. American Journal of Physical Anthropology 148(3):379–388.

Milella M, Mariotti V, and Belcastro M. 2011. You Can't Tell a Book by its Cover: The Effects of Age, Sex and Physical Activity on Theseal Changes in an Italian Contemporary Skeletal Collection. 80th Annual Meeting of the American Association of Physical Anthropologists. Minneapolis, MN.

Milner GR, Anderson E, and Smith VG. 1991. Warfare in Late Prehistoric West-Central Illinois. American Antiquity 56(4):581–603.

Moore WM, Silverberg MM, and Read MS. 1972. Nutrition, Growth and Development of North American Indian Children. Washington, DC: U.S. Government Printing Office.

Morris EH. 1939. Archaeological Studies in the La Plata District, Southwestern Colorado and Northwestern New Mexico. Washington, DC: Carnegie Institution of Washington, Pub. 519.

Ortner DJ. 2003. Identification of Pathological Conditions in Human Skeletal Remains. New York: Academic Press.

Ortner DJ, and Putschar WG. 1985. Identification of Pathological Conditions in Human Skeletal Remains. Smithsonian Contributions to Anthropology 28:1–488.

Ortner SB. 2006. Anthropology and Social Theory: Culture, Power, and the Acting Subject. Durham, NC: Duke University Press.

Osterholtz AJ, Bethard JD, Gonciar A, and Nyaradi Z. 2014. Possible Prenatal and Perinatal Scurvy at Telekfalva, Romania. Annual Meeting of the American Association of Physical Anthropologists.

Oxenham M, and Tayles N. 2006. Bioarchaeology of Southeast Asia. Cambridge: Cambridge University Press.

Palkovich AM. 1980. The Arroyo Hondo Skeletal and Mortuary Remains. Santa Fe, NM: School of American Research Press.

Perry MA, and Buikstra J. 2012. Introduction. Bioarchaeology and Behavior: The People of the Ancient Near East. Gainesville: University Press of Florida. p 1–7.

Powell ML. 1988. Status and Health in Prehistory: A Case Study of the Moundville Chiefdom. Washington, DC: Smithsonian Institution Press.

Powell ML, Bridges PS, and Mires AMW, editors. 1991. What Mean These Bones? Studies in Southeastern Bioarchaeology. Tuscaloosa: The University of Alabama Press.

Rose JC, Condon KW, and Goodman AH. 1985. Diet and Dentition: Developmental Disturbances. In: Gilbert RI, Jr., and Mielke JH, editors. The Analysis of Prehistoric Diets. Orlando, FL: Academic Press. p 281–305.

Scheuer JL, and Black S. 2000. Developmental Juvenile Osteology. San Diego, CA: Academic Press.

Scheuer JL, and Black S. 2004. The Juvenile Skeleton. Amsterdam: Elsevier.

Selye H. 1976. The Stress of Life. New York: McGraw-Hill.

Sheridan SG. 1999. 'New Life the Dead Receive': The Relationship between Human Remains and the Cultural Record for Byzantine St. Stephen's. Revue Biblique 106(4): 574–611.

Sheridan SG. 2002. Scholars, Soldiers, Craftsmen, Elites? Analysis of the French Collection of Human Remains from Qumran. Dead Sea Discoveries 9(2):199–248.

Shollmeyer KG, and Turner CG, II. 2004. Dental Caries, Prehistoric Diet, and the Pithouse-to-Pueblo Transition in Southwestern Colorado. American Antiquity 69(3):569–582.

Spencer SD. 2013. Violence in the Lower Illinois River Valley (ca AD 700–1250): An Examination of Injuries at Schild Utilizing Taphonomy, Paleopathology and Forensic Science [Dissertation]. Bloomington: Indiana University.

Steckel RH, and Rose JC, editors. 2002. The Backbone of History: Health and Nutrition in the Western Hemisphere. Cambridge: Cambridge University Press.

Stodder ALW, Martin DL, Goodman AH, and Reff DT. 2002. Cultural Longevity in the Face of Biological Stress: The Anasazi of the American Southwest. In: Steckel RH, and Rose JC, editors. The Backbone of History: Health and Nutrition in the Western Hemisphere. Cambridge: Cambridge University Press. p 481–505.

Stuart-Macadam P. 1987. Porotic Hyperostosis: New Evidence to Support the Anemia Theory. American Journal of Physical Anthropology 74:521–526.

Stuart-Macadam P, and Kent S, editors. 1992. Diet, Demography, and Disease. New York: Aldine de Gruyter.

Sutton MQ, Sobolik KD, and Gardner JK. 2010. Paleonutrition. Tucson: University of Arizona Press.

Swedlund AC. 1994. Issues in Demography and Health. In: Gumerman GJ, and Gell-Mann M, editors. Understanding Complexity in the Prehistoric Southwest. Reading, MA: Addison-Wesley Publishing Company.

Thompson JL, Alfonso-Durruty MP, and Crandall JJ. 2014. Tracing Childhood: Bioarchaeological Investigations of Early Lives in Antiquity. Gainsville: University Press of Florida.

Tishkoff SA, and Verrelli BC. 2003. Patterns of Human Genetic Diversity: Implications for Human Evolutionary History and Disease. Annual Review of Genomics and Human Genetics 4(1):293–340.

Titiev M. 1972. The Hopi Indians of Old Oraibi. Ann Arbor: University of Michigan Press.

Tung TA. 2012. Violence, Ritual, and the Wari Empire: A Social Bioarchaeology of Imperialism in the Ancient Andes. Gainesville: University Press of Florida.

Ubelaker DH. 1999. Human Skeletal Remains: Excavation, Analysis, Interpretation, third edition. New Brunswick, NJ: Aldine Transaction.

Villotte S, and Knüsel CJ. 2013. Understanding Entheseal Changes: Definition and Life Course Changes. International Journal of Osteoarchaeology 23(2):135–146.

Waldron T. 2009. Paleopathology. Cambridge: Cambridge University Press.

Walker PL. 1989. Cranial Injuries as Evidence of Violence in Prehistoric Southern California. American Journal of Physical Anthropology 80(3):313–323.

Walker PL. 1996. Integrative Approaches to the Study of Ancient Health: An Example from the Santa Barbara Channel Area of Southern California. In: Pérez-Pérez A, editor. Notes on Population Significance of Paleopathological Conditions: Health, Illness and Death in the Past. Barcelona: Fundació Uriach. p 97–105.

Walker PL. 1997. Wife Beating, Boxing, and Broken Noses: Skeletal Evidence for the Cultural Patterning of Violence. In: Martin D, and Frayer DW, editors. Troubled Times: Violence and Warfare in the Past. Amsterdam: Gordon and Breach. p 145–175.

Walker PL. 2001. A Bioarchaeological Perspective on the History of Violence. Annual Review of Anthropology 30:573–596.

Walker PL, Bathurst RR, Richman R, Gjerdrum T, and Andrushko VA. 2009. The Causes of Porotic Hyperstosis and Cribra Orbitalia: A Reappraisal of the Iron-Deficiency-Anemia Hypothesis. American Journal of Physical Anthropology 139:109–125.

Walker PL, and Erlandson JM. 1986. Dental Evidence for Prehistoric Dietary Change on the Northern Channel Islands, California. American Antiquity 51(2):375–383.

Wedel VL, and Galloway A. 2014. Broken Bones: Anthropological Analysis of Blunt Force Trauma. Springfield, IL: Charles C Thomas.

Wells C. 1964. Bones, Bodies, and Disease: Evidence of Disease and Abnormality in Early Man. London: Thames and Hudson.

West WR, Jr. 1993. Research and Scholarship at the National Museum of the American Indian: The New "Inclusiveness." Museum Anthropology 17(1):5–8.

White TD. 1992. Prehistoric Cannibalism at Mancos 5MTUMR-2346. Princeton, NJ: Princeton University Press.

White TD, Folkens PA, and Black MT. 2012. Human Osteology, third edition. Burlington, MA: Academic Press.

Zuckerman MK, Turner BL, and Armelagos GJ. 2012. Evolutionary Thought in Paleopathology and the Rise of the Biocultural Approach. In: Grauer AL, editor. A Companion to Paleopathology. Malden, MA: Blackwell Publishing. p 34–57.

3

PREGNANCY AND BIRTH IN ANCIENT AMERICA

Thinking about pregnancy, birth, and the first year of life for moms and babies for cultures in the past is very challenging. From the bioarchaeological record, it can be partially inferred from patterns in morbidity and mortality for infant and adult female human remains. Additional lines of evidence come from the archaeological context. Because almost all of the indigenous groups living in ancient America have living descendants today, their oral histories and traditions may also provide some clues to what pregnancy, birth, and the first year of life were like in ancient times. Ethnohistoric, archival, and ethnographic information is sometimes useful for broadening an understanding of these momentous life history events. However, information from historic and contemporary writings about Native Americans cannot be mapped directly onto the past and they are not necessarily good analogies for the past (Figure 3.1). Ethnographic and historic documents can only be used as guides to formulating a set of *possibilities* for what might have shaped events in the past. All indigenous cultures have undergone both large and small changes in the intervening years between their ancestral past, their tumultuous history with colonial powers, and their contemporary existence today in the U.S.

Life-history theory provides a framework for thinking about human adaptation and human variation with an eye to including stages of infancy, childhood, adolescence, and adulthood into explaining some of the differences that are measured or observed for different cultures and at different points in the evolutionary history of humans. Typically what is studied in life-history analyses are things such as birth, growth, diet, morbidity and mortality, and the biocultural processes tied to these events (Hill 1993). Reproductive strategies figure prominently in life history theory because the timing of births, birth spacing, fertility, and infant and maternal mortality figure importantly in the maintenance and vitality of communities

FIGURE 3.1 Hopi Indian mother carrying her baby on her back outside an adobe dwelling, circa 1900 (CHS-3740). By Pierce, C.C. (Charles C.), 1861–1946 [Public domain], via Wikimedia Commons.

(Chisholm 1993). Some of these human events and processes can be reconstructed for past societies, but many details are missing for past people.

Yet, of this much we can be sure: Humans living in every corner of the world during every period going back thousands of years likely dealt with social dynamics defined by cultural ideologies linked to formalities about mating, pregnancy, birth, and health status – as people do today (Trevathan 2011). Thus, baseline information about pregnancy and birth can be used to formulate more specific questions about health during life-history events for various periods and cultures in the past. The birth of a child within the interwoven axes of biology, culture, and environment is a major event. Cultural and environmental factors entwine in ways that affect conception, the infant while in utero and sharing resources with the mother, and then during and after birth when every aspect of care regarding the child is bounded by ideology, subsistence and diet, social organization and politics, customs and ritual, and religious and metaphysical beliefs (Stone and Walrath 2006; Trevathan and McKenna 1994).

The complexity of women's roles in ancient societies cannot be underscored enough. As Adams and Garcia (2006: 125) summarize their notion regarding the lives of Chumash Indian women in historic times:

> Women were the basis of village life. They kept the village going by giving birth, caring for children, gathering and processing acorns, prickly pear cactus fruits and other plant foods, and many other activities. They were responsible for the health of their families and cared for and nurtured their children, husbands, parents and relatives.

It is difficult to capture this kind of interwoven complexity for women in the past. The best that can be done is to use data derived from human remains and the archaeological context to hint at the range of possibilities for how this played out in the ancient past.

This chapter provides a selection of studies on ancient groups from the four core areas (California coast, Pueblo Southwest, Mississippian/Lower Illinois River Valley, and the Georgia Bight) regarding what pregnancy, birth and the first year of life might have been like for mother and infant in ancient America. This overview is by no means extensive or complete. It represents a sampling of the kinds of information bioarchaeologists use to think about moms and babies in times and places for which there are no written records. An examination of birth and infant health leads directly to thinking about maternal health during pregnancy and just after giving birth. These are controversial issues even today that are fraught with questions about the role of mothers in shaping their infant's health and welfare and the various ways that parenting activities affect the health of their children. For example, these kinds of issues for ancient children are addressed in the edited volume titled *Tracing Childhood, Bioarchaeological Investigations of Early Lives in Antiquity* (Thompson et al. 2014). Cross-cultural case studies from the ancient world are presented on the ways that children are shaped by their culture but also how children shape the cultures they live in.

In general though, there simply are not many focused analyses of infancy and birth in the bioarchaeological literature. There are a number of practical reasons why there are so few studies of infant health in the ancient world. The first is that many skeletal collections contain few infant remains because of the problems already discussed regarding size and fragility. Infant bones are difficult to measure due to breakage and the fact that they are not yet fused. A further challenge is that the death assemblage represents an accumulation of individuals who died over sometimes hundreds of years. A final problem is that cemetery-based studies do not represent the healthy or "average" infant but, rather, those who died.

This final challenge involves having a glimpse into causes of death but not as much insight into healthy infants and children. We essentially have access to the ancient morgue, but not to the living, healthy, growing infants who went on to become the adults and elderly in any given culture. Bioarchaeologists see infants and children with abnormal changes and lesions on their bones having to do with killers such as infectious disease, anemia, scurvy, and rickets (Lewis 2007).

Background and some things to consider

In bioarchaeology, the traditional term used for any individual under the age of 18 to 20 (the age at which growth in height mostly ceases for both males and females) is subadult. More recently, there has been a shift to rename the encompassing category as nonadult (see Lewis 2006: 2) to avoid the negative connotation of "sub" in subadult. The smallness and fragility of newborn and infant bones make them much more difficult to excavate and to retrieve for analysis (Baker et al. 2005: 16). At the Libben site in northwestern Ohio, Lovejoy and his colleagues (1977) used fine mesh screens to make sure that small bones from preterm and term infants were recovered from a large ossuary site and, in doing so, were able to retrieve an unheard of high number of infant and children's bones (discussed later in this chapter).

Methods for the assignment of sex for nonadult human remains exist but there are not yet any standards that can be applied to most populations to assign sex. As Lewis (2007: 48) summarizes it, "sex estimations from nonadult skeletons are notoriously difficult, making associated anthropological techniques unreliable, or forcing us to add greater error ranges to our results in order to account for unknown sex." She goes on to say that sex estimations in full skeletons from adults can reach as high as a 95% accuracy rate, whereas current methods for estimating sex from infant dentition, skull, or pelvis reaches only 70%. Sex is typically not estimated for subadults for these reasons.

Estimating of age at death is a crucial starting point for the analysis of human remains, and there are many methods to do so (see Chapter 2). Age is largely based on assumed biological characteristics associated with growth and development. Certain biological features appear at particular phases of growth associated with stages such as infancy, childhood, and adult categories (Baker et al. 2005; Scheuer and Black 2000). Changes in growth can be very dramatic during certain ages but these changes in growth can be altered by poor nutrition and disease. Providing an exact biological (or chronological) age is very difficult, but bioarchaeologists are fairly accurate at providing developmental age, allowing us to examine some of the problems with growth and development that might have been experienced by infants.

Paleodemography is the study of the structure of ancient populations based on age and sex to reconstruct what kinds of stressors might have caused early death in different age and sex categories. Bioarchaeologists work with populations of human remains that can essentially provide a death profile, that is, how many individuals died in each age category. This kind of information is useful in knowing how many individuals died at what age. The challenge in using the age distribution of nonadults for a given population revolves around the problems of understanding all the ways that the sample may be biased. From a living population that experiences deaths over time, to the ways that those dead are buried, to the natural alterations that may destroy bone and teeth over time, to which archaeological sites are excavated and how thoroughly they are done so, and finally to what is actually found, retrieved, and analyzed is a "torturous" path (Milner et al. 2008: 571). These kinds of loss of information are important to try to account for. In general, the larger the skeletal population, the more likely it is that the dead are somewhat representing the pattern as it was experienced in real time by the original culture.

Infant mortality rate is the number or percentage of infants who die before their first birthday. One pattern that holds across many different ancient cultures in the New World is that infant mortality was relatively high, estimated to be around 25% (Storey 1985: 520) compared with overall rates in the U.S. today that are around 6% (Haelle 2014). Life expectancy at birth is a function of the distribution of deaths across various age categories for cultures. Life expectancy at birth is based on the mean age at death or the construction of survivorship for all age categories (Milner et al. 2008). Roksandic and Armstrong (2011) provide an easy-to-understand methodology for constructing mean age at death and other aspects of survivorship and chances of making it to old age in any given age group. They rely on developmental stages to divide the age categories for nonadults. As discussed earlier, these include infancy, early childhood, late childhood, adolescence, young, full and mature adulthood, and senile adulthood. This chapter focuses on two related age categories: infancy (birth to about 2 years of age) and young adult females.

A variety of other things likely affected infant survival in the past. Neonates die today from a variety of causes but they are all preventable and include such things as diarrhea, pneumonia, and birth complications (Figure 3.2). Infants are vulnerable to the maternal uterine environment as well as to the environment into which they are born. Infant abuse or child maltreatment may have happened in the past as it does today, but this is very difficult to identify for past populations (Gaither 2012).

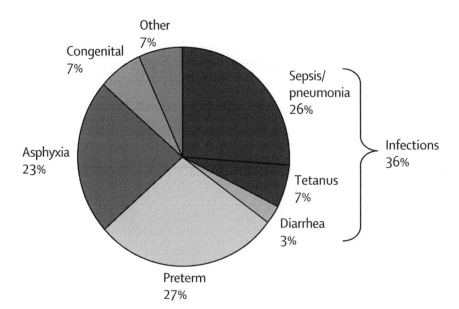

FIGURE 3.2 Distribution of deaths for neonates in the first 28 days of life assessed on a global level for the year 2000. From Joy E. Lawn, Simon Cousens, and Jelka Zupan, "4 Million Neonatal Deaths: When? Where? Why?" *The Lancet* 365, no. 9462 (2005): pp. 891–900. Reprinted with permission.

Definitions of child maltreatment varies from culture to culture, but physical abuse can sometimes by established by the appearance of depression fractures on the cranium or broken ribs or long bones (Martin and Harrod 2015). Infanticide (the intentional killing of infants) and abortion (the intentional killing of the fetus) also may have played a role in past societies but that information is difficult (but not impossible) to reconstruct from bioarchaeological data (Lewis 2007: 92–93). Here one would rely on the finding of preterm infant human remains and the context within which they are located.

What are some issues related to pregnancy, birthing, and maternal health that bioarchaeologists can grapple with? There are a few things beyond the assessment of the health of adult females that provide some clues to the pregnancy and birth experience that include examination of the birth canal size and changes in the pelvis brought on by pregnancy. While bioarchaeologists use the pelvis to distinguish between males and females, it has also revealed important obstetrical information that sheds light on pregnancy and birth. The male pelvis architecture generally creates a smaller inner space (the aspects of the birth canal in females), and the male pelvis shape is more narrow because of the size and angle of the iliac crest of the hip structure (White et al. 2011: 417). Historically, biological anthropologists and osteologists have focused primarily on the pelvic distinctions between males and females and have neglected to evaluate pelves in an obstetric light (Stone In Press).

The female bony pelvis serves several roles (Figure 3.3). Besides housing the birth canal, it has developed throughout human evolution to accommodate

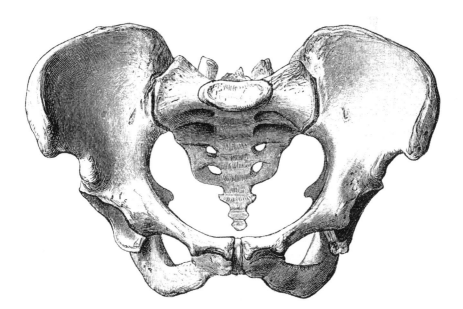

FIGURE 3.3 Female pelvis showing the normal dimensions of the birth canal. "Gray242" by Henry Vandyke Carter – Henry Gray (1918) *Anatomy of the Human Body.*

bipedality. Nutritional factors, of course, play a part in the development of the pelvis (Walrath 2003). The inlet is the bony passageway through which the fetus must first descend. Often the inlet dimensions are used clinically to identify a contracted pelvis. The pelvic inlet is considered to be contracted if its shortest anteroposterior (from to back) diameter is less than 100 millimeters, or if the greatest transverse (side-to-side) diameter is less than 120 centimeters. The brim index (calculated as the anteroposterior diameter $\times$ 100/transverse) is used to describe the overall character of the pelvic inlet and to assign a pelvis to one of the "parent pelvic types" established by Caldwell and Moloy (1938) (see Walrath [2003] for an examination of these dimensions and their implications for female labor and birth). A brim index greater than 95 is classified long oval or anthropoid in which the anteroposterior diameter is greater than the transverse. An index of 90 to 95 is classified as round or gynecoid, and this is where the anteroposterior and transverse diameters are nearly equal. A brim index of less than 90 is classified as flat transverse oval or platypelloid shape, and this is where the anteroposterior is less than the transverse diameter.

What this all means is that females who were nutritionally deprived during growth or who have had certain diseases that have rendered the pelvis contracted may have difficulties during labor (Konje and Lapido 2000). Tague (1994) provided some early studies on pelvic morphology for ancient populations and Stone (In Press) has followed this up with a broader study that clarified the ways that various cultural practices including workloads, diet, nutrition, gender roles, disease, and other factors work to sometimes make pregnancy difficult or even deadly for some females.

Childbirth, also referred to as parturition, has long been thought to leave its marks on the female pelvis. Some researchers report the finding of "parturition pits" along the ventral portion of the pelvis as proof of a female having given birth, but close scrutiny of this literature has failed to support the notion that there are these kinds of specific skeletal alterations that can be traced directly to childbirth (Ubelaker and de la Paz 2012). While things such as parturition pits are sometimes caused by childbirth, other activities also can cause the exact same thing because these pits have been found on some male pelves as well as on females who have never given birth.

Examples of death during childbirth are very rare in the bioarchaeological record. Arriaza and colleagues (1988) reported on 18 (out of 187) females from ancient Chile (dating from about 1300 BC to AD 1400) appeared to have died from the complications of childbirth. These human remains had excellent preservation with naturally mummified tissues still intact, and the unborn or partially born infants were preserved in the cavity of the adult female's skeleton where the uterus would have been. The authors suggest that acute diseases or cultural practices relating to the birth process may have resulted in the death of both mother and fetus. This was a remarkable and rare find because of the large number of individuals retrieved from these ancient cemeteries and to the excellent preservation. Maternal deaths are often related to hemorrhage, hypertension, and sepsis, all of which are preventable problems, but they are often facilitated by prolonged and obstructed labor, poor nutrition and poor health, or the presence of disease states that compromise the mother (Say et al. 2014).

Maternal health during pregnancy can be compromised by poor nutrition and hard work. Forms of raiding among different indigenous groups in America often were done to take women and children as captives (Cameron 2013). In these cases, captive women and their children could make accommodations and be integrated into households and communities as they were for the ancestral Hodenosaunee (formerly the Iroquois) (Wilkinson and Van Wagenen 1993) or captive women could be kept as outsiders and forced to do hard physical labor as they were in some ancestral Pueblo communities (Martin et al. 2010). Gender roles and sexual division of labor (discussed in Chapter 5) also play a role in how healthy pregnant women may be given their expected roles in subsistence and food production (Larsen 1998). Pregnancy can negatively affect the oral biology of women, and they can be prone to getting more caries (cavities) (Watson et al. 2010). While caries are not necessarily life threatening, they can go on to become large and abscessed, and this can lead to systemic infections.

Harris and Ross (1987: 49) provide a review of ethnographic literature on women in agricultural societies and the kinds of stresses and strains that they are under. With agricultural intensification, females in adulthood labor under the pressure to increase their economic productivity along with decreasing their spacing of births. This places a burden on women to partition their activities among a number of competing tasks. Agricultural females tend to work 7 days a week for approximately 10.8 hours a day to complete all the farming, household, food production, and child-care tasks in their domain (Harris and Ross 1987: 50). These data amassed from historic and contemporary agriculturally based groups are useful in understanding some of the constraints placed on pregnancy and birth in ancient agricultural groups.

Life-history approaches for understanding ancient patterns of maternal and infant outcomes are useful for understanding all the ways that human groups worked to offset poor health and early death. For example, Walker and Johnson (2002) have shown that agrarian societies often have reproductive cycles that are synchronized in ways that maximize mother and infant health. They found that for indigenous groups in the U.S., conception times peaked in July with a second weaker peak in February. These correspond to peak birthing seasons in late spring and fall when food is likely to be more diverse and plentiful. Often ritualized ceremonies around marriage are performed in midsummer when the crops are planted and growing and take less time to cultivate and protect. Low conception during the time of harvesting in the autumn makes good sense because there is a lot of work involved and the harvest must be completed before the first winter frost.

There are certainly many other things to consider when thinking about pregnancy and birth in the ancient world, but these are some of the more major areas that have at least been approached by bioarchaeologists, but much more work is still left to be done in this area of research. Consider this an invitation to delve more into the area by formulating new research questions that can be answered with bioarchaeological data. This is a wide-open area of study as can be surmised from this brief overview. What is known about pregnancy and birth in ancient America is unfortunately not very much, but the focus on the core areas provides some aspects of what moms and their babies were up against.

Vignettes

California coast

Although in a seemingly lush coastal and island environment, the California coastal region was anything but that. The ancient Chumash communities experienced a number of environmental changes that decreased resources and the ability of people to have enough to eat. Over time, there was a definite increase in anemia in infants (Walker 1985). There was an aggregation of people in areas with limited resources, and this likely also caused contamination of freshwater sources with enteric bacteria.

The prevalence of porotic hyperostosis in a population with a heavy dietary dependence on marine resources shows that among prehistoric American Indians, this condition is not always associated with an iron- and protein-deficient diet of cultigens. It seems likely that high nutrient losses associated with diarrheal disease are often more significant in the underlying causes of anemia (porotic hyperostosis) than a low dietary intake of essential nutrients (Walker 1986). In most of these communities along the coast of California or on the islands off the coast, Walker documented cases of anemia in individuals aged at about 3 to 4 years, but these were in a healed state, suggesting that anemia was present and a problem for infants during the first years of life. Those that survived showed only the healed lesions later in life. Walker also found that individuals who are anemic early in life die before reaching adulthood at a higher rate than individuals who never experienced anemia (1986: 349).

The problems of anemia from a combination of poor diet and bacterial infections were not just located in the infants and children. For young males aged 18 to 30, about 24% of them died with cases of anemia whereas for age-matched females in their peak reproductive years, 35% died with cases of anemia. At any given time then, about a third of the reproductively aged females were experiencing anemia, which can exacerbate problems with pregnancy and delivery. Having anemia means that the blood is not delivering oxygen as well as it should be, so there will be periods of tiredness if the condition becomes chronic. Most pregnant females take iron supplements today to ensure that they have plenty in their system to meet the needs of the fetus (McArdle et al. 2014).

While much more information has been provided about ancestral Chumash health during the period of contact and missionization in the California coastal regions, Walker and Johnson (2002: 66) provide some possible insights into other practices concerning newborns. They state that "elderly Chumash consultants interviewed . . . at the beginning of the 20th century verified that infanticide was practiced in the 'old days' when deformed babies were born and that abortions were sometimes performed by 'eating medicine.'"

In a study of historic use of medicinal plants used by Chumash women, Adams and Garcia (2006) demonstrated that a number of naturally growing plants in the California coastal areas were relied on for a number of ailments specific to reproductive-aged females. For example, Iris root was used to accelerate the birthing process because of its chemical properties, and chewing the root of the viola plant could ease labor pains. Passage of the afterbirth was facilitated by a decoction made of *Trichostema* leaves that Chumash women historically drank (Adams and Garcia 2006: 128). The authors further note that there were many restrictions placed on adults after the birth of an infant including that the "husband could not touch his wife until the baby could stand on its feet by itself" (2006: 127).

This brief overview of data from the skeletal remains of newly born infants and young adult females suggests that even in a place which provided fishing and the possibilities of foraging and agriculture, there were hardships brought on by changes in the climate that made food resources and drinking water more scarce, and these hardships likely made it difficult to ensure that each pregnancy and birth was successful and that infants all survived. There was population growth over time, so the frequency of maternal and/or infant deaths did not contribute to the decline in population size, but it must have had an impact on creating subgroups of mothers and their babies, who were more vulnerable to disease and early death.

Pueblo Southwest

The ancient American Southwest was a challenging place to be a farmer, especially in the area around the Colorado Plateau with its higher elevation. A large number of archaeological sites from the periods AD 900 up to contact have created a very large database of indigenous lifeways (Cordell 1997). One area, Black Mesa, was populated by farmers living in small groups in what was a remote, marginal area. These people are the ancestors to the contemporary Hopi people who still live on the same mesa tops in that region of northern Arizona. The population cultivated maize, gourds, and beans, and supplemented their diet by gathering natural vegetation such as wild grasses, cacti, and pinon nuts. Their diet also included the meat of smaller animals such as rabbits and prairie dogs that were found in the region (Martin et al. 1991). Because of the marginal and sometimes harsh Southwestern environment, the Black Mesa people were just able to meet their dietary requirements, a precarious nutritional situation that was detrimental to the health of newborns and to some mothers.

For newborns and infants living in settled desert farming communities, life was tough. Looking at long-bone lengths plotted against dental age, infants living on Black Mesa show a period of rapid growth until the age of 2 and then growth is much slower than it should be suggesting the beginning of weaning stress (discussed in the next chapter). Comparing the growth of infants from Black Mesa with others indigenous groups (the Arikara from South Dakota and Dickson Mounds, Illinois) the growth of Black Mesa infants is below that of other ancient children as well as that of children today (Martin et al. 1991: 87).

Enamel hypoplasias from the deciduous teeth of the infants from Black Mesa likewise reveal troubles for the newborns. From the deciduous dentition we can observe a special segment of the population – newborns and infants that failed to survive. Several that died soon after birth showed dental defects that corresponded with enamel growth during the third trimester suggesting that the uterine environment was stressed, likely because of morbidity or undernutrition of the mother (Martin et al. 1991: 103). Also, in the first year of life, 83.3% of the infants had periosteal reactions (infections) on their long bones at the time of death. The death of infants this young suggest that the vagaries of life in a marginal area for agriculture may have contributed to infant morbidity and mortality.

One example of the ways that paleopathological analyses can be used to reconstruct maternal morbidity and mortality comes from the Black Mesa sample of females with complete pelves (hip bones) aged between 20 and 40 years. The study was designed to see if any of females dying in their young adulthood years had constricted or flattened birth canals. Measurements from these pelves were compared with age-matched males from the group and well-nourished contemporaries (Martin 2000: 280; Martin and Seefeldt 1991). The Black Mesa female pelves were compared to the female pelves from the archaeological populations of Indian Knoll, Pecos Pueblo, and Libben (Tague 1989). In general, when comparing the young females with older females (those that did not die young) and age-matched males, young females had predominantly obstetric measurements that were transverse oval (or platypelloid) with a brim index of 78.4. Females who lived through the childbearing years had a brim index of 81.1, indicating a rounded, gynecoid shape.

One individual stood out in this analysis of obstetrical dimensions. A Black Mesa female aged 15 to 18 had a highly contracted and asymmetrical pelvic inlet. Her inlet anteroposterior (front to back) dimension is radically different when measured from the middle of the sacral promontory to the left pubis (8.3 cm) as to the right pubis (7.1 cm). It is doubtful that a fully developed fetus could pass through this contracted pelvic inlet without a high probability of maternal and perinatal morbidity (Martin and Seefeldt 1991). This study further suggested that many of the Black Mesa females had contracted pelvic inlets – common to those who lack optimum levels of nourishment – which is a condition that can lead to any number of obstetric complications, including maternal and perinatal mortality.

Females are obviously capable of giving birth successfully to their babies under all kinds of trying and adverse conditions, so the interpretation of these data point to a tipping point for maternal health (Figure 3.4). Stone (In Press) provides a systematic review of all of the circumstances that can predispose some young mothers to early death. Almost all of these are located in the political-economic and social structures of the culture that include inadequate dietary resources, long periods

IN THE CRADLE-BASKET

FIGURE 3.4 A Hopi mother with her infant, titled "In the cradle-basket." While the birth process may have been difficult for some women in the past, it is likely that the majority of infants were successfully delivered. Credit: Charles Deering McCormick Library of Special Collections, Northwestern University Library; *Edward S. Curtis's "The North American Indian,"* 2003. http://digital.library.northwestern.edu/curtis/ The North American Indian (1907–1930) v.12, The Hopi ([Seattle]: E.S. Curtis; [Cambridge, MA: The University Press], 1922), Facing page 56.

of hard work, abuse and neglect while still-growing young girls, and a variety of other negative conditions. These likely played a role in the past as well affecting the ability of some mothers and babies to survive. Because population size generally increased over time in the ancient Pueblo Southwest, it is clear that females successfully birthed many infants. But it is important to remember that the environmental constraints on successful farming likely placed some individuals at risk for poorly developed skeletal structures such as the pelvis, and this may have led to problems in birthing for some.

Mississippian/Lower Illinois River Valley

At Dickson Mounds people began transitioning to agriculture from their ancestral tradition of foraging around AD 1150 and by AD 1300 were fully committed farmers. Blakey and Armelagos (1985) showed that stress (as measured by enamel hypoplasias) did occur for some infants during the prenatal period and peaked in the month immediately following birth. Children whose teeth showed prior periods of stress before birth tended to live for shorter periods and to die earlier than did those children who did not experience in utero stress (Larsen 1987: 367). Therefore, health of the mother was determined to be an important factor in the health of the newborn infant in terms of health risks and survival in the Mississippian groups transitioning to or having adopted agriculture. Especially at places like Dickson Mounds and the larger ceremonial center of Cahokia, females had to partition their time between taking care of their infants and children and processing maize, which often meant long hours at the grinding stations (Figure 3.5).

For infants in their first year of life, there was a generally low frequency (10%) of anemia (porotic hyperostosis) during the transitional period where farming was not yet the only mode of subsistence, but the frequency rises to 33% in the agricultural period (Goodman et al. 1984).

FIGURE 3.5 A diorama of a Cahokia woman grinding maize, an activity that many spent long hours doing to feed their families. By Herb Roe – www.chromesun.com (own work).

For 1- to 2-year-olds, the rate of anemia for transitional period infants is 21%, and this increases to 47% for the agriculturalists. This is attributed to the benefits of a more varied diet that likely included more animal protein for foraging and transitional groups (Buikstra 1984: 227).

North of the Mississippian/Lower Illinois River Valley region in Ohio near Lake Erie, a large Late-Woodland habitation site (the Libben Site) was excavated that yielded 452 infants and children out of a total sample of 1,327 articulated skeletons. This is a remarkably high number of nonadults in part because of the excavation strategy and the fine mesh screening that was used to recover even the smallest infant bones resulting in a very representative population (Lovejoy et al. 1977). Premature infant bones (two lunar months) representing likely mis-carriages were retrieved, making this a quite unique finding for ancient American habitation areas. The Late Woodland period (AD 800–1100) is typically seen as being based on foraging, with little evidence for corn agriculture, and so this site provides a snapshot of life in ancient America prior to the shift to maize cultivation.

The frequency and distribution of porotic hyperostosis lesions indicative of some type of anemic condition were carefully studied using very refined age cate-gories for the site of Libben. For infants between birth and 6 months, none showed evidence of anemia and those infants aged between 6 months and 1 year, about one-quarter had signs of anemia at the time of death. However, for infants aged between 1 and 3, the frequency of anemia jumps to 72% with most cases (88%) showing active (not healed) lesions (Mensforth et al. 1978: 29). These same infants, when examined for nonspecific infectious responses on the long bones (periosteal reactions), showed that half of them also were experiencing that health problem and that half of those showed active cases (no healing; Mensforth et al. 1978: 34). The distribution of these combined lesions showed that there was a synergistic inter-action between infants being initially exposed to nonspecific infections and this could be anything from staph (*Staphylococcus*) (Figure 3.6) and strep (*Streptococcus*) to rickets and scurvy. Thus, infants were being exposed to life conditions that caused an anemic response. These mortality rates suggest that the ages between birth and 2 to 3 years were crucial in avoiding infectious pathogens as well as conditions resulting from dietary problems or the poor absorption of nutrients. This could be due to diarrhea and other childhood illnesses that move food too quickly through the system for nutrients to be absorbed.

This study from an earlier period than the Mississippian where the subsis-tence was more diverse and likely had more animal protein and woodland plants shows that infants were still quite at risk for being exposed to everyday bacte-rial pathogens that cause a systemic response and to anemia that can be caused by many things including diet and complications from other childhood symp-toms of poor health such as diarrhea. Lovejoy and colleagues (1977) projected that there was likely a mean family size of 3.8 and that life expectancy at birth was 20 years (which is well within normal for many precolonial populations in ancient America). The survivorship data for all subadults showed that the highest rate of

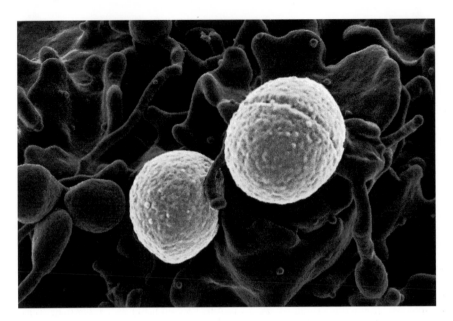

FIGURE 3.6 *Staphylococcus aureus* outside a white blood cell. This is a very common bacterium that in healthy people usually causes no health problems. However, it can trigger skin infections, respiratory problems, and even food poisoning. By National Institutes of Health (NIH). Credit: NIAID via Flickr, http://creativecommons.org/licenses/by/4.0/.

infant and child mortality was during birth to 3 years, where it has been estimated that about two-thirds of them died by the age of 3 (Mensforth et al. 1978: 44). While some research does show that a foraging and hunting lifestyle was generally better for overall health when compared to later groups who adopted agriculture, this study shows that being born in ancient America was fraught with the possibilities of poor health, which lead to sickness and then death.

Georgia Bight

Larsen (1984, 1998) examined preagricultural groups (before AD 1150) and agricultural groups (AD 1150 onward) to see what kinds of changes in health may be associated with the shift to agriculture. What makes this area different is that some of the groups living on islands and coastal regions relied more on hunting, gathering, and fishing in addition to farming and this is a departure from other core areas looked at in this section. There were only a total of 7 newborn to age 2 infants in the preagricultural sample (representing 4.6% of the total population), and 12 in the agricultural sample (6.8% of the population).

In a variety of studies that focused primarily on adults, over time and across the region, Larsen and Ruff (2011) documented a range of variability in adult health and overall adaptation. This variability had to do with the nature of the landscape in the eastern part of the U.S. during the periods prior to colonization. While health generally declined following the foraging to farming transition (Larsen 1987) in this region, there was considerable variation due to local circumstances having to do with lifestyle and resource acquisition (Larsen and Ruff 2011: 310). It is difficult to tease out what pregnancy and birth were like for the large number of groups living in the Georgia Bight, but in subsequent chapters the lives of children and adults in this large and diverse region are better known. Newborns are scarce in the skeletal collections, and this suggests that in most places, infant mortality was not as significant as other regions where environmental marginality played a larger role in health issues for newborns.

To sum up

Life in America for the earliest inhabitants of the core regions discussed above suggest that environmental factors (coastal, island, desert, river valley, inland) and subsistence activity (foraging, mixed economy, agriculture, intensified agriculture) had a lot to do with the general health of moms and their babies. Climate change as documented for the California coastal and island peoples as well as for the American Southwest made farming, fishing, and gathering sometimes inadequate in providing the full range of caloric and nutrient essentials necessary for young mothers and their newborn infants. Although this is not surprising, the details obtained from the skeletal records based on enamel hypoplasias, growth of the long bones, the mother's obstetric dimensions and rates of anemia together help provide an interpretation for why some females in young adulthood and some newborn infants did not survive.

An anthropological approach to thinking about the role of pregnancy and birth in the life history of females from any period demands that adaptation be viewed within a framework of flexibility and resilience. If we are to really comprehend the positions of women in different societies, much more specific information on the long range and cyclic patterns of their lives is needed. While some of this information can be gleaned from the skeletal remains as summarized here, these data are limited and not without problems. However, their existence affords a number of opportunities for studying women and reproduction in a broader temporal and spatial context for ancient America.

The data here for the core areas show that some females during peak reproductive years are predisposed to a higher risk of morbidity and mortality due to the stresses placed on them. And, some newborns also were at higher risk because of the vagaries of infections and nutritional problems that affected their survival rates. The picture that emerges from these studies is at odds with the older notion (and stereotype) of ancient populations in which all women were assumed to be biologically attuned to bear children easily and at full fecundity levels. In reality, the effects of nutritional stress and disease, in the absence of supplements and antibiotics, placed some mothers and some babies at risk. The implications for such a situation speak directly to the need for assessing the range of variability in human groups for being able to accommodate and deal with stressors in their particular setting back then and today.

References

Adams JD, and Garcia C. 2006. Women's Health among the Chumash. Evidence-Based Complementary and Alternative Medicine 3(1):125–131.

Arriaza B, Allison M, and Gerszten E. 1988. Maternal Mortality in Pre-Columbian Indians of Arica, Chile. American Journal of Physical Anthropology 77(1):35–41.

Baker BJ, Dupras TL, and Tocheri MW. 2005. The Osteology of Infants and Children. College Station: Texas A&M University Press.

Blakey ML, and Armelagos GJ. 1985. Deciduous Dental Defects in Prehistoric Americans from Dickson Mounds: Prenatal and Postnatal Stress. American Journal of Physical Anthropology 66:371–380.

Buikstra J. 1984. The Lower Illinois River Region: A Prehistoric Context for the Study of Ancient Diet and Health. In: Cohen MN, and Armelagos GJ, editors. Paleopathology at the Origins of Agriculture. New York: Academic Press. p 215–234.

Caldwell WE, and Moloy HC. 1938. Anatomical Variations in the Female Pelvis: Their Classification and Obstetrical Significance: (Section of Obstetrics and Gynæcology). Proceedings of the Royal Society of Medicine 32(1):1–30.

Cameron CM. 2013. How People Moved among Ancient Societies: Broadening the View. American Anthropologist 115(2):218–231.

Chisholm JS. 1993. Death, Hope, and Sex: Life-History Theory and the Development of Reproductive Strategies. Current Anthropology 1993:1–24.

Cordell LS. 1997. Archaeology of the Southwest, second edition. San Diego, CA: Academic Press.

Gaither C. 2012. Cultural Conflict and the Impact on Non-Adults at Puruchuco-Huaquerones in Peru: The Case for Refinement of the Methods Used to Analyze Violence against Children in the Archeological Record. International Journal of Paleopathology 2(2–3):69–77.

Goodman AH, Lallo J, Armelagos GJ, and Rose JC. 1984. Health Changes at Dickson Mounds. In: Cohen MN and Armelagos GJ, editors. Paleopathology at the Origins of Agriculture. New York: Academic Press. p 271–305.

Haelle T. 2014. U.S. Infant Mortality Rate Worse than Other Countries. CBSNews. http://www.cbsnews.com/news/u-s-infant-mortality-rat-worse-than-other-countries.

Harris M, and Ross EB. 1987. Food and Evolution: Toward a Theory of Human Food Habits. Philadelphia: Temple University Press.

Hill K. 1993. Life History Theory and Evolutionary Anthropology. Evolutionary Anthropology: Issues, News, and Reviews 2(3):78–88.

Konje J, and Lapido OA. 2000. Nutrition and Obstructed Labor. The American Journal of Clinical Nutrition 77(1):35–41.

Larsen CS. 1984. Health and Disease in Prehistoric Georgia: The Transition to Agriculture. In: Cohen MN, and Armelagos GJ, editors. Paleopathology at the Origins of Agriculture. New York: Academic Press. p 367–392.

Larsen CS. 1987. Bioarchaeological Interpretations of Subsistence Economy and Behavior from Human Skeletal Remains. In: Schiffer MB, editor. Advances in Archaeological Method and Theory, Volume 10. San Diego, CA: Academic Press. p 339–445.

Larsen CS. 1998. Gender, Health, and Activity in Foragers and Farmers in the American Southeast: Implications for Social Organization in the Georgia Bight. In: Grauer AL, and Stuart-Macadam S, editors. Sex and Gender in Paleopathological Perspective. Cambridge: Cambridge University Press. p 165–187.

Larsen CS, and Ruff CB. 2011. 'An External Agency of Considerable Importance': The Stresses of Agriculture in the Foraging-to-Farming Transition in Eastern North America. In: Pinhasi R, and Stock JT, editors. Human Bioarchaeology of the Transition to Agriculture. New York: Wiley. p 293–316.

Lewis ME. 2006. The Bioarchaeology of Children: Perspectives from Biological and Evolutionary Anthropology. Cambridge: Cambridge University Press.

Lewis ME. 2007. The Bioarchaeology of Children: Perspectives from Biological and Forensic Anthropology. Cambridge: Cambridge University Press.

Lovejoy CO, Meindl RS, Pryzbeck TR, and Barton TS. 1977. Paleodemography of the Libben Site, Ottawa County, Ohio. Science 198(1977):291–293.

Martin DL. 2000. Bodies and Lives: Biological Indicators of Health Differentials and Division of Labor by Sex. In: Crown PL, editor. Women and Men in the Prehispanic Southwest: Labor, Power and Prestige. Sante Fe, NM: School of American Research Press. p 267–300.

Martin DL, Goodman AH, Armelagos GJ, and Magennis AL. 1991. Black Mesa Anasazi Health: Reconstructing Life from Patterns of Death and Disease. Carbondale: Southern Illinois University Press.

Martin DL, and Harrod RP. 2015. Bioarchaeological Contributions to the Study of Violence. Yearbook of Physical Anthropology 156:116–145.

Martin DL, Harrod RP, and Fields M. 2010. Beaten Down and Worked to the Bone: Bioarchaeological Investigations of Women and Violence in the Ancient Southwest. Landscapes of Violence 1(1):Article 3.

Martin DL, and Seefeldt WD. 1991. Prehistoric Obstetrics: Why Anasazi Women Died Young on Black Mesa, Arizona (AD 800–1150). 60th Annual Meeting of the American Association of Physical Anthropology, Milwaukee, WI.

McArdle HJ, Gambling L, and Kennedy C. 2014. Iron Deficiency during Pregnancy: The Consequences for Placental Function and Fetal Outcome. Proceedings of the Nutrition Society 73(1):9–15.

Mensforth RP, Lovejoy CO, Lallo JW, and Armelagos GJ. 1978. Part Two: The Role of Constitutional Factors, Diet, and Infectious Disease in the Etiology of Porotic Hyperostosis and Periosteal Reactions in Prehistoric Infants and Children. Medical Anthropology: Cross-Cultural Studies in Health and Illness 2(1):1–59.

Milner GR, Wood JW, and Boldsen JL. 2008. Advances in Paleodemography. In: Katzenberg MA, and Saunders SR, editors. Biological Anthropology of the Human Skeleton, second edition. Hoboken, NJ: John Wiley & Sons. p 561–600.

Roksandic M, and Armstrong SD. 2011. Using the Life History Model to Set the Stage(s) of Growth and Senescence in Bioarchaeology and Paleodemography. American Journal of Physical Anthropology 145(3):337–347.

Say L, Chou D, Gemmill A, Tunçalp Ö, Moller A-B, Daniels J, Gülmezoglu M, Temmerman M, and Alkema L. 2014. Global Causes of Maternal Death: A WHO Systematic Analysis. The Lancet Global Health 2(6):e323–e333.

Scheuer JL, and Black S. 2000. Developmental Juvenile Osteology. San Diego, CA: Academic Press.

Stone PK. In Press. Biocultural Perspectives on Maternal Mortality and Obstetrical Death from the Past to the Present. Yearbook of Physical Anthropology.

Stone PK, and Walrath D. 2006. The Gendered Skeleton: Anthropological Interpretations of the Boney Pelvis. In: Gowland R, and Knüsel CJ, editors. The Social Archaeology of Funerary Remains. Oxford: Oxbow Books. p 168–178.

Storey R. 1985. An Estimation of Mortality in a Pre-Columbian Urban Population. American Anthropologist 87(3):519–535.

Tague RG. 1989. Variation in Pelvic Size between Males and Females. American Journal of Physical Anthropology 80:59–71.

Tague RG. 1994. Maternal Mortality or Prolonged Growth: Age at Death and Pelvic Size in Three Prehistoric Amerindian Populations. American Journal of Physical Anthropology 95:27–40.

Thompson JL, Alfonso-Durruty MP, and Crandall JJ. 2014. Tracing Childhood: Bioarchaeological Investigations of Early Lives in Antiquity. Gainesville: University Press of Florida.

Trevathan WR. 2011. Human Birth: An Evolutionary Perspective. Piscataway, NJ: Transaction Publishers.

Trevathan WR, and McKenna JJ. 1994. Evolutionary Environments of Human Birth and Infancy: Insights to Apply to Contemporary Life. Children's Environments 1994:88–104.

Ubelaker DH, and de la Paz JS. 2012. Skeletal Indicators of Pregnancy and Parturition: A Historical Review. Journal of Forensic Sciences 57(4):866–872.

Walker PL. 1985. Anemia among Prehistoric Indians of the American Southwest. In: Merbs CF, and Miller RJ, editors. Health and Disease in the Prehistoric Southwest. Tempe: Arizona State University. p 139–164.

Walker PL. 1986. Porotic Hyperostosis in a Marine-Dependent California Indian Population. American Journal of Physical Anthropology 69(3):345–354.

Walker PL, and Johnson JR. 2002. For Everything There Is a season: Chumash Indian Births, Marriages, and Deaths at the Alta California Missions. Human Biologists in the Archives: Demography, Health, Nutrition and Genetics in Historical Populations 35(2002):53–77.

Walrath D. 2003. Rethinking Pelvic Typologies and the Human Birth Mechanism 1. Current Anthropology 44(1):5–31.

Watson JT, Fields M, and Martin DL. 2010. Introduction of Agriculture and its Effects on Women's Oral Health. American Journal of Human Biology 22(1):92–102.

White TD, Black MT, and Folkens PA. 2011. Human Osteology. San Diego, CA: Academic Press.

Wilkinson RG, and Van Wagenen KM. 1993. Violence Against Women: Prehistoric Skeletal Evidence from Michigan. Midcontinental Journal of Archaeology 18:190–216.

4
GROWING UP IN ANCIENT AMERICA

Archaeologically, childhood has often been an understudied aspect of life, but this is rapidly changing (particularly within bioarchaeology; for numerous studies, see Bluebond-Langner and Korbin 2007; Halcrow and Tayles 2008; Kamp 2001; Thompson et al. 2014). Lewis (2007) dedicates an entire book to the topic. Titled *The Bioarchaeology of Children* it examines ancient health focusing on the kinds of things that make infants and children vulnerable to disease and death from a wide variety of mostly Old World settings. She combines modern clinical and biological information on this segment of the life-history trajectory and summarizes what we can hope to learn from ancient children's skeletons.

Lewis focuses on weaning and dietary stress as primary areas that make early childhood so dangerous. Halcrow and Tayles (2008) provide a detailed overview of how to read the skeletons of children for important indicators of stress and pathology and how to consider the complex biocultural context within which children grow up. Weaning as a culturally determined activity is one of those complex variables that must be understood for ancient cultures. Children have a full set of deciduous dentition by the age of 2 to 3 (Ubelaker 1989: 65), and it is at this age that many groups begin to initiate supplemental feeding. It is the most advantageous time to permanently switch from breast milk to the staple foods of the group (Figure 4.1). The first permanent teeth begin to show up at around age 6, and this corresponds to full development of the immune system (Lewis 2007: 101). Thus, focusing on what it was like for children in the early childhood years between the ages of 2 through 6 make sense because this was an important and distinctive time while growing up. As the data on mortality patterns discussed earlier suggest, children who survive this period have a good chance of making it to adulthood, as late childhood and adolescence are far less risky.

FIGURE 4.1 Hopi children. Weaning from mother's breast milk to food is a critical time in children's growth and development. Credit: Charles Deering McCormick Library of Special Collections, Northwestern University Library; Edward S. Curtis's *The North American Indian,* 2003. Digital ID, ct12077, http://digital.library.northwestern.edu/ curtis/ The North American Indian (1907–1930) v.12, The Hopi ([Seattle]: E.S. Curtis; [Cambridge, Mass.: The University Press], 1922), facing page 36.

Collecting robust data on what it was like to grow up in ancient America is challenging on many levels. Children are difficult to study in the archaeological record for several reasons. First, children may not be buried in the same place as adults, and this may make their burials more difficult to locate. This may mean that they are not recovered systematically during the normal course of excavation. Second, children's bones are thinner and more fragile and the younger they are, the more fragile the skeletal material is likely to be (Scheuer and Black 2000: 14). In this case, normal taphonomic processes over time may render the bones fragmentary or completely missing. This can lead to the underutilization and underrepresentation of nonadult bones in analyses because they are incomplete or bone surfaces are poorly preserved. Third, excavation of burials is time-consuming and laborious. Often screening of the burials is not done to save time, but very small bones may simply not be recovered. At the Libben site, Lovejoy and colleagues (1977) used a very fine mesh screen to ensure that premature and full-term infants and children were recovered. Finally, if a population is undergoing social changes such as the introduction or intensification of agriculture, the population may be demographically unstable. This instability may complicate assessments of overall mortality rates for the population (Perry 2005).

Background and some things to consider

Following from the previous chapter that examined infant morbidity and mortality from birth to about the age of 2, the focus here is on that portion of nonadults aged from about 2 years onward into the late teen years. As discussed, the perinatal/infant mortality rates for ancient people in the New World are relatively high when compared with modern rates. The rates for early childhood (ages 2 to 6) are likewise high (13%–24%) as calculated for selected precolonial groups from the New World (Storey 1985: 526). In the U.S. today, the mortality rate for children under the age of 5 is 7% (World Bank 2014). Although this period (particularly ages 2–6 or so) is often referred to as the weaning years when referring to ancient populations, it is very difficult to know exactly the age at which weaning occurred at any given place or time (Reynard and Tuross 2015). Thus, the reasoning behind the continued relatively high mortality rates in children from weaning age onward necessitates the inclusion of other alternative factors that may contribute to illness and death. Early childhood survivors seem to do much better in late childhood (ages 6–10) and adolescence (ages 10–18). Estimates of mortality rates drop for these two age groups (5%–14%) (Storey 1985: 526), and these rates are more in line with U.S. teenager mortality rates (15%–19%; USA Life Expectancy 2013). Therefore, the most vulnerable years for children in the ancient world appears to be in the first 6 years of life. This chapter focuses on early childhood to flesh out what some of the risk factors would have been.

While challenging and difficult to interpret, bioarchaeological data derived from children's burials can reveal a great deal about some of the contingencies and risks involved in survival. Using a life-history approach to what can be known about ancient people's bodies and lives provides a way to peer into the past at different points along the trajectory of birth to death for individuals, and comparing several core areas provides a way to envision variability among contemporaneous groups. Life history does not always map onto chronological age as discussed earlier, but it is just as valuable to use developmental indicators of growth and aging. For example, using modern forensic techniques, a child's long-bone length may make them appear to be older or younger than their chronological age because of a variety of things (e.g., diet, health, genetics, environment, and activity level) that affect growth of long bones (Ubelaker 1989: 69). While dental eruption provides a fairly accurate chronological age up to about 18 years of age, epiphyseal union (the cessation of growth in long bone length) also can be an indicator of chronological age.

For these reasons, this chapter focuses on early childhood (ages 2–6), late childhood (6–10), and adolescence (10–18) following the suggested age categories of Roksandic and Armstrong (2011: 341). These stages are based on distinct biological events having to do with dental and skeletal markers of development. Early childhood begins around the time that the deciduous dentition is full erupted at 2 years and ends with the emergence of the first permanent teeth, typically the first molar or central incisors at around 10 years of age. Late childhood begins with the eruption of the first permanent teeth through to the eruption of the permanent canine, typically around 10 years of age. Adolescence begins with this eruption and ends with the epiphyseal union of the long bones, typically in the late teens (see various methodologies presented in Buikstra and Ubelaker 1994). Using these three distinct age categories to think about growing up in ancient America takes advantage of the timing of weaning at around 2 (which can place infants and children at risk for disease) and the timing of the fully matured immune system at around 6 (which protects children from some diseases).

Childhood and adolescence are dynamic stages of life where an individual begins to function as an autonomous being and learns the rules of their own society and how to function within it. Within this period, there are prominent changes to both biology/physiology and to cultural identity. Weaning is regarded as a process for which the initiation of and length is culturally determined, but it always involves the shifting from an exclusively breast-milk diet to the traditional foods relied upon by that culture (Dettwyler 1995). It is therefore not tied to a specific age but to a process that may occur at different times for different groups. This is typically a physiologically traumatic transition and occurs at a time when an infant's immune system is not yet fully mature (Lewis 2007). Breast milk is rich in carbohydrates and lactose as well as zinc and iron. Iron, in particular, is necessary for the production of both hemoglobin and myoglobin. All of these are crucial for normal growth and development. In addition to nutrients, breast milk provides passive immunity to the suckling infant for a wide variety of diseases (Lewis 2007). During the transition from breast milk to solid foods, children become exposed to an increasing number of bacterial and parasitic vectors through the combination of the lack of maternal immunological support and the exposure to new foods. This may lead to malnutrition or nutritional stress for the child. It is clear from modern studies that this is a dangerous time, and would have been doubly so in the past prior to the introduction of vaccines and the intervention of Western medicine for such things as diarrheal diseases.

Weaning is traditionally inferred osteologically by the presence of linear enamel hypoplasias (see Chapter 2) on the permanent dentition but newer methods are emerging that analyze nitrogen isotope ratios determined from biochemical studies of archaeological bones (Reynard and Tuross 2015). Linear enamel hypoplasias have been used for a long time, and these defects in the permanent dentition occur during childhood but persist into adulthood, so they are an indication of childhood physiological disruption. When examined on a population level, patterns emerge that highlight the likelihood of the timing of the physiological disruption during early childhood, and this can be a way to examine the social timing of weaning (considered to be a major physiological disruption) within that group. For example, Wall (1991) found a clustering between the ages of 2 and 3 years in individuals from precontact

California. This was interpreted as the typical age of weaning for the group. Because the growth of teeth is highly controlled by genetics the hypoplastic defects on the teeth can be estimated to have occurred during half-year increments, and a chronology of when the defects occurred can be reconstructed. Goodman and Rose (1990) provide the methodology for this, and it has been utilized by many bioarchaeologists in their studies of childhood health.

After weaning, growth and development continues at fairly predictable rates, but while teeth are under strong genetic timing for growth, bones are much more effected by many things that can slow or stop growth and development (Stinson 2012). Children's bones start out as cartilage models in utero and, in the third trimester, begin to ossify. This process of ossification permits the highly vascularized bones to grow both in length and width until the ages of 18 for females and 21 for males. By those ages, compact bone at the articular ends fuse at the epiphyseal plate. The growing skeleton is subject to environmental, nutritional, and disease stresses throughout the growth and development period, and signs of infectious disease and nutritional problems become evident on the bones of children who died. See Chapter 2 for additional details about the identification of these nutritional deficiencies and infectious processes and how they are identified. For example, when the age at death is secured by dental eruption, long-bone length for that age can be compared to that developed using standards based on well-nourished modern populations and this can provide evidence of growth faltering (Pinhasi and Stock 2011).

Another major physiological change occurring during childhood and adolescence is that of puberty. Skeletally, this is visible in the emergence of both primary and secondary sexual characteristics around the age of 16 (discussed in Chapter 2) and as these changes progress they permit the assignment of biological sex to skeletons (White et al. 2011). After puberty, primary and secondary sexual characteristics become more pronounced with the fusion of the elements of the pelvis and the development of muscle attachments. It is typically thought that the social status of "adult" was likely attained at a younger age than in modern western society (Schwartz 2012).

Vignettes

California coast

The California coast and the associated Channel Islands provide a counterpoint to the other core groups discussed in this volume. They were not agricultural, but instead foraged and fished as a means of subsistence. The Channel Island chronologies are usually split into early versus late components. Health comparisons have been conducted between these two groups.

The presence and timing of linear enamel hypoplasias have been used to infer childhood stress (or physiological disruptions) and when that stress occurred (Figure 4.2). Linear enamel hypoplasias have been shown to be higher in agriculturalists.

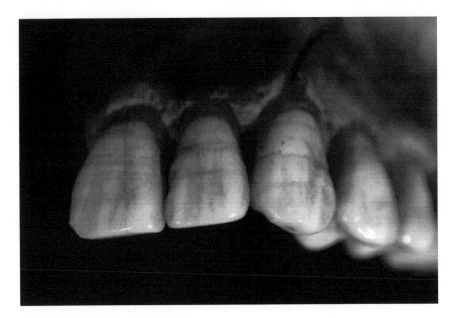

FIGURE 4.2 This photo shows the linear enamel hypoplasias (LEH) that are visible in adult teeth but that were effected by some type of stress while those teeth were forming in early childhood (between the ages of 1–6). Specimen ID: AFIP 1002959. Source collection: Anatomical division. From National Museum of Health and Medicine, Otis Historical Archives via Flickr, http://creativecommons.org/licenses/by/4.0/.

Cohen and Armelagos (1984: 573; reprinted 2013) reviewed 19 case studies of ancient populations undergoing the shift from foraging to agriculture and summarized the findings this way:

> [T]he incidence of physiological stress increases greatly and average mortality rates increase appreciably ... most of these agricultural populations have high frequencies of porotic hyperostosis and cribra orbitalia, and there is a substantial increase in the number and severity of enamel hypoplasias and pathologies associated with infectious disease.

Although this pattern of increasing poor health is well documented, interpretations of why this is seen have been challenged over the years, and newer evidence from isotopes and better diagnostic criteria of disease has challenged some of the premises about what makes agriculture a less healthy human endeavor than foraging (Pinhasi and Stock 2011).

In contrast to the agriculturalists of the Lower Illinois River Valley or the Southwest, the prevalence of linear enamel hypoplasias decreases with time for coastal California from 33% to 17% (Kerr 2004). Different islands were more subject to stressors than others as well. For example, San Nicolas Island individuals have more hypoplasias than other islands, indicating that children living there were exposed to more stress than the other islands.

In line with the decrease in linear enamel hypoplasias over time, there is also a reduction of caries (cavities) rates. Walker and Erlandson (1986) attribute this shift to a change from carbohydrate-rich tubers and roots to a more marine-based diet in the later periods of occupation. Geography also played a role in caries rates. In his dissertation, Bartelink (2006) compared caries rates between Sacramento Valley and the San Francisco Bay groups. He found that those groups living in the Sacramento Valley had higher caries rates regardless of period than those living in the San Francisco Bay, a difference attributed to the greater reliance on marine resources along the coast (San Francisco Bay).

There are sex differences in the expression of lesions related to stress and diet for all groups. One such difference can be seen in the expression of cribra orbitalia for the adult samples indicating that as children, males and females were exposed to different stresses (Lambert 1994). They possibly ate substantially different diets or had access to food sources in different amounts. Lambert (1994) also found that the percentage of individuals exhibiting cribra orbitalia (a condition of anemia) increased from the early to the late periods, from 13.8% to 30.6% of the total population. This may be related to climate change or to resource depletion brought on by population increases (Rick et al. 2005). As ecological conditions worsened and food became scarcer, the entire population showed more and more signs of nutritional stress. But women's health suffered the most. It is also during this later period that violence becomes more prevalent. The same is true for dental pathologies such as antemortem tooth loss (Bartelink 2006). Children and adolescents also were exposed to violent interaction. Lambert (1994, 1997) found that individuals older than 10 years were more likely to exhibit trauma than those younger than the age of 10. This suggests a shift in the social identity of individuals at that age. They were included in activities after the age of 10 that exposed them to increased violent interaction, either with other adolescents or with the adult population.

When a child died, they would have probably been buried within a shell midden mound. These mounds would have also held domestic refuse, artifacts, house remains, and artifacts (Lightfoot and Luby 2012). Lambert (1993) notes that in mortuary samples from this area, children and adolescents were less common than adults. This may indicate that nonadults were buried using a different mortuary program and were not recovered as part of the normal excavations. The inclusion of at least some nonadults in the same mortuary program as adults, however, is intriguing. It suggests that there are possibly multiple burial programs present, and children were included in some but not all. This may indicate a ranked society (such as seen in the Lower Illinois River Valley; see the following discussion) or that burial customs were highly regionalized.

Based on the data gleaned from larger analyses, a snapshot of what life was like in ancient California for children presents a nuanced picture. They would have been weaned onto starchy foods and marine resources, but this process was likely different for males and females. Adult females tend to have worse overall health indicators for stress, suggesting that they may have been exposed to more stress as children (Goodman and Armelagos 1988). Diet after weaning would have been dependent on local access. If they lived near the coast, they would have relied heavily on marine resources; if they lived farther from the coast, they would have relied more on starchy roots and tubers. Rites of passage occurred in their late childhood or early adolescence that would have changed their social standing within the community. In this case, that seems to have exposed them to increased levels of interpersonal violence.

Pueblo Southwest

Children and adolescents have been a significant focus of bioarchaeologists in the Southwest (Figure 4.3). As a result, we can piece together what it was like to

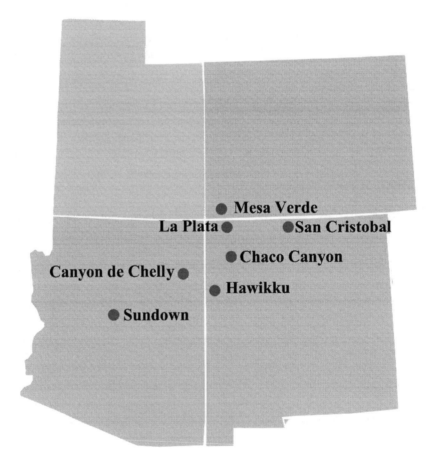

FIGURE 4.3 Map showing the locations of all sites mentioned that had child burials that are reviewed in this chapter.

experience childhood and adolescence. For the nonadult population as a whole (aged newborn through 15 years) living in northern New Mexico at the site of La Plata (approximately AD 1200), a little more than half (61.1%) show signs of anemia (Martin et al. 1991). Comparing this with groups living approximately the same time in the Southwest, this is among the lower frequencies reported for children, with Chaco Canyon showing a rate of 83% and the Mesa Verde region showing a rate of 87.8% (Stodder 1987; 1989: 179). Danforth and colleagues (1994) report that four out of five nonadults aged 2 or under (80%) at this later Pueblo site in Arizona had lesions at the time of death (although the frequency for the total population is about 23%). Canyon de Chelly shows a frequency of 55.1% (Walker 1985: 143). For sites later in time dated to around AD 1400 such as San Cristobal and Hawikku, Stodder (1990: 223) reports frequencies of 87% and 74%, respectively.

Interpreting the data on porotic hyperostosis as an indicator of anemia involves a simultaneous understanding of a number of factors. Early interpretations of porotic hyperostosis linked it exclusively to an iron-poor diet, but it is now assumed that diet per se may play a less prominent role in the expression of anemia in a population. The complex interaction of micronutrients and iron absorption are only a part of the picture. There is often a synergistic effect between dietary deficiencies and susceptibility to transmissible infectious diseases.

In the Southwest, the co-occurrence of porotic hyperostosis in nonadults with periosteal reactions (lesions indicative of systemic infectious disease) is relatively frequent. Out of 15 cases where both cranial and postcranial material were available to assess for lesions of porotic hyperostosis and periosteal reaction for the La Plata children, 50% show both porotic hyperostosis and periosteal reactions, suggesting a comorbid relationship (Martin et al. 1991). Evidence suggests that infectious disease finds a more "willing" host in the anemic individual, and Keusch and Farthing (1986: 145) demonstrate that iron-deficiency anemia can predispose children to respiratory and gastrointestinal infections. For the Black Mesa population, co-occurrence was 61.9% for the nonadults, but the patterning was quite different from that of the La Plata.

The site of Sundown, near Prescott (Arizona), has a small assemblage of skeletal remains that have been analyzed by Merbs and Vestergaard (1985). These date to a period of occupation between AD 1100 and 1200. Though the number of individuals is small, the proportions are somewhat telling and give an idea about infant and child mortality. Of the 24 individuals recovered, 16 were younger than 12 years of age when they died. Nine were between 0 and 3 years, four between 3 and 6 years of age when they died, and three between the ages of 6 and 12. At least some of those in the youngest category may be the result of weaning deaths. Nine of these individuals had signs of stress in the form of porotic hyperostosis and cribra orbitalia. The individuals with active porotic hyperostosis had a younger age at death than those without it, suggesting that the stress leading to porotic hyperostosis may have been a contributing factor to their deaths. Additionally, these young individuals tended to have multiple indicators of stress, with both porotic hyperostosis and cribra orbitalia present.

Childhood deaths occurring after weaning may be at least partly due to under- or malnutrition. As noted by Taylor (1985), a diet consisting primarily of maize and beans (the primary crops cultivated by groups in the Southwest) are relatively low in protein, high in carbohydrates, and provide only minimal amounts of vitamin C. Protein would have been present in the diet in the form of both hunted and domesticated animals. But during weaning, high-protein foods would likely not have been consumed. Palkovich (1985: 133) defines children as "high risk" in terms of mortality and disease risk.

The Sundown site also illustrates another pattern common to the study of adolescents in the archaeological record: they are sparse. There are no individuals from the Sundown site between the ages of 12 and 18 years. By age 12, individuals have survived childhood stress and are not faced with significant endemic diseases that have a significant impact on mortality. At Black Mesa, only 17 of the 172 individuals had an age at death of between 12 and 18 years of age, making up 9% of the total burial population (Martin et al. 1991).

In a study (almost 50 years ago) of Pueblo Indian children living in New Mexico, Corbett (1968) demonstrated that there was a high incidence of iron deficiency anemia in young children visiting the local medical clinic. At 15 months, 100% of the children had lower than normal mean corpuscular hemoglobin concentrations. Rates tapered off to between 40% and 60% in older children. He also found a co-occurrence of anemia and respiratory infections in 73% of the children. These data from historic Pueblo villages suggest that environmental (deserts) and culture (agricultural lifestyle) underlie the frequencies of anemia and infections (Figure 4.4).

Regardless of its root cause, anemia in even slight to moderate rates can be considered to be a red flag for childhood health. The symptoms of anemia (which do not preserve in the archaeological record) are pale skin, brittle nails, fatigue, apathy, poor temperature regulation, and loss of appetite. Learning ability, work performance, and immune status can be significantly compromised by poor iron stores.

Once weaning was successfully accomplished, children were exposed to a multitude of infectious diseases and pathogens. Martin and colleagues (1985) note the presence of pathological changes to the bones consistent with endemic exposure to infectious disease. Juveniles with less-developed immune systems would have been especially susceptible to these.

There is no discernable patterning in location of burials at Black Mesa, meaning that children and adolescents were given the same burial treatments as adults. Burials of children between the ages of 1 and 9 at Black Mesa are mostly single interments, with individuals semiflexed, flexed, extended, or disarticulated. Few differences were identified in the patterning of grave goods or burial locations either (Martin et al. 1991). This suggests a far more egalitarian social structure, with the full inclusion of children and adolescents as full community members (as opposed to more ranked social structure visible in the Mississippian/Lower Illinois River Valley; see the following discussion).

FIGURE 4.4 Looking across rows of corn from a historic Hopi agricultural plot. The vagaries of subsisting largely on maize agriculture in the Southwest are made clear by the close timing of frost-free days for growth and the challenges of dry farming in a desert region. Photo by Ansel Adams, U.S. National Archives and Records Administration, 1941. Courtesy of Department of the Interior, National Park Service, branch of Still and Motion Pictures, via Wikimedia Commons.

For the nonadult portion of the La Plata Valley population, 5 out of 19 (26.3%) possible cases demonstrated lesions indicative of generalized nonspecific infection. For children with periosteal reactions of the long bones, the majority was moderate in expression and was about equally represented by active and healing status at the time of death. It is difficult to assess the age of onset of infectious disease in this subgroup because of missing information in the younger age categories, but two of the five cases of periosteal reaction are in children aged 1.5 to 2, and the other three cases are in older children aged 3 to 5. Four of the five cases co-occur with porotic hyperostosis. Frequencies of nonspecific infections for a number of Southwest villages range from a low of 2.7% at Mesa Verde (Miles 1966) to a high of 17% at Chaco Canyon (Stodder 1989).

Tuberculosis, a chronic infectious disease, is documented for two individuals from La Plata. One of these cases was a child of about 9 years of age who showed a pattern of fusion and lesions in the vertebrae that suggest tuberculosis. Although the vertebral elements are highly fragmentary and poorly preserved, evidence of destruction and resorption of the articular facets, and lytic lesions on the body of some of the thoracic vertebrae represent a pattern that has been linked to tuberculosis. On several of the thoracic vertebrae, the inferior and superior articular facets exhibit osteolytic destruction. The severity of destruction has caused the collapse of the thoracic body, and the exposed cancellous bone is dense and shows sclerotic development.

Tuberculosis in other precontact Southwest specimens has been largely associated with sites dating to the later periods (AD 1300–1450; Merbs 1989). Stodder (1990) found cases at both San Cristobal and Hawikku, and she suggests that there may have been an epidemic wave of tuberculosis (which is highly contagious and immunocompromised individuals are most at risk). The clustering of several cases of tuberculosis at San Cristobal suggested to her a highly compromised group.

The experience of childhood would have changed significantly with the introduction of agriculture. As part of a foraging society in the Southwest, weaning would likely have occurred later than would have occurred if one were growing up in an agricultural society. In the ancient Southwest, agriculture was the primary mode of subsistence from at least AD 800 up to historic times. Weaning would have taken place somewhere between 1 and 2 years of age. For agriculturalist, weaning

FIGURE 4.5 Hopi children. Adapted from the original (cropped). Photograph "Hopi Children" circa 1906, courtesy of the Library of Congress (http://hdl.loc.gov/loc.pnp/cph.3c12223). Open access.

food was likely a paste that consisted of corn or other cultivated grains. However, all the evidence for ancient health of children suggests that as many as 50% did not survive into the teenage years. Once weaning was accomplished the diet of children appears to have been essentially the same as the adult diet and does not appear to vary by sex (as it did in ancient California). Childhood and adolescence would have been a time of gaining more and more social roles as an individual grew, likely becoming a full member of society sometime after puberty (Figure 4.5). Children who made it through childhood into adolescence had a good chance of making it into adulthood since there are so few teenagers in the archaeological record.

Mississippian/Lower Illinois River Valley

A large number of earthen mounds were noted by the early colonial settlers to the areas in and around modern day St. Louis that include the Mississippi River and the Lower Illinois River. Some of these mounds, such as Monk's Mound (Figure 4.6) were generally unknown to the populace of the 1800s that these mounds contained hundreds of indigenous American burials. In the early 1930s and onward, archae-ologists would excavate many of these, but there are still many earthen mounds throughout the area that have been made into historic areas and national parks (Goodman and Armelagos 1985).

The transition from a hunter-gatherer lifestyle to an agricultural subsistence base has significant health impacts. Cook (1976) examined the lengths of the femur shafts from both groups in Illinois. A similar study was conducted by Goodman and colleagues (1984) for the groups buried at Dickson Mounds. Both studies showed slower growth of the long bones in agricultural groups when compared with hunter-gatherers of a similar age (based on dental development). Both groups of researchers attribute this growth slowdown to an increased exposure to nutri-tional stress for the agriculturalists.

Even within agriculturalists, there are health differences between the beginnings of agriculture and later, when agriculture is intensified to feed larger populations. The intensification of agriculture in the late Woodland brought with it some sig-nificant changes for life during childhood. Cook (1979) noted a significant increase in childhood mortality, particularly when the early late Woodland was compared to the terminal late Woodland periods. In other words, with more agricultural inten-sification, came a higher likelihood of dying during childhood. Work at Dickson Mounds supports this interpretation (Goodman et al. 1984). Weaning deaths are also included in this pattern and may be attributable to high-carbohydrate weaning foods that provide relatively poor nutrition (Cook 1979; Powell 1992). In study-ing the Libbon population, there was a significant relationship between decreased life expectancy and the presence of linear enamel hypoplasias. This decreased life expectancy is due to damage to the immune system brought on by weaning in some individuals.

With respect to health, the transition to solid foods may be exacerbated by the transition of the group as a whole to a more intensified agricultural subsistence

FIGURE 4.6 What a burial mound in the Mississippian region looked like in historic times. This photo is of Monks Mound located at Cahokia from an 1887 illustration. "Cahokia monks mound McAdams 1887" by William McAdams – *Records of Ancient Races in the Mississippi Valley* by William McAdams (1887). Licensed under Public Domain via Wikimedia Commons.

base. Cook (1979) found that long-bone growth was slower when compared to dental development for individuals in the Late Woodland period who died between the ages of 1 and 5 years. Additionally she was able to show that decreased cortical thickness of the long bones themselves may be associated with weaning, particularly in later periods.

Diet was likely high in carbohydrates, both during weaning and afterward. Alfonso-Durruty and colleagues (2014) examined the amount of carious lesions, antemortem tooth loss, and wear on both nonadults and adults. They found that wear was generally light and that the degree of carious lesion formation indicated that not only was the diet high in carbohydrates, but it was also relatively soft (based on the lesser degree of wear).

Weaning at Dickson Mounds probably occurred around the second year of life, based on the presence of linear enamel hypoplasias occurring at that age. Evidence of nutritional stress can also be found in the long bones. Goodman, Armelagos, and Clark (1984) found two periods during childhood and adolescence when individuals were experiencing more stress than other times. The first time dates to between 2 and 3 years, possibly related to weaning stress. The second time is around 13 years of age. This second stressful period may be indicative of a social change relating to the onset of puberty, including the assumption of different social roles or a change in diet based on age.

Although children were exposed to violence, they were far less likely to be the victims of interpersonal violence. For example, during analysis of the Norris Farms site in Illinois, only two individuals younger than 15 years of age exhibited antemortem trauma (Milner 1995; Milner et al. 1991). For nonadults at Dickson Mounds, nonadults in the late Woodland have a higher frequency of fractures than those in the terminal late Woodland period, indicating a shift in social practices during this transition (Goodman et al. 1984).

If a child died, the method of burial varied based on the local cultural traditions. For Mississippian Moundville, the inclusion of infants and juveniles in the elite burials surrounded by elite grave goods gives an indication that social rank was ascribed at birth. Associations with families were important, particularly at a time before the child would have been able to gain their own cultural capital (Powell 1992). At Gibson Mounds (in Illinois), children in central burial pits were found buried with adult males and with exotic grave goods (grave goods manufactured outside the community). In this community, children were buried only with adult males, which Buikstra (1976) indicates a social linkage between the adult males and the young that did not exist between children and adult females. A second burial program also exists, in which individuals are buried in a more egalitarian manner, where grave goods appear to have been allocated based on age and sex alone. The inclusion of adult males and children in the more exclusive portion of the burial program has been interpreted as showing social differentiation and ranking within different portions of society (Buikstra 1976).

Children and adolescents have been extensively studied for this area. Weaning would likely have occurred between the ages of 1 and 3 years and would have included the shift to locally available cultigens such as chenopodium. After weaning, diet would have been the same for both males and females. Children were likely exposed to endemic diseases, particularly those inhabiting the river bottoms and those in contact with agricultural processes. Treponemal diseases would have also been endemic and could have been passed to children. As soon as an individual would have been able to walk and move within the community, exposure to infectious pathogens could have occurred. To a certain extent, exposure to these pathogens would have led to a more robust immune system. It is likely that exposure to infectious pathogens and endemic disease that occurred after the child's immune system was robust would have been at least partially responsible for the lower numbers of individuals between the ages of 12 and 18 dying.

If the death of a child or adolescent did occur, the bodies may have been treated differently. Infants and very small children may have been used as foundational burials for structures or burial mounds. Adult burial customs decreed a period of processing within a central tomb prior to secondary deposition in the mound surrounding the central chamber. In many cases, underneath the central chamber lies an infant or small-child burial. It is generally believed that the last burial to occur within the burial mound was that of an important individual. If there is a child in the central tomb, it is always accompanied by an adult male, likely indicating a special relationship between males and children. This might suggest a patriarchal social structure. Child and adolescent burials are also as secondary depositions, just like the adults. This suggests that they were considered to be important members of the group. Unlike in the Southwest, subfloor burials were not a common practice reserved for children.

Georgia Bight

The earliest human remains from this area date to around 1100 BC, when populations were highly mobile and subsisted on foraged and hunted terrestrial and marine resources. After about AD 700, populations were far more reliant on cultigens such as maize (Larsen 1998).

The transition from foraging to agriculture has, as with other areas, biological consequences. In his study of more than 600 burials dating to both foragers and agriculturalists along the Georgia coastal region, Larsen (1981) found that there were changes in both the teeth and bones of individuals, with a general reduction in the size of premolars and molars in women. In an additional study, Larsen (1983) examined the size of deciduous dentition during this transition. Deciduous teeth become smaller when populations change to agriculture. He attributes this change to the inability of the individuals to reach their full genetic potential (i.e., the largest possible tooth size) because of a more marginal diet. Although both sexes experience a general increase in carious lesions with the introduction of agriculture, the greatest increase occurs among women (Larsen 1998). This suggests that men and women were eating different diets, with women consuming more carbohydrates than men. Larsen (1998) draws an association between gendered labor, where men were still heavily involved in hunting activities. It is presently unclear at what age the diet for women and men diverge; that is, what age did boys begin to provision with the men?

In terms of diet, Larsen (1987) notes that groups living along the coast utilized more marine fishes, which may have helped to include more protein into the diet than may have been available to other groups included in this chapter. He attributes the relatively lower rates of porotic hyperostosis in coastal agricultural populations compared to other prehistoric agriculturalists to the availability of more protein.

In terms of burial traditions, the Georgia Bight groups maintained shell mounds. Burial appears to have been conducted along matrilineal lines (Thomas et al. 1979; 2008). Burials become increasingly elaborate, ultimately including Hopewell trade goods. In their comprehensive report about the human burials, Thomas et al. (1979) provide breakdowns of the demography of the individuals interred. They make a distinction between intrusive secondary burials and primary burials within the mound structures. For the Seaside Mound group, primary burials included both adults and juveniles, but only one child (aged 6–8 years) was listed as an intrusive secondary burial. They note the presence of at least 55 adults, but only 6 nonadults are listed for the Cunningham and Seaside Mound groups. This suggests that children may have been subject to a different burial program than the adults.

The majority of synthetic work for the Georgia coastal populations has been centered on exploring the lives of adults. Relatively poor preservation of skeletal materials in general makes large-scale generalizations about lived experience difficult. For juvenile remains, which typically have poorer preservation than do adult remains, this problem is compounded. It is therefore more difficult to understand the lived experience of childhood and adolescence. What is clear from published data is that children experienced nutritional stress. It is unclear at what age gendered labor would have become a social reality. It is likely that young children stayed with their mothers and would have been exposed to similar diets, but eventually, boys would have begun hunting and this would have led to a change in diet for them, with the girls continuing with the other women. This could have led to higher caries rates amongst adolescent girls depending on when this gender-specific trend began.

To sum up

Being a child in ancient America would have been dangerous and risky for some. After successful weaning, exposure to the world would have meant exposure to infectious agents and a possibly insufficient diet. Exploring the social world of children is still a difficult prospect, particularly through the lens of human remains. While studies have been conducted using ceramics and toys archaeologically (e.g., Kamp et al. 1999), it is generally believed that indicators such as entheses (muscle markers) are unreliable for individuals younger than 18 years. Typically, health indicators about stress, trauma, and exposure to infectious diseases (as in the preceding case studies) are the only empirical data that can be reliably used.

There is no doubt that the death of a child was a momentous and important life-history event that was marked with rituals and social activities. The burial of children under house floors has been interpreted as a desire to keep the child close to the family in multiple regions under study. Childhood is a time of enculturation, when children learned what it means to be part of their community. They begin to acquire the skills necessary to take over adult roles, including gender-specific work skills and ritual activities. They go through rites of passage, gain cultural knowledge, and become full members of society.

The experience of childhood varied greatly, as seen in the case studies. Whether a group was agricultural or foraging or ate maize or consumed marine resources had a differential impact on the health of children. Agricultural groups weaned their children with different foods, and agricultural children were exposed to different diseases and social stresses.

The vignettes provided show a variety of ecological and social adaptations. Ecologically, groups took advantage of the resources at their disposal, from rich agricultural lands in the Mississippian/Lower Illinois River Valley to dry farming in the Pueblo Southwest and the exploitation of marine resources along the California coast. A great variety of social complexity is inferred from these data in such things as differential burial of infants (possibly indicating they were not seen as full members of the society) in the Southwest to rich elaborate burials of infants and children and the use of infants as dedicatory burials in the Mississippian. These are reflective of ideological differences in the use of cultural constructs to apportion resources and maintain social cohesion. In this way, burials can be seen as a form of social capital that ties people to specific locations and legitimizes a predominant social order (Osterholtz 2015; Sofaer 2006).

References

Alfonso-Durruty M, Bauder J, and Giles B. 2014. Dental Pathologies and Diet in the Middle Woodland Burials from Helena Crossing, Arkansas. North American Archaeologist 35(1):87–108.

Bartelink EJ. 2006. Resource Intensification in Pre-Contact Central California: A Bioarchaeological Perspective on Diet and Health Patterns among Hunter-Gatherers from the Lower Sacramento Valley and San Francisco Bay [Dissertation]. College Station: Texas A&M University.

Bluebond-Langner M, and Korbin JE. 2007. Challenges and Opportunities in the Anthropology of Childhoods: An Introduction to "Children, Childhoods, and Childhood Studies." American Anthropologist 109(2):241–246.

Buikstra J, and Ubelaker DH. 1994. Standards for Data Collection from Human Skeletal Remains. Fayetteville: Arkansas Archaeological Survey.

Buikstra JE. 1976. Hopewell in the Lower Illinois Valley: A Regional Approach to the Study of Biological Variability and Mortuary Activity. Evanston, IL: Northwestern University Archaeological Program.

Cohen MN, and Armelagos GJ, editors. 1984. Paleopathology at the Origins of Agriculture. New York: Academic Press.

Cook DC. 1976. Pathologic States and Disease Process in Illinois Woodland Populations: An Epidemiologic Approach [PhD dissertation]. Chicago: The University of Chicago.

Cook DC. 1979. Part Four: Subsistence Base and Health in Prehistoric Illinois Valley: Evidence from the Human Skeleton. Medical Anthropology 3(1):109–124.

Corbett TH. 1968. Iron Deficiency Anemia in a Pueblo Indian Village. Journal of the American Medical Association 205:136.

Danforth ME, Cook DC, and Knick SG, III. 1994. The Human Remains from Carter Ranch Pueblo, Arizona: Health in Isolation. American Antiquity 59(1):88–101.

Dettwyler KA. 1995. A Time to Wean: The Hominid Blueprint for the Natural Age of Weaning in Modern Human Populations. In: Stuart-Macadam P, and Dettwyler KA, editors. Breastfeeding: Biocultural Perspectives. Chicago: Transaction Publishers. p 39–73.

Goodman AH, and Armelagos GJ. 1985. Disease and Death at Dr. Dickson's Mounds. Natural History 94(9):12–18.

Goodman AH, and Armelagos GJ. 1988. Childhood Stress and Decreased Longetivity in a Prehistoric Population. American Anthropologist 90:936–944.

Goodman AH, Martin D, Armelagos GJ, and Clark G. 1984. Indications of Stress from Bones and Teeth. In: Cohen MN, and Armelagos GJ, editors. Paleopathology at the Origins of Agriculture. New York: Academic Press. p 13–49.

Goodman AH, and Rose JC. 1990. Assessment of Systemic Physiological Pertubations from Dental Enamel Hypoplasias and Associated Histological Structures. Yearbook of Physical Anthropology 33:59–110.

Halcrow SE, and Tayles N. 2008. The Bioarchaeological Investigation of Childhood and Social Age: Problems and Prospects. Journal of Archaeological Method and Theory 15:190–215.

Kamp KA. 2001. Where Have All the Children Gone?: The Archaeology of Childhood. Journal of Archaeological Method and Theory 8(1):1–34.

Kamp KA, Timmerman N, Lind G, Graybill J, and Natowsky I. 1999. Discovering Childhood: Using Fingerprints to Find Children. American Antiquity 64(2):309–315.

Kerr SL. 2004. The People of the Southern Channel Islands: A Bioarchaeological Study of Adaptation and Population Change in Southern California [PhD dissertation]. Santa Barbara: University of California.

Keusch GT, and Farthing MJ. 1986. Nutrition and Infection. Annual Reviews in Nutrition 6:131–154.

Lambert PM. 1993. Health in Prehistoric Populations of the Santa Barbara Channel Islands. American Antiquity 58(3):509–521.

Lambert PM. 1994. War and Peace on the Western Front: A Study of Violent Conflict and its Correlates in Prehistoric Hunter-Gatherer Societies of Coastal California [Unpublished PhD dissertation]. Santa Barbara: University of California.

Lambert PM. 1997. Patterns of Violence in Prehistoric Hunter-Gatherer Societies of Coastal Southern California. In: Martin DL, editor. Troubled Times: Violence and Warfare in the Past. Amsterdam: Gordon and Breach. p 77–109.

Larsen CS. 1981. Skeletal and Dental Adaptations to the Shift to Agriculture on the Georgia Coast. Current Anthropology 22(4):422–423.

Larsen CS. 1983. Deciduous Tooth Size and Subsistence Change in Prehistoric Georgia Coast Populations. Current Anthropology 24(2):225–226.

Larsen CS. 1987. Bioarchaeological Interpretations of Subsistence Economy and Behavior from Human Skeletal Remains. In: Schiffer MB, editor. Advances in Archaeological Method and Theory, Volume 10. San Diego, CA: Academic Press. p 339–445.

Larsen CS. 1998. Gender, Health, and Activity in Foragers and Farmers in the American Southeast: Implications for Social Organization in the Georgia Bight. In Grauer AL, and Stuart-Macadam P, editors. Sex and Gender in Paleopathological Perspective. Cambridge: Cambridge University Press. p 165–187.

Lewis ME. 2007. The Bioarchaeology of Children: Perspectives from Biological and Forensic Anthropology. Cambridge: Cambridge University Press.

Lightfoot KG, and Luby EM. 2012. Mound Building by California Hunter-Gatherers. In: Pauketat T, editor. The Oxford Handbook of North American Archaeology. Oxford: Oxford University Press. p 212–223.

Lovejoy CO, Meindl RS, Pryzbeck TR, and Barton TS. 1977. Paleodemography of the Libben Site, Ottawa County, Ohio. Science 198(1977): 291–293.

Martin DL, Goodman AH, Armelagos GJ, and Magennis AL. 1991. Black Mesa Anasazi Health: Reconstructing Life from Patterns of Death and Disease. Carbondale: Southern Illinois University Press.

Martin DL, Piacentini C, and Armelagos GJ. 1985. Paleopathology of the Black Mesa Anasazi: A Biocultural Approach. In: Merbs CF, and Miller RJ, editors. Health and Disease in the Prehistoric Southwest. Tempe: Arizona State University. p 104–114.

Merbs CF. 1989. Trauma. In: Iscan MY, and Kennedy KAR, editors. Reconstruction of Life from the Skeleton. New York: Alan R. Liss. p 161–199.

Merbs CF, and Vestergaard EM. 1985. The Paleopathology of Sundown, A Prehistoric Site Near Prescott, Arizona. In: Merbs CF, and Miller RJ, editors. Health and Disease in the Prehistoric Southwest. Tempe: Arizona State University. p 85–103.

Miles JS. 1966. Orthopedic Problems of the Wetherill Mesa Populations. Wetherill Mesa Studies, Publications in Archaeology 7G. Washington, DC: National Parks Service.

Milner GR. 1995. An Osteological Perspective on Prehistoric Warfare. In: Beck LA, editor. Regional Approaches to Mortuary Analysis. New York: Plenum Press. p 221–244.

Milner GR, Anderson E, and Smith VG. 1991. Warfare in Late Prehistoric West-Central Illinois. American Antiquity 56(4):581–603.

Osterholtz AJ. 2015. Bodies in Motion: A Bioarchaeological Analysis of Migration and Identity in Bronze Age Cyprus (2400–1100 BC) [Dissertation]. Las Vegas: University of Nevada.

Palkovich AM. 1985. Interpreting Prehistoric Morbidity Incidence and Mortality Risk: Nutritional Stress at Arroyo Hondo Pueblo, New Mexico. In: Merbs CF, and Miller RJ, editors. Health and Disease in the Prehistoric Southwest, Anthropological Research Papers, No. 34. Tempe: Arizona State University. p 128–138.

Perry MA. 2005. Redefining Childhood through Bioarchaeology: Toward an Archaeological and Biological Understanding of Children in Antiquity. Archeological Papers of the American Anthropological Association 15(1):89–111.

Pinhasi R, and Stock JT, editors. 2011. Human Bioarchaeology of the Transition to Agriculture. Chichester, NJ: Wiley-Blackwell.

Powell ML. 1992. In the Best of Health? Disease and Trauma among the Mississippian Elite. Archeological Papers of the American Anthropological Association 3(1):81–97.

Reynard LM, and Tuross N. 2015. The Known, the Unknown and the Unknowable: Weaning Times from Archaeological Bones Using Nitrogen Isotope Ratios. Journal of Archaeological Science 53:618–625.

Rick TC, Erlandson JM, Vellanoweth RL, and Braje TJ. 2005. From Pleistocene Mariners to Complex Hunter-Gatherers: The Archaeology of the California Channel Islands. Journal of World Prehistory 19:169–228.

Roksandic M, and Armstrong SD. 2011. Using the Life History Model to Set the Stage(s) of Growth and Senescence in Bioarchaeology and Paleodemography. American Journal of Physical Anthropology 145(3):337–347.

Scheuer L, and Black SM. 2000. Developmental Juvenile Osteology. San Diego, CA: Elsevier Academic Press.

Schwartz GT. 2012. Growth, Development, and Life History throughout the Evolution of Homo. Current Anthropology 53(S6):S395–S408.

Sofaer J. 2006. The Body of Material Culture: A Theoretical Osteoarchaeology. Cambridge: Cambridge University Press.

Stinson S. 2012. Growth Variation: Biological and Cultural Factors. Human Biology: An Evolutionary and Biocultural Perspective. New York: John Wiley & Sons. p 587–635.

Stodder ALW. 1987. The Physical Anthropology and Mortuary Practice of the Dolores Anasazi: An Early Pueblo Population in Local and Regional Context. In: Petersen KL, and Orcutt JD, editors. Dolores Archaeological Program: Supporting Studies: Settlement and Environment. Denver, CO: Bureau of Reclamation, Engineering and Research Center. p 336–504.

Stodder ALW. 1989. Bioarchaeological Research in the Basin and Range Region. In: Simmons AH, Stodder ALW, Dykeman DD, and Hicks PA, editors. Human Adaptations and Cultural Change in the Greater Southwest. Wrightsville: Arkansas Archaeological Survey Research Series, no. 32. p 167–190.

Stodder ALW. 1990. Paleoepidemiology of Eastern and Western Pueblo Communities [Unpublished PhD dissertation]. Boulder: University of Colorado.

Storey R. 1985. An Estimation of Mortality in a Pre-Columbian Urban Population. American Anthropologist 87(3):519–535.

Taylor MG. 1985. The Paleopathology of a Southern Sinagua Population from Oak Creek Pueblo, Arizona. In: Merbs CF, and Miller RJ, editors. Health and Disease in the Prehistoric Southwest. Tempe: Arizona State University. p 115–118.

Thomas DH, Andrus CFT, Bishop GA, Blair E, Blanton DB, Crowe DE, DePratter CB, Dukes J, Francis P, and Guerrero D. 2008. Native American Landscapes of St. Catherines Island, Georgia. Part 3; Anthropological Papers of the American Museum of Natural History, no. 88, pt. 3.

Thomas DH, Larsen CS, Clark GR, DePratter CB, and Lunsford AM. 1979. The Anthropology of St. Catherines Island. 2, The Refuge-Deptford Mortuary Complex. Anthropological Papers of the AMNH; no. 56, pt. 1.

Thompson JL, Alfonso-Durruty MP, and Crandall JJ. 2014. Tracing Childhood: Bioarchaeological Investigations of Early Lives in Antiquity. Gainesville: University Press of Florida.

Ubelaker DH. 1989. Human Skeletal Remains, Excavation, Analysis, Interpretation. Washington, DC: Taraxacum.

USA Life Expectancy. 2013. USA Teen Death Rate. USA Life Expectancy. http://www.worldlifeexpectancy.com/usateen-death-rate.

Walker PL. 1985. Anemia among Prehistoric Indians of the American Southwest. In: Merbs CF, and Miller RJ, editors. Health and Disease in the Prehistoric Southwest. Tempe: Arizona State University. p 139–164.

Walker PL, and Erlandson JM. 1986. Dental Evidence for Prehistoric Dietary Change on the Northern Channel Islands, California. American Antiquity 51(2):375–383.

Wall CE. 1991. Evidence of Weaning Stress and Catch-Up Growth in the Long Bones of a Central California Amerindian Sample. Annals of Human Biology 18:9–22.

White TD, Black MT, and Folkens PA. 2011. Human Osteology. San Diego, CA: Academic Press.

World Bank. 2014. Mortality Rate, Under-5 (per 1,000 Live Briths). World Bank. http://data.worldbank.org/SH.DYN.MORT.

5

ADULT LIFE IN ANCIENT AMERICA

Given the challenges posed by teasing out the data on neonates, infants, children, and adolescents, presenting summary data on adults between the ages of 20 and 50 is less so because adult human remains preserve better and are well represented in most final resting places for the dead. There is a quite vast literature on health in ancient America that focuses primarily on adults, and so this chapter provides only a selection of that literature on adult health for the four core culture areas. The adult years are the most economically productive years of an individual's life. Pregnancy has been addressed in Chapter 3, but this chapter addresses the issues of maternal health on a larger scale, examining age at death distributions in the various populations and the effects of population increases typically seen with the introduction of agriculture.

In particular, diet, nutrition, and exposure to infectious diseases are important features of the ancient landscape in terms of health. But interpersonal violence also is something that adults were routinely exposed to. For this reason, both health and violence are explored in separate sections for each region. The role of resource specialization and intensification, whether in the form of agriculture or the intensification or exploitation of marine resources, is also explored. Generally, intensification of subsistence activities has significant impacts on the wear and tear of the body, and living in close, packed quarters also facilitates the transmission of communicable bacterial diseases.

Background and some things to consider

How people go about their lives is largely a function of culture, which includes a wide range of technological, behavioral, and ideological systems (Goodman et al. 1988). In terms of ancient health, it is important to understand as much about the cultural patterns as possible to understand which cultural customs buffered against poor health and which customs may have promoted disease. For example, ancestral Pueblo people lived in enclosed rock shelters at Mesa Verde in Colorado in the 1200s. Although these shelters offered protection from the elements, predators, and enemies, the small, enclosed spaces also facilitated the exchange of communicable diseases such as *Staphylococcus* and *Streptococcus*, as well as respiratory ailments from poorly ventilated hearths, as seen in the rates of infectious disease with the children from this site.

The development of agriculture in North America was an important cultural innovation that allowed the majority of the groups a greater production of calories relative to human expenditure. Thus, agriculture would seem to provide a buffer against undernutrition. However, there is a strong correlation between agricultural living and nutritional stress combined with higher infectious disease rates (see Cohen and Armelagos 1984 for examples of these correlations for a number of New and Old World ancient groups). Ecological and demographic changes associated with intensified farming no doubt had a profound influence on the health of the most vulnerable such as infants and weaning-age children. Individuals are more or less vulnerable to disease depending on a number of factors having to do with their general fitness, immunity, age, reproductive status, exposure to previous diseases, and other variables that can compromise health (Finch 2012). Individuals experiencing malnutrition, for example, are less resistant to infectious diseases, and infectious disease can further lower nutritional status.

Fortunately for the paleopathologist, the biological effects of nutrition and disease are the primary indicators of stress outlined in Chapter 2. Although it is crucial to document these changes at the individual level, from an anthropological perspective it is equally important to realize that health and adaptation have significance that extends beyond the individuals to the population and community. Nutritional inadequacy or undernutrition in adults has different community-level effects than in children. For example, for subsistence-based communities in Mexico where reliance on maize and a lack of health-care facilities studies have revealed that undernutrition causes many problems for adults. It has a negative effect on work capacity, fertility, morbidity, and mortality and is associated with secondary disruptions to the social, political, and economic structure of a community (Allen 1984). In turn, these cultural and population-level changes cause further changes in the environmental and cultural systems. Foraging with its richer and more diverse diet with meat and a wide range of wild plants and nuts was decidedly better for health. Once agriculture becomes a way of life, the diet is dramatically changed.

In general, for preindustrial populations, there are data to suggest that it was difficult to live in the kinds of hygienic homes associated with living in the 1900s. High rates of infection and limited access to really effective medicine would have placed everyone at a disadvantage relative to today. In fact, one of the primary causes of mortality throughout human evolution was likely infections and the association of high early mortality and shorter life spans provide insight into thinking about what life was like prior to the 1900s (Finch 2012). While there were likely many plants that afforded medicinal and palliative benefits to those who were sick, their effects would have been limited when diseases were compounded by nutritional and other stressors (Vogel 2013).

Osteoarthritis is among the oldest and most commonly known diseases affecting humans. Measuring the amount of arthritic involvement with skeletal remains is sometimes difficult because of the potentially large number of areas to be assessed (each vertebra and all joint systems) and the range of variation in bony response among individuals. While many factors may contribute to the breakdown of skeletal tissue, the primary cause of osteoarthritis is related to aging, biomechanical wear and tear and functional stress (Ortner and Putschar 1981). Biomechanical stress is most apparent at the articular surfaces of long bone joint systems and is referred to as degenerative joint disease (DJD). The patterning of DJD has been linked to behavioral factors and individuals who habitually engage in activities that put strain on the joint systems. In general, early Native Americans appeared to sustain osteoarthritis in rates comparable with individuals today, although the earlier rate of onset and decreased life span of their ancient ancestors may have served to compress the observable cases into a shorter time frame within the life span.

Traumatic lesions found on ancient adults the world over encompass a broad range of clinical classifications that include fractures, crushing injuries, wounds caused by weapons and other devices, dislocations, and an assortment of degenerative problems such as exostoses, osteochondritis dissecans, and spondylolysis (Ortner and Putschar 1981). These types of injury are primarily caused by physical force or by contact with sharp or blunt objects. The cause of traumatic lesions can often be determined by analyzing the intensity and direction of the force. Interpretations concerning trauma are generally more direct than other kinds of pathologies, especially if the age, sex, and health status of the individuals are known. For example, if the traumatic lesion occurs with periosteal reaction and infectious inflammation, a severe condition that originally involved the soft tissue, as well as the bone, is implied. Simple fractures that do not break through the soft tissue and skin rarely becomes infected (Merbs 1989). Also, the degree to which a trauma has healed provides a clue to the relationship between the event and the possible contribution of the trauma to morbidity and mortality.

Fractures in long bones, ribs, and vertebrae are the most frequently reported of the traumatic lesions in the paleopathology literature (Merbs 1989) and the most easily assessed. Fractures can be classified into a number of categories ranging from micro stress fractures to greenstick breaks to comminuted and complete breaks. However, the response of bone to any kind of fracture is the same. There is immediate vascularization and new bone forms within a few days after the break occurs. Calcium salts are released from dead bone fragments and from the living bone and are used in calcifying the callous matrix that forms a binding and connecting sheath around the two fractured ends. Within two weeks, calcification is underway, and the internal remodeling and reorganization of the bone callus begins. The healing process can last for months or years, depending on the age and health of the individual and the severity of the break (Ortner and Putschar 1981). Even a poorly aligned or unaligned bone will eventually mend itself if infection does not interfere with the healing process. The process occurs much more quickly in children than in adults. Union of two bone ends can be complete in four to six weeks in children, while in adults the process can take four or five months (Merbs 1989).

Depression fractures occur most frequently on adult crania and have been reported for many specimens in the archaeological record (Ortner and Putschar 1981). Merbs (1989) defines a depression fracture as one produced by a force applied to just one side of a bone whereas compression fractures are produced when there is force from two sides; however, these distinctions can be difficult to make in archaeological specimens and shallow holes in the cranium are often referred to as depression fractures. Depression fractures usually result from a blow to the head by a blunt object. On the cranium, this results in a depression in the outer bony table, and if the skin is broken, there will be some infectious response as well. The pathophysiological responses are similar in cranial fractures: there is a coagulation of blood at the site with resultant formation of new bone at the fracture site. After the site has completely remodeled and healed, there will usually remain a telltale depression in the cranium at the original site usually remains.

Bones that are in the process of healing need to be cautiously interpreted. The rate of repair and remodeling is modified by age, type of fracture, where the fracture occurs, degree of vascularization, amount of motion between the broken ends, and presence of infection (Merbs 1989). Infection at the site of the bone fracture can seriously hamper repair, and the determination of the timing of the fracture on archaeological specimens is rarely possible without determining the nature of the healing process in conjunction with a wide number of variables having to do with the individual. Careful observation of the entire skeleton of individuals with trauma can aid in the understanding of not only the timing of the event but also related health problems. For example, a healed fractured femoral neck may contribute significantly to osteoporosis and osteoarthritis in adjacent bones (Merbs 1989). Asymmetry in body proportions may occur when unaligned bones heal making compensatory biomechanical changes necessary. These kinds of secondary changes are important to note because they could contribute significantly to our understanding of the quality of life and changes in health that may accompany a traumatic lesion.

The extent to which fractures disable and deform individuals can sometimes be assessed, and this information can be very important in understanding community health dynamics. Adults crippled by unaligned fractures could be less productive in subsistence activities. Furthermore, lifelong accumulated adjustments in the forms of limping and an inefficient gait would also enhance osteoarthritic changes in joints and other health problems. The medical aspects of trauma in precontact groups are largely speculative, although Merbs (1989) has reviewed a number of cases in which "bone setting" was clearly a skill some groups possessed.

Specific types of trauma can provide a direct inference about behavioral patterns. Certain activities predispose individuals to certain types of accidental or intentional trauma. Moreover, various forms of interpersonal violence (warfare, scalping, mutilation, lacerations, cannibalism) and of surgical intervention (trephination, amputation) can sometimes be specifically identified (Merbs 1989; White 1992). Fractures of the forearm (radius and ulna) can reveal information about the activities of the group. A common fracture seen in many archaeological specimens is at the distal end where the wrist is located, and these are generally referred to a Colles fractures. They result when an individual who is falling extends the arms to break or soften the fall. Fractures that occur farther up along the forearm may result from the raising of the arm in front of the face to ward off a blow (these are called parry fractures).

The patterning of the nutritional stress, dietary problems, disease, and trauma within a population can be very enlightening regarding understanding how the built and modified environments that people lived in linked them to or protected them from these. Thinking about what it was like to live as adults in ancient America is aided by understanding the burden of sickness within communities and the prevalence of suboptimal living conditions. The occurrence of multiple injuries, injuries from artifacts and weapons, and the demographic pattern by age and sex can provide insights into the use of force or violence in a society or the potential problems in lifestyle and subsistence activities that lead to accidents.

Vignettes

California coast

Health

As noted earlier, prehistoric peoples of the California coast were hunter-gatherers who focused primarily on exploitation of marine resources. They also ate terrestrial resources, particularly in the Sacramento valley. Exchange was also an important element to their societies (Arnold 1992). To some extent, the exploitation of specific resources was dependent upon the ecology of the region they inhabited. The coast of the mainland provided more carbohydrate-rich plant foods, while the island middens show that those residing there were more dependent upon large fish and sea mammals (Orr 1968). Environmental change can sometimes also be seen in dietary shifts. Some groups, such as those on Santa Rose Island show a shift from higher carbohydrate diets towards a more ocean-based diet.

This is evidenced by a change in the degree of wear visible on the teeth as well as a change in caries rates. High carbohydrate foods (particularly those that require processing prior to eating) are correlated with more dental caries, which are more prominent in earlier periods, and a higher degree of dental wear. These changes did not affect males and females equally. Through time, carious lesions of both sexes declined so that both males and females had approximately the same number. In earlier periods, females are more heavily affected by carious lesions than are males, however (Lambert and Walker 1991: 966). This may be related to the changes in oral chemistry of females during pregnancy (see Chapter 3). For example, about 14% of males and 16% of females had caries in the molars in the later marine group as compared to earlier periods, which showed approximately 24% for males and 30% for females for the same teeth.

FIGURE 5.1 Fishing was an important aspect of life, and would have been accomplished through either fishing from the coast or through the use of watercraft. "Fishing with a gaff-hook-Paviotso." Credit: Charles Deering McCormick Library of Special Collections, Northwestern University Library; *Edward S. Curtis's "The North American Indian,"* 2003. Adapted (color corrected) from the original source: Southern California Shoshoneans. The Diegueños. Plateau Shoshoneans. The Washo [portfolio]; plate no. 538.

Porotic hyperostosis is a typical marker of health and anemia. When all periods are combined, women had greater expression of anemia. For example, in the 18–30 age category, 23% of males showed evidence of anemia, compared with 34% of the females. For the 30–45 age category, it was 28% of males and 37% of females. For older individuals, this trend reverses. For the 45+ age category, 40% of males and 35% of females showed evidence of anemia. In general, anemia is pervasive within the population. However, some women may be more prone to anemia due to additional blood loss associated with menstruation, pregnancy, and childbirth (Hollimon 1991: 464).

To examine change through time with respect to health, Lambert (1993) recorded the presence of periosteal reactions for all adult burials. There are significant changes over time in the number and demography of individuals with periosteal reactions. The number of individuals with periosteal reaction increases throughout

FIGURE 5.2 Seed gathering was a common activity and would have provided valuable carbohydrates for the population. "Gathering Seeds – Coast Pomo" by Edward S. Curtis. Adapted (cropped) from the original source: Library of Congress Prints and Photographs Division (b&w film copy neg., cph 3c16525) http://hdl.loc.gov/loc.pnp/cph.3c16525. Public domain.

the early and middle periods but declines during the late period. Overall males are more affected with periosteal reaction than females. Through time, female periosteal reaction frequencies increase from 40% in the early period to 73% in the late period. For males, this pattern is reversed, with 60% in the early period and 27% in the late period (Hollimon 1991: 465). The reason for this pattern is unclear, but Lambert and Walker (1991) are careful to note that this does not indicate that the overall health of the population becomes healthier with time. Looking at these data in conjunction with dental evidence of childhood stress, the lower frequency of periosteal reactions in men may simply indicate that males may have been engaged in maritime activities removed from densely populated communities and that they may not have been exposed to the same pathogens as the females. The increase in female frequency may indicate a greater exposure to communicable diseases. There is evidence of sexual division of labor within these populations; this social patterning underlies health differences between males and females (Hollimon 1991).

Osteoarthritis is evident in these populations as well. The frequency of arthritis generally increased through time, suggesting subsistence activities relating to intensive marine harvesting and perhaps trading came at a cost to the adults. Although, later-period females showed reduction in arthritis of the vertebral column and knees as compared to earlier periods, this may be a result of a change in women's roles with women more actively involved with gathering terrestrial resources than males in earlier periods (Walker and Hollimon 1989). During the late period, males have more osteoarthritis in the wrist and elbow compared with early period males. The shoulder and hands in early period males are more arthritic than later period males, however. Changes in weaponry and fishing equipment may underlie some of this variation. Harpoons were used during the early period, and the bow and arrow were more common over time (Walker and Hollimon 1989: 180).

In summary, males and females were under different constraints with respect to health. The sexual division of labor allowed for different health to develop among males and females, a pattern that appears to have begun in childhood (see Chapter 4). Females, because of the biological processes associated with menstruation, childbirth, and lactation, were more likely to be nutritionally stressed than males. As Hollimon notes, the consequences relating to differential health status "allow us to examine economic roles of women and men in this prehistoric society, and discuss the risks they faced by virtue of their activities" (1991: 468).

Violence

Violence was a common element of prehistoric California life. Warfare, as well, seems to have played a role in social organization and the formation of chiefdoms over time. Given the important role of violence, understanding its effects on males and females through time is instrumental for a holistic view of human activity. Cranial depression fractures that were fully healed at the time of death suggest that during periods of environmental instability and climate change, violent interactions increased. Beginning with the Late Middle period (around AD 900), the frequency of these fractures increased through time and seems to be linked to population growth and environmental instability (Walker 1989). For example, 19.3% of all adult crania had cranial depression fractures. By sex, 24% of the males and 10% of the females sustained head wounds. Together, 7% of those with cranial fractures had more than one healed fracture. Walker (1989) hypothesized that these may be intentional injuries made in times of fighting, warfare, or other types of interpersonal violence. Many of these injuries are to the face and frontal bone, suggesting face-to-face conflict; additionally the majority occur on the left side of the cranium, suggesting a right-handed attacker (Lambert 1997). Those involved may have included high-status males and females. Cranial injuries are most common in the archaeological sites with low marine activity, suggesting a relationship between increased violence and decreased marine resources. The violence likely not meant to be lethal but, rather, a performance to influence social behavior. Lambert (1997: 89) argues that these nonlethal conflicts serve to diffuse tensions without causing death, which may be preferred over more lethal solutions to social conflict. This is particularly true when important relationships were at stake.

Violence toward women may present a different pattern. Lambert (1997: 89) notes that the location varies more in women than men and that this lack of pattern and lower frequency suggest that males and females were not involved in the same types of violence. She argues instead that these may be the result of violence perpetrated on women by women. Alternatively, she suggests that these may be the result of intimate partner violence, which lacks systematic rules. Regardless of the cause, differences existed in how men and women experienced violent interactions.

Around the same time that interpersonal violence increases, an increase in the presence of projectile injuries and wounds occurs. Weapons were designed to kill, requiring good aim. It is believed that this type of wound is more indicative of warfare. This might also indicate between-group violence (as opposed to the cranial trauma more likely to be related to intragroup social control). Examples of projectile wounds include embedded points found within vertebrae. The group most largely affected by this violence is young adult males between of the ages of 15 and 40 (Lambert 1997: 96). Females of similar age are less than half as likely to be the victim of this type of violence. There is no indication of massacres and individuals with wounds were recovered from community cemeteries that followed the normal burial program. Projectile injuries are similar to those described for known examples of modern tribal warfare (Lambert 1997: 98).

Lethal and nonlethal violence in the California context seem mostly related to the availability of resources. While it is understood that violence is multifaceted in its causes and cannot be strictly linked a single cause (e.g., climate change), for the precolonial California groups, there is a distinct linkage (Walker and Thornton 2002: 514–515). It is likely that violence between groups was related to resource stress. It is also likely that intragroup violence was similarly linked. Intragroup violence may have had a greater role to play, however, in developing hierarchy and negotiating status.

Pueblo Southwest

Health

With thousands of years of continuous living in the Southwest, the Pueblo groups offer insight into survival and adaption through periods of climate change and cultural upheaval. An impressive wealth of data exists for many aspects of Pueblo early history; thousands of archaeological sites have been excavated, and the reconstruction of environment, climate, culture, trade networks, population movement, settlement patterns, housing, subsistence activities, and other facets of life exists in the published literature (Cordell and McBrinn 2012). The Southwest provides an unusually rich database for exploring relationships among availability of resources, resource allocation, alliance formation, risk sharing, population density, settlement, and other variables likely to have a role in health and well-being.

The feature of the Pueblo Southwest that stands out most from other regions in the U.S. is that the people were largely desert farmers (Figure 5.3). Agriculture was adopted in some form or another by the Pueblo I period (around AD 900) and the people continued to utilize maize agriculture as a primary mode of subsistence up to the time of contact with the Spanish colonists in the 1500s (Cordell and McBrinn 2012). The marginal and unpredictable nature of the local environments in the Southwest played an important role in shaping subsistence economies. Nelson and colleagues (2012) present an excellent overview of why this is such an important area to study in terms of what can be learned regarding the lives and lifestyles of farmers in already marginalized areas for agriculture.

In reconstructing health for the adults living in the Southwest, it is clear that many of the health problems facing people worldwide today were endemic and vexing difficulties for those in the past as well. As example, iron deficiency anemia was ubiquitous among adults (and infants and children too as discussed in Chapters 2 and 3). Anemia was a constant throughout the occupation of the Southwest (Walker 1985) and remains a health problem in more contemporary times (Story et al. 2000). Tuberculosis has been demonstrated to exist in a number of Southwestern

FIGURE 5.3 Dry farming in the Arizona desert. "Corn Field, Indian Farm near Tuba City, Arizona, in Rain, 1941." Photo by Ansel Adams, U.S. National Archives and Records Administration, 1941, via Wikimedia Commons.

skeletal series such as San Cristobal (Stodder 2012), and it and other infectious diseases are a recurrent and growing problem today (Asturias et al. 2000: 351). Marden and Ortner (2011) reported on a case of treponematosis (a form of nonvenereal syphilis) for the ancient community living in Chaco Canyon, New Mexico.

Nutritional anemia is found in adults across the Southwest from the earliest periods. For example, at Canyon de Chelly, 88% of the individuals (this includes children and adults) show involvement (Walker 1985). The underlying cause of nutritional anemia is not attributed only to the consumption of iron-poor maize. Walker (1985) argued that iron-deficiency anemia is the end result of a complex interaction between factors such as food intake, metabolism, malnutrition, and infectious disease. Thus, these lesions signal problems with consumption and/or utilization of certain nutrients, but does not provide information directly on the source of the problem. Walker (1985: 153) concludes that "[t]he remarkable prevalence of osseous lesions indicative of anemia among prehistoric Southwest Indians apparently resulted from the interaction of a complex set of biological and cultural variables relating to nutrition and infectious disease. Lack of iron in the diet, prolonged breast feeding, diarrheal and helminth infections, and living conditions conducive to the spread of disease all appear to have contributed to the prevalence of (anemia)."

Health problems for adults seemed to have worsened when compared from the Pueblo I period (AD 900) through to Pueblo III (AD 1350). Stodder (2012) presents a summary of disease in the ancient Southwest and provides a review of patterns of mortality, growth disruption, nutritional problems, and other indicators of morbidity. Tying this into climatic, ecological, nutritional, and political changes occurring at the end of the later period, Stodder's interpretation is one that suggests that community health became increasingly compromised over time.

Akins (1986) and Harrod (2012) present a paleopathological analysis of the Chaco Canyon human remains. Although Chaco Canyon could have supported thousands of individuals, only several hundred burials have been excavated. Both Akins and Harrod were interested in delineating differences in health for high-status (Pueblo Bonito) and low-status (small site) individuals. According to Akins, Chaco Canyon inhabitants suffered from what she terms "subsistence stress" as indicated by growth disruption, high rates of nutritional anemia, and degenerative diseases (1986: 135). Akins further reports that for individuals from high-status burials it is likely that authority-holding elites had greater access to nutritional resources and enjoyed better health (1986: 137–140). Although there is some indication of better health, both groups experienced considerable degenerative diseases throughout adulthood.

In addition to studies on the Chaco Canyon burials, human skeletal remains from the Kayenta region of northeastern Arizona were examined. Wade (1970) analyzed 165 burials showing that for adults, health in general was poor, with a slight trend toward increased stress in the later periods. For Black Mesa, the paleopathology of adults showed similar trends, with cases of infection, anemia, growth disruptions, and degenerative osteoarthritic disease that were persistent throughout the occupation of the mesa (Martin et al. 1991).

In terms of dental disease, the frequency for caries at Grasshopper approaches 20% (Fenton 1998: 109). These data are in line with earlier sites such as Black Mesa (26%), Navajo Reservoir (15%), and Salmon Ruin (20%) (Martin et al. 1991). Dental health, represented by the percentage of individuals in each assemblage with one or more carious teeth, was poor in Southwestern populations. However, the rate of caries actually declines with increasing cohort age in most dental assemblages from the region, because high rates of occlusal wear and attrition and frequent antemortem tooth loss overtake the rate of caries formation. This is exemplified by the contrast between the Dolores sample, which has a preponderance of young adults and a 71% caries prevalence, and the Black Mesa population which has an equal imbalance in the opposite direction – more older individuals and a much lower caries rate (Martin et al. 1991).

Pueblo groups in the northern Four Corners region, living in densely population cliff shelters at Mesa Verde, created an environment highly conducive to the spread of contagious diseases such as respiratory illness and dysentery (Kunitz 1970). Sedentism associated with agriculture also brings populations in close contact with their wastes. Often disposal of excrement in or near the source of potable water increases the potential for contamination. Studies of coprolites from these settlements reveal at least eight species of helminthic parasites (Reinhard 1988). In the ancient Southwest, rabbits and coyotes likely carried tick-borne fevers, Q-fever, rabies, tularemia, Giardia, and sylvatic plague (Schlossberg 2001). Van Blerkom (1997) provides an inclusive list of viruses thought to have been present in the Southwest prior to contact, and these include staphylococcal and streptococcal viruses, some forms of herpes and hepatitis, poliomyelitis, pertussis, and rhinoviruses.

The health of ancestral Pueblo adults thus varied in time and space, as did the nature of their communities and settlement patterns. Based on paleoepidemiological data, the health trends in Southwestern populations may be summarized in the following ways. Ubiquitous nutritional and health challenges led to growth disruptions, anemia, and infectious disease. In the later, larger pueblos endemic diseases including treponematosis and tuberculosis were increasingly common, possibly reaching epidemic proportions in some precontact settlements experiencing significant disruption.

Violence

Injury and trauma on individual skeletal remains has been noted in the literature as well suggesting that along with health problems involving anemia and infections, violence was a fact of life throughout the Pueblo I through III periods (AD 900–1350). There is an abundance of bioarchaeological evidence from large and small sites for low-level warfare combined with other forms of ritualized violence such as dismemberments and massacres that may have been enacted to support a stratified social order. Disarticulated, unburied, cut, and burned human bones are linked to group executions, mutilation of bodies (men, women, and children), and cannibalism (Turner and Turner 1999).

While there are some criticisms of some of the interpretations and differences of opinion about the meaning of all of the violence discussed for the ancient Southwest, there is a great deal of evidence for violence (Dongoske et al. 2000). In general, most scholars agree that increasingly impoverished environmental conditions in the 12th and 13th centuries served as a stimulus for a range of manifestations of violence (Harrod and Martin 2014). There is archaeological evidence for fortified sites, palisades, defensive architecture, aggregation of communities, and structures such as watchtowers (LeBlanc 2000). Warfare (which in the ancestral Pueblo literature is described as raiding, ambush, intercommunity violence, and intra-ethnic or tribal clashes) and fear of attack are provided as the most likely reasons for the defensive architecture used in the periods leading up to the 10th century (LeBlanc 1999: 119).

The osteological record supports large-scale village massacres in places such as Castle Rock (Kuckelman et al. 2002), Cowboy Wash (Billman et al. 2000), and Sacred Ridge (Stodder et al. 2010). However, the assemblages and burials found at these sites are not comprised of simply dead bodies struck down while fighting. There is a remarkable range of variability in the kinds of corpse treatment (by both the perpetrators of the attack and possibly returning survivors), rituals for burial of the dead that are unique to this period, and cases of violent deaths. In addition, there is skeletal evidence documenting victims of violent interactions who escaped death. Healed (nonlethal) traumatic injuries and head wounds are present at many sites as well. Stodder (1989: 187) compiled a frequency chart for a number of Southwestern groups, and she documents relatively high rates of cranial injury. For the Transwestern Pipeline series (ca. AD 1200), Hermann (1993) notes that several adult females had cranial depression fractures as well as a number of lower-body healed fractures. At Carter Ranch (AD 1200) Danforth and colleagues (1994) summarize trauma for the following individuals, although sex was not specified. One-quarter of 24 adults had healed fractures. There are two nasal fractures, one associated with a broken jaw and the other with a broken humerus; two radius fractures; a clavicular fracture; and a femur fracture. The fractures are interpreted to have resulted from blows to the body (Danforth et al. 1994: 96).

A number of prehistoric human skeletal assemblages exhibit signs of dismemberment and disarticulation, perimortem damage, and thermal alteration (Figure 5.4). These assemblages (which include children and adults, males and females) have been variously interpreted to represent acts of cannibalism (Turner and Turner 1999; White 1992), witchcraft killings (Darling 1999), warfare (LeBlanc 1999), ritualized dismemberment (Ogilvie and Hilton 1993), and political massacres used to increase social control (Osterholtz 2013). Allen and colleagues (1985) analyzed ten cases of scalping at Navakwewtaqa (AD 1200–1300) and Grasshopper Ruin (AD 1300). Some of the individuals who had been scalped showed depression fractures as well. For example, at Navakwewtaqa, there were four males ranging in age from 25 to 40 who were scalped, and three females ranging in ages from 25 to 35. One female had a depression fracture on the left frontal, and one had an ovoid shaped hole on the left parietal, suggesting penetration by a weapon and the

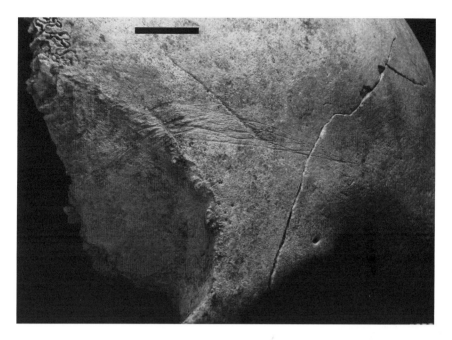

FIGURE 5.4 Cut marks consistent with scalping from the site of Sacred Ridge on the right temple area. Photo by Anna J. Osterholtz.

probable cause of death. At Grasshopper, two males were scalped, and one young female aged 15 exhibited a depression fracture. Most of these individuals were buried with many grave goods such as bowls, beads, awls, and crystals. The authors suggest that this "indicates that it was members of these two communities themselves who were the victims of the practice [scalping]" (Allen et al. 1985: 30).

For Pueblo groups living in northern New Mexico (ca. AD 1200), a detailed study was conducted for a sample of 66 individuals (Martin et al. 2001). In terms of violence-related injuries, young children were free of fractures and trauma. Three young adult males had healed cranial depression fractures (all slight in expression), and three older males had postcranial fractures (a healed broken rib, a healed broken finger, and a healed broken wrist). Six females had healed cranial depression fractures that ranged from moderate to very severe in expression. The ages of the women ranged from 20 to 38 (peak reproductive years). Three of the women had multiple head wounds, and in four women with head wounds, there were also traumatic lesions on the body as well (healed fractured ribs, shoulder, vertebrae, and hip). Compared to the males, the inventory of healed fractures for women is longer and more extensive and involves multiple wounds for several of the women. These women clearly formed a subgroup of victims of violence and may represent captives abducted from neighboring villages (Martin et al. 2010). The evidence for severe and multiple trauma on women suggest strongly that in addition to warfare, other forms of violence were also being practiced.

Although it shows up in different forms and different times in different places, it was a ubiquitous and persistent part of daily life. Massacres, dismemberments, burning, possible cannibalism, scalping, intentional injury, and limited hand-to-hand combat have all been documented, and these cases of violence represent relatively large-scale and integrated systems of political and cultural dynamics involving things such as oppression, coercion, and conflict resolution (Martin et al. 2010). It is possible that to maintain unanimity and harmony across diverse (economically, linguistically, and ideologically) Pueblo communities, violence in culturally specific forms may have been necessary. There have been so many publications about violence in the ancient Southwest that it is not possible to report on every piece of evidence, but much of the variability and kinds of data available are compiled in the edited volume by Nichols and Crown (2008).

The indigenous peoples of the Southwest have always been in a state of growth, adaptation, migration, decline, and movement. The themes of resilience, flexibility, movement, and hardship tempered with respect for the power of nature and climatic events in their everyday lives are strongly entwined in their oral narratives (Echo-Hawk 2000). Hotez (2008) suggests that this region of the U.S. has long been a challenging and difficult place to live even today.

Mississippian/Lower Illinois River Valley

The record of research in the Mississippian and Lower Illinois River Valley is voluminous with hundreds of excavated sites producing thousands of burials that have been studied. It is also an area where there is a rich context for daily life and changes over time with a large amount of artifacts and architectural remains. Much like the Pueblo Southwest, this is a region where archaeologists have been working for a long time, and so there is little hope to do justice to summarizing all that is known about adult health and patterns of violence (Cook 2012).

This region in the periods leading up to the 1300s is important for understanding both the costs of the transition to agriculture from foraging as well as the effects of the increasing reliance on maize agriculture over time. In addition to this, this region was host to some of the larger and more densely populated early towns in the U.S. These larger communities were ruled over by chiefdoms that extracted tribute and created inequality among the local populace particularly at places such as Cahokia outside of St. Louis in Missouri (Pauketat 1994).

Health

North of Cahokia on the Illinois River was the site of Dickson Mounds, which included several burial mounds from which more than 3,000 burials were recovered. Dickson Mounds was part of what is called "the Mississippian tradition," which is a network of agricultural groups that spreads throughout most of the region (Goodman and Armelagos 1985). The dead were buried consistently in burial mounds over time, so researchers have been able to look at the shifting health effects of the transition to agriculture and intensification of maize dependence over time. Infections in the form of periosteal reaction increased dramatically between the earlier groups and the later ones, and this has been attributed to people living in close and cramped quarters sharing transmissible bacterial infections such as staph and strep (Goodman et al. 1984). The frequencies jumped from 26% in the early groups to 84% in the later agriculturalists. Anemia was also a major health problem for primarily children and young adult females (Lallo et al. 1977). The patterning of this suggests it results from a combination of nutritional problems and other things that can compromise the absorption of dietary mineral such as diarrhea.

Osteoarthritis was present in adults aged older than 35 with the age of onset being earlier for the later intensive agriculturalists (Martin et al. 1979). Even though osteoarthritis is a function of age and wear and tear on the joint systems, it is also influenced by cultural and ecological variables. In this case, agriculturalists at Dickson Mounds carried out more strenuous activities causing these degenerative conditions to begin earlier in their adulthood (around the age of 25–30) and to affect more adults (70%) than the earlier foraging/transitional groups where only 40% of the adults had osteoarthritis. Individuals with multiple joint involvements statistically demonstrated a higher percentage of infectious lesions as well (Martin et al. 1979: 61).

Overall, health decreased over time in the Mississippian region. Goodman and Armelagos (1985) showed that adults who were stressed as children lived shorter lives on average. Life expectancy at birth was 26 years in the early groups, and it decreased to 19 in the later Mississippian periods. The causes of poorer health are due to increased population density and sedentism (Goodman et al. 1984). In addition to this, people at Dickson Mound may have been trading food surplus from their bountiful region to the city of Cahokia in exchange for highly prized items such as copper-covered ear spools and marine shell necklaces. As Goodman and Armelagos state, "the trading of needed food for items of symbolic value, to the point where health is threatened, may not seem to make sense," but in fact, people do this all the time (1985: 15). This kind of trading suggests the possibility for inequality as well, where some individuals are positioned to control the flow of goods while others must work hard to produce items for trade.

Tracking status and health in antiquity is often difficult because we must rely on settlement patterns to distinguish central from peripheral groups, and mortuary behavior to distinguish high- from low-status individuals (Figure 5.5). As an example, Powell (1988) presents a detailed analysis of status and health for prehistoric Mississippian cultures at Moundville in Alabama. Moundville was highly stratified, and these divisions within the cultural system were assumed to have had an impact on health for different segments of the population. Although elite males were found to be taller than nonelite males, no stature differences were found for females. Furthermore, there were no statistically significant differences in the rates of infections or nutritional pathologies among the different groups. Based on an analysis of strontium, elite males were suggested to have had a diet richer in meat. Powell contrasts these findings among different status groups with neighboring

FIGURE 5.5 A diorama of a Cahokia elite personage. Adapted from the original photo by Herb Roe – www.chromesun.com (own work).

chiefdoms. At Chucalissa, elite males were found to have more fractures than any other subgroup (Powell, 1988: 194). Powell's detailed analysis of status and health for the prehistoric Mississippian chiefdoms provides a cautionary note that the relationships among variables may be complex and not easily identified.

Violence

In the Southwest, conflict was not very well organized or patterned, although there is plenty of evidence for violence. For cities like Cahokia, there was very organized warfare complete with rules of military engagement that was lorded over other smaller and less organized neighbors in the region. Pauketat summarizes these differences when he states that "[b]efore Cahokia, tensions between kin groups or villages would occasionally boil over into small-scale conflicts of blood feuds, a few people might have lost their scalps and their lives in the occasional skirmish or ambuscade, but organized military action was essentially unknown up to 1050 (at Cahokia)" (2009: 165). This captures well the difference between what is called endemic warfare in the Southwest with the kinds of warfare practiced in the Mississippian region. Cahokia likely had standing armies composed of warriors who used mace-like war clubs and shields to carry out combat against their foes.

A review of 109 Mississippian settlements indicated that they were palisaded from about 1050 onward and prior to that less than 5% had these safety structures (Milner 1999: 123). This period has been discussed in great depth as being a time of raging warfare across the region. The appearance of fortified settlements and chiefdoms (a political structure based on kinship and formed by rigid hierarchies) during this time suggested fierce competition among various groups (Steinen 1992). Powell (1992) details the high prevalence of trauma in the elite males that reflects their role in warfare and their attainment of high status through being victorious in battles.

Milner provides an exhaustive summary of victims of violence for the Mississippian region using the following criteria, "embedded points in bones, distinctive purposeful trauma such as cranial vault fractures from celts, or signs of mutilation including scalping" (1999: 112). He found that for one cemetery from Norris Farms 16% of the 264 individuals buried there were violently killed, all but two were adults, and most were males. Blunt force trauma from heavy weapons or being shot with arrows was the major cause of death. Milner points out that victims were bludgeoned more than it would take to kill them and that bodies were mutilated due to the removal of scalps, limbs, and heads (1999: 114). Milner notes that the individuals who died violently at Norris Farms were also those most afflicted by other pathologies such as osteoarthritis, and so the ability to fight off the attacks or flee was hindered by poor health.

Koziol (2012) uses the treatment of captives and slaves as an example of the ways that trauma can vary significantly among individuals within the same group. Her research focused on Mound 72 at Cahokia, where captives and slaves were likely buried after being forced to participate in a theatrical and ritualized performance involving torture and execution (Figure 5.6). As she states, "the Mound 72 story goes beyond representations of elite hierarchy and enactments of hero-figures" (2012: 237). A large number of females (118) were buried together and biological distance studies have shown that these women were not local to the Cahokia area. Female captives came from outside the communities, likely through warfare and raiding, and lived for a relatively short time at Cahokia before being killed. Females were sacrificed in a performance that would have had many witnesses from Cahokia in attendance.

Chronic warfare in the Mississippian region caused heavy loss of life, up to one-third of all adult deaths (Milner et al. 1991). It also played a role in captive taking and sacrifice of large numbers of adults captured from other groups within the region.

FIGURE 5.6 Artist's re-creation of the sacrifice at Mound 72. Adapted from the color representation by Herb Roe – www.chromesun.com (own work).

Georgia Bight

The Georgia Bight is unique in that this region combines both a transition from hunter-gatherer to agricultural lifeways and a concentration on marine resources. Environmental change, in the form of rising sea levels, is also a factor in the development of social complexity and the decision of where to place settlements. Remains included in the following summary are from both coastal and barrier island assemblages; the locations of these sites presents diversity in terms of subsistence. For examples, the exploitation of marine resources is more likely to occur in the barrier islands groups than on the mainland.

Health

In discussing health in the precontact George Bight, Larsen and colleagues provided chapters in an examination of Catalina de Gaule that focused on demography, oral health, anemia, and infection (Larsen 1990a: 165). With respect to demography, there is a general trend toward increased birth rates with the introduction of agriculture around AD 1150 (Larsen et al. 2002: 414). This increased birth rate is consistent with larger aggregated communities and increased fertility associated with sedentism and agricultural economies.

Dental caries are used as an indicator of carbohydrate consumption. Diet in preagricultural groups (1100 BC – AD 1150) consisted of both marine and terrestrial foods, but most foods were relatively low in carbohydrates. This translates to lower rates of dental caries. Agriculture, particularly maize agriculture is associated with higher rates of dental caries. With the introduction of agriculture, there is a total increase in the percentage of teeth with dental caries from 1.2% (preagricultural) to 9.6% (agricultural). As was seen with the California coast, males and females were unequally affected by caries. Even in the preagricultural groups, women tended to have more caries (1.1% of females had caries while only .3% of males were affected). After agriculture, women also exhibited more (12.8% compared to 8.3% of male teeth). Larsen and colleagues (2002: 421) conclude that females were eating more carbohydrates than males were and relate this dietary difference to sexual division of labor. It is also possible to interpret these data as evidence of increased biological stress related to biological processes only experienced by women, namely, menstruation, pregnancy and childbirth, and lactation (see Chapter 2 in this volume).

The transition to agriculture is also examined through the examination of signs of anemia. Generally, precontact groups experienced low rates of porotic hyperostosis and cribra orbitalia. Walker and Thornton (2002: 423–424) assert that since the rates of cribra orbitalia actually decrease with the introduction of agriculture, this should not be seen as a factor in assessing anemia within these groups. Preagricultural groups do see a general drop in the rates of cribra orbitalia from 5.7% to 3.1% with the introduction of agriculture, but this pattern is skewed by the inclusion of juvenile (less than 10 years of age) data. Juveniles show a decrease from 38.5% to 6.1% with the introduction of agriculture. When just the adults are considered, there is an increase of a rate of 0% to 2.4% for both males and females. This suggests that the overall drop is related to childhood nutrition and may indicate that children were substantially stressed and did not survive long enough to exhibit skeletal changes.

When examining periosteal reactions of the tibia, the transition to agriculture has a tremendous impact. Agriculture and the aggregation of populations expose the population to crowd diseases, possibly contaminated water supplies, and other health challenges. In preagricultural groups, the overall rate of periosteal reactions is 9.5%, increasing to 19.8% in agricultural groups. As with dental health, males and females are differently affected. Males increase from 9.3% to 23.6%, while females increase from 4.3% to 24.1%. In preagricultural groups, therefore, men may have been exposed to different disease vectors than women were, but the similar rates of infection indicate that men and women were both exposed to disease (Larsen et al. 2002: 414).

Powell (Larsen 1990b; Larsen et al. 2002: 425) conducted a detailed examination of remains from the Irene Mound site and found evidence of endemic treponematosis and tuberculosis for the agricultural group inhabiting the site between AD 1150 and 1450. Both these diseases are typically associated with sedentary agricultural groups as they rely on crowds to maintain a pathogenic load (Larsen 1990b). Tuberculosis is endemic in large populations. Individuals are typically exposed during infancy or childhood; if the immune response is insufficient, lesions may develop within the lungs and lymph nodes. These may become calcified within the lungs,

but the pathogen may remain active for years. If an individual is subsequently rein-
fected or subjected to significant stresses later, the capsules may rupture, spreading
the infection throughout the body. Lesions associated with tuberculosis can be
found throughout the skeleton but typically focus on vertebrae and ribs.

Treponemal infections begin through skin lesions during childhood and can last
for years. As with tuberculosis, skeletal lesions are rare. Powell found that 80 out
of 235 individuals (34%) exhibited lesions consistent with treponemal infection.
Ten individuals exhibited lesions consistent with tuberculosis; these individuals
exhibited a lower mean age at death than the rest of the population by approximately
5 years (Powell 1990: 34).

Osteoarthritis was also examined. In general, there is an overall decrease in
the prevalence of degenerative joint disease with the introduction of agriculture. Two significant changes from pre- to postagriculture rates are the lumbar
vertebrae, which show an overall decrease from 41.9% to 24.5%, and the wrist,
which shows a decrease from 5.9% to 1.1%. However, when the individual joints
are examined, there is a single instance of increased with the introduction of
agriculture. In males, there is a slight increase in the frequency of thoracic DJD
from 16.7% to 19.2% (Larsen et al. 2002: 429). This pattern is different from that
visible in other culture areas covered by this text with the change to agriculture.
Examining differences between males and females show differences in behavior
based on the prevalence of DJD. For the lumbar spine, in preagricultural groups,
males are more likely to exhibit degenerative changes (50% of males and 38.5%
of females). This same pattern holds true for the shoulder (17.7% of males and
5.2% of females) and the wrist (15.4% of males and 2.3% of females). In agricultural groups, males are also more affected for all joints examined. For the
shoulder, approximately 10.1% of males exhibited changes while only 2.9% of
females exhibited changes. Through examination of these data, sexual division
of labor can be inferred, even with the change of subsistence base. However, it is
important to note that age was not controlled for in this study, so there is no way
of knowing if one group or the other had more or fewer younger adults, which
would skew the frequencies downward.

As with other areas, the transition to agricultural subsistence had real and profound effects on health. Men and women experienced these changes differently,
likely indicative of gendered patterns of activity and possibly different diets. Of
interest in this area is the identification of diseases such as treponematosis and
tuberculosis with the introduction of agriculture. The exposure to treponematosis
is likely due to tilling fields and picking up pathogens through skin lesions. Tuberculosis requires a significant population to remain active, something that would not
have been possible during preagricultural times when populations were small and
highly mobile. Of interest is the drop in rates of osteoarthritis with agriculture for
this group, a pattern not seen in other culture areas. However, these researchers did
not control for age, and so it is unclear if some of the trends might be more related
to having more or fewer young adults in the samples for each period (Larsen
et al. 2002).

Violence

Violent interaction has been split into an analysis of accidental injuries and intentional trauma. The only instances of accidental injuries were identified in the preagricultural group. Only seven instances were identified, all fractures to the distal radius or the ulna. Intentional trauma was found in both preagricultural and agricultural populations. Trauma to the face and nasal bones increases slightly with the introduction of agriculture, from 0% to .4%. Cranial vault fractures decrease, though, from 2.9% to 1.6%. Larsen and colleagues (2002: 432) also describe weapon wounds to the arm, the hand, and the leg. Frequencies for all of these decreases with the introduction of agriculture. One individual, an adult female from Sea Island Mound dating to the preagricultural period shows signs of partially healed scalping. Yet widespread endemic raiding or warfare during the period between AD 1000 and 1400 do not seem to have been pronounced as they were in other core areas discussed.

To sum up

The challenges faced by doing these kinds of summaries include the tendency to oversimplify the life situations of these ancient Americans instead of appreciating the coexisting realities and complexities present in their everyday lives. At the same time that people experienced celebrations, marriages, and births, there was also danger, uncertainty, and suffering due to climate change, warfare, and resource depletion. Based on their material culture, it is clear that there were systems of knowledge in place regarding agriculture, medicine, astronomy, math, philosophy, metaphysics, and economics, to name but a few. Cultures differ in basic and in subtle ways; their patterns of thinking, logic, perception, construction of social categories, their goals and values, ideals, morals, and general psychology. Learned ideologies provide deep structures that underlie these patterns. Every culture has specific rules about what is appropriate to eat and how to behave. Almost all of these things must be inferred using the bioarchaeological and archaeological findings. Therefore, the data presented in this chapter on adults are only modest and incomplete vignettes offered to better understand what it was like to be an adult in ancient cultures of America.

And in focusing on health, it is important to keep in mind that we are not talking about a Western experience of disease and illness in which physicians can dispense powerful medications such as aspirin, antibiotics, and antidiarrheal tonics. None of the dead can rise and answer our questions about what they were able to utilize in their natural environment for medicines. But from all that they have left behind, their imperishable home artifacts and gear along with bits and pieces of themselves can be used to provide broad brushstrokes about what their lives were like.

This chapter has covered a lot of material, both in terms of geographical and temporal variation but also in terms of cultural dynamics over time. Adulthood is an important time frame to study, and it tends to be the focus of many bioarchaeological analyses. This is likely for several reasons: (1) adult remains tend to be the most highly mineralized and therefore preserve better than the bones of the very young or the very old; (2) they tend to form the majority of those individuals recovered during the course of excavations, particularly if juveniles are buried according to different burial customs; and (3) they are useful in understanding elements of childhood, particularly in the identification of childhood stress, and so they are typically used for the analysis of multiple life stages.

The studies for the core areas represent a very small fraction of the published and unpublished literature that is available on disease and ancient Americans, but we were careful to select those that we felt had the strongest cases for seeing patterns. It is useful to know that common and highly prevalent microorganisms that cause illness do initiate changes in the morphology of bone tissue, such as anemia, *staph* and *strep* infections, respiratory ailments, gastrointestinal problems, and diarrhea.

Patterns of death and disease are not random occurrences. They are intimately linked to every facet of lifestyle from diet and climate to occupation, social structure, and religion (Wells 1964: 87). Although death is the ultimate indicator of maladaptation, its timing and its patterning within populations reveal a variety of challenges in the physical and social environment. By focusing on multiple indicators of stress combined with the ecological and cultural context the adult health profiles presented here reveals important aspects of life in the ancient world.

References

Akins NJ. 1986. A Biocultural Approach to Human Burials from Chaco Canyon, New Mexico, Reports of the Chaco Center, No. 9. Santa Fe, NM: National Park Service.

Allen LH. 1984. Functional Indicators of Nutritional Status of Whole Individuals or the Community. Clinical Nutrition 3:169–175.

Allen WH, Merbs CF, and Birkby WH. 1985. Evidence for Prehistoric Scalping at Nuvak-wewtaqa (Chavez Pass) and Grasshopper Ruin, Arizona. In: Merbs CF, and Miller RJ, editors. Health and Disease in the Prehistoric Southwest. Tempe: Anthropological Research Papers, No. 34, Arizona State University. p 23–42.

Arnold JE. 1992. Complex Hunter-Gatherer-Fishers of Prehistoric California: Chiefs, Specialists, and Maritime Adaptations of the Channel Islands. American Antiquity 57(1):60–84.

Asturias E, Brenneman GR, Petersen K, Hashem M, and Santosham M. 2000. Infectious Disease. In: Rhoades ER, editor. American Indian Health. Baltimore: Johns Hopkins University Press. p 347–369.

Billman BR, Lambert PM, and Leonard BL. 2000. Cannibalism, Warfare, and Drought in the Mesa Verde Region during the Twelfth Century A.D. American Antiquity 65(1):145–178.

Cohen MN, and Armelagos GJ, editors. 1984. Paleopathology at the Origins of Agriculture. New York: Academic Press.

Cook DC. 2012. Paleopathology in the American Mid-Continent. In: Buikstra J, and Henderson C, editors. The Global History of Paleopathology. New York: Oxford University Press. p 259–265.

Cordell LS, and McBrinn ME. 2012. Archaeology of the Southwest, third edition. Walnut Creek, CA: Left Coast Press.

Danforth ME, Cook DC, and Knick, SG, II. 1994. The Human Remains from Carter Ranch Pueblo, Arizona: Health in Isolation. American Antiquity 59(1):88–101.

Darling JA. 1999. Mass Inhumation and the Execution of Witches in the American Southwest. American Anthropologist 100(3):732–752.

Dongoske KE, Martin DL, and Ferguson TJ. 2000. Critique of the Claim of Cannibalism at Cowboy Wash. American Antiquity 65(1):179–190.

Echo-Hawk RC. 2000. Ancient History in the New World: Integrating Oral Traditions and the Archaeological Record in Deep Time. American Antiquity 65(2):267–290.

Fenton TW. 1998. Dental Conditions at Grasshopper Pueblo: Evidence for Dietary Change and Increased Stress. Tucson: The University of Arizona.

Finch CE. 2012. Evolution of the Human Lifespan, Past, Present, and Future: Phases in the Evolution of Human Life Expectancy in Relation to the Inflammatory Load. Proceedings of the American Philosophical Society 156(1):9–44.

Goodman AH, and Armelagos GJ. 1985. Disease and Death at Dr. Dickson's Mounds. Natural History 94(9):12–18.

Goodman AH, Brooke Thomas R, Swedlund AC, and Armelagos GJ. 1988. Biocultural Perspectives on Stress in Prehistoric, Historical, and Contemporary Population Research. American Journal of Physical Anthropology 31(S9):169–202.

Goodman AH, Lallo JW, Armelagos GJ, and Rose JC. 1984. Health Changes at Dickson Mounds, Illinois (950–1300 AD). In: Cohen MN, and Armelagos GJ, editors. Paleopathology at the Origins of Agriculture. New York: Academic Press. p 271–306.

Harrod R, and Martin DL. 2014. Bioarchaeology of Climate Change and Violence: Ethical Considerations. New York: Springer.

Harrod RP. 2012. Centers of Control: Revealing Elites among the Ancestral Pueblo during the "Chaco Phenomenon." International Journal of Paleopathology 2(2–3):123–135.

Hermann NP. 1993. Burial Interpretations. In: Cohen C, Bunds D, and Cella N, editors. Across the Colorado Plateau: Anthropological Studies for the Transwestern Pipeline Expansion Project. Anthropology. Albuquerque, NM: Maxwell Museum of Anthropology. p 77–95.

Hollimon SE. 1991. Health Consequences of Divisions of Labor among the Chumash Indians of Southern California. In: Walde D, and Willows ND, editors. Archaeology of Gender. Calgary, Alberta, Canada: University of Calgary Archaeological Asssociation. p 462–469.

Hotez PJ. 2008. Neglected Infections of Poverty in the United States of America. PLoS Neglected Tropical Diseases 2(6):e256.

Koziol KM. 2012. Performances of Imposed Status: Captivity at Cahokia. In: Martin DL, Harrod RP, and Pérez VR, editors. The Bioarchaeology of Violence. Gainesville: University of Florida Press. p 226–250.

Kuckelman KA, Lightfoot RR, and Martin DL. 2002. The Bioarchaeology and Taphonomy of Violence at Castle Rock and Sand Canyon Pueblos, Southwestern Colorado. American Antiquity 67:486–513.

Kunitz SJ. 1970. Disease and Death among the Anasazi. El Palacio 76:17–22.

Lallo JW, Armelagos GJ, and Mensforth RP. 1977. The Role of Diet, Disease, and Physiology in the Origin of Porotic Hyperostosis. Human Biology 1977:471–483.

Lambert PM. 1993. Health in Prehistoric Populations of the Santa Barbara Channel Islands. American Antiquity 58(3):509–521.

Lambert PM. 1997. Patterns of Violence in Prehistoric Hunter-Gatherer Societies of Coastal Southern California. In: Martin DL, editor. Troubled Times: Violence and Warfare in the Past. Amsterdam: Gordon and Breach. p 77–109.

Lambert PM, and Walker PL. 1991. Physical Anthropological Evidence for the Evolution of Social Complexity in Coastal Southern California. American Antiquity 65:963–973.

Larsen CS, editor. 1990a. The Archaeology of Mission Santa Catalina de Gaule: 2 Biocultural Interpretations of a Population in Transition. New York: The American Museum of Natural History.

Larsen CS. 1990b. Chapter 1. Biological Interpretation and the Context for Contact. In: Larsen CS, editor. The Archaeology of Mission Santa Catalina de Gaule: 2 Biocultural Interpretations of a Population in Transition. New York: The American Museum of Natural History. p 11–25.

Larsen CS, Crosby AW, Griffin MC, Hutchinson DL, Ruff CB, Russel KF, Schoeninger MJ, Sering LE, Simpson SW, Takács JL, et al. 2002. A Biohistory of Health and Behavior in the Georgia Bight: The Agricultural Transition and the Impact of European Contact. In: Steckel RH, and Rose JC, editors. The Backbone of History: Health and Nutrition in the Western Hemisphere. Cambridge: Cambridge University Press. p 406–439.

LeBlanc SA. 1999. Prehistoric Warfare in the American Southwest. Salt Lake City: The University of Utah Press.

LeBlanc SA. 2000. Regional Interaction and Warfare in the Late Prehistoric Southwest. In: Hegmon M, editor. The Archaeology of Regional Interaction: Religion, Warfare, and Exchange Across the American Southwest. Boulder: University Press of Colorado. p 41–70.

Marden K, and Ortner DJ. 2011. A Case of Treponematosis from Pre-Columbian Chaco Canyon, New Mexico. International Journal of Osteoarchaeology 21(1):19–31.

Martin DL, Akins NJ, Goodman AH, and Swedlund AC. 2001. Harmony and Discord: Bioarchaeology of the La Plata Valley. Santa Fe: Museum of New Mexico, Office of Archaeological Studies.

Martin DL, Armelagos GJ, and King J. 1979. Degenerative Joint Disease of the Long Bones fom Dickson Mound. Henry Ford Hospital Medicine Journal 27:60–64.

Martin DL, Goodman AH, Armelagos GJ, and Magennis AL. 1991. Black Mesa Anasazi Health: Reconstructing Life from Patterns of Death and Disease. Carbondale: Southern Illinois University Press.

Martin DL, Harrod RP, and Fields M. 2010. Beaten Down and Worked to the Bone: Bioarchaeological Investigations of Women and Violence in the Ancient Southwest. Landscapes of Violence 1(1):Article 3.

Merbs CF. 1989. Trauma. In: Iscan MY, and Kennedy KAR, editors. Reconstruction of Life from the Skeleton. New York: Alan R. Liss. p 161–199.

Milner GR. 1999. Warfare in the Prehistoric and Early Historic Eastern North America. Journal of Archaeological Research 7:105–151.

Milner GR, Anderson E, and Smith VG. 1991. Warfare in Late Prehistoric West-Central Illinois. American Antiquity 56(4):581–603.

Nelson MC, Hegmon M, Kintigh KW, Kinzig AP, Nelson BA, Anderies JM, Abbott DA, Spielmann KA, Ingram SE, and Peeples MA. 2012. Long-Term Vulnerability and Resilience: Three Examples from Archaeological Study in the Southwestern United States and Northern Mexico. In: Cooper J, and Sheets P, editors. Surviving Sudden Environmental Change: Understanding Hazards, Mitigating Impacts, Avoiding Disasters. Boulder: University Press of Colorado. p 197–220.

Nichols DL, and Crown PL, editors. 2008. Social Violence in the Prehispanic American Southwest. Tucson: University of Arizona Press.

Ogilvie MD, and Hilton CE. 1993. Analysis of Selected Human Skeletal Material from Sites 423–124 and -131. In: Cohen C, and Bunds D, editors. Across the Colorado Plateau: Anthropological Studies for the Transwestern Pipeline Expansion Project. Albuquerque, NM: Maxwell Museum of Anthropology. p 97–128.

Orr PC. 1968. Prehistory of Santa Rosa Island. Santa Barbara, CA: Santa Barbara Museum of Natural History.

Ortner DJ, and Putschar W. 1981. Identification of Pathological Conditions of Human Skeletal Remains. Washington, DC: Smithsonian Institution Press.

Osterholtz AJ. 2013. Hobbling and Torture as Performative Violence: An Example from the Prehistoric Southwest. Kiva 78(2):123–144.

Pauketat TR. 1994. The Ascent of Chiefs – Cahokia and Mississippian Politics in Native North America. Tuscaloosa: University of Alabama Press.

Pauketat TR. 2009. Cahokia: Ancient America's Great City on the Mississippi. New York: Viking-Penguin.

Powell ML. 1988. Status and Health in Prehistory: A Case Study of the Moundville Chiefdom. Washington, DC: Smithsonian Institution Press.

Powell ML. 1990. Chapter 2. On the Eve of the Conquest: Life and Death at Irene Mound, Georgia. In: Larsen CS, editor. The Archaeology Mission Santa Catalina de Guale: 2 Biocultural Interpretations of a Population in Transition. New York: The American Museum of Natural History. p 24–35.

Powell ML. 1992. In the Best of Health? Disease and Trauma Among the Mississippian Elite. Archeological Papers of the American Anthropological Association 3(1):81–97.

Reinhard KJ. 1988. Cultural Ecology of Prehistoric Parasitism on the Colorado Plateau as Evidenced by Coprology. American Journal of Physical Anthropology 77:355–366.

Schlossberg D. 2001. Infections from Leisure-Time Activities. Microbes and Infection 3(6):509–514.

Steinen KT. 1992. Ambushes, Raids, and Palisades: Mississippian Warfare in the Interior Southeast. Southeastern Archaeology 1992:132–139.

Stodder ALW. 1989. Bioarchaeological Research in the Basin and Range Region. In: Simmons AH, Stodder ALW, Dykeman DD, and Hicks PA, editors. Human Adaptations and Cultural Change in the Greater Southwest. Wrightsville: Arkansas Archaeological Survey Research Series, no. 32. p 167–190.

Stodder ALW. 2012. The History of Paleopathology in the American Southwest. In: Buikstra JE, and Roberts CA, editors. The Global History of Paleopathology: Pioneers and Prospects. Oxford: Oxford University Press. p 285–304.

Stodder ALW, Osterholtz AJ, Mowrer K, and Chuipka JP. 2010. Processed Human Remains from the Sacred Ridge Site: Context, Taphonomy, Interpretation. In: Perry EM, Stodder ALW, and Bollong CA, editors. Animas-La Plata Project: XV-Bioarchaeology. Phoenix, AZ: SWCA Environemntal Consultants. p 279–415.

Story M, Strauss K, Gilbert TJ, and Brousard BA. 2000. Nutritional Health and Diet-Related Conditions. In: Rhoades ER, editor. American Indian Health. Baltimore: Johns Hopkins University Press. p 201–220.

Turner CG, II, and Turner JA. 1999. Man Corn: Cannibalism and Violence in the Prehistoric American Southwest. Salt Lake City: University of Utah Press.

Van Blerkom LM. 1997. Zoonoses and the Origins of Old and New World Viral Diseases: A Reappraisal. In: Romanucci-Ross L, Moerman DE, and Tancredi LR, editors. The Anthropology of Medicine. New York: Bergin and Garvey. p 143–168.

Vogel VJ. 2013. American Indian Medicine. Tulsa: University of Oklahoma Press.

Wade WD. 1970. Skeletal Remains of a Prehistoric Population from the Puerco Valley, Eastern Arizona. Boulder: University of Colorado.

Walker PL. 1985. Anemia among Prehistoric Indians of the American Southwest. In: Merbs CF, and Miller RJ, editors. Health and Disease in the Prehistoric Southwest. Tempe: Arizona State University. p 139–164.

Walker PL. 1989. Cranial Injuries as Evidence of Violence in Prehistoric Southern California. American Journal of Physical Anthropology 80(3):313–323.

Walker PL, and Hollimon SE. 1989. Changes in Osteoarthritis Associated with Development of a Maritime Economy among Southern California Indians. International Journal of Anthropology 4(3):171–183.

Walker PL, and Thornton R. 2002. Health, Nutrition, and Demographic Change in Native California. In: Steckel RH, and Rose JC, editors. The Backbone of History: Health and Nutrition in the Western Hemisphere. Cambridge: Cambridge University Press. p 506–523.

Wells C. 1964. Bones, Bodies, and Disease: Evidence of Disease and Abnormality in Early Man. London: Thames and Hudson.

White TD. 1992. Prehistoric Cannibalism at Mancos 5MTUMR-2346. Princeton, NJ: Princeton University Press.

6

GROWING OLD IN ANCIENT AMERICA

Scientific research on human aging has focused on changes in physiological and psychological functioning as part of what is considered the normal process of aging (Goldsmith 2014). As stated previously, life expectancy in nonindustrialized societies was likely in the 40s; since the 1800s it has doubled, and the rapid increases in life span within the last 50 years has been attributed to medical, cultural, and environmental factors (Finch 2012). It is not clear what the average lifespan was for precolonial groups in ancient America, but there is evidence that in some groups, individuals did live into their 60s (Martin et al. 1991). Anthropologists have a particularly focused view of aging that puts it largely within a biocultural framework, and a new review of anthropological approaches to understanding has recently forwarded a number of cross-cultural case studies to show the value of doing so (Rubenstein et al. 2014). Although biological wear and tear may explain some of the changes in functioning, it is becoming increasingly clear that cultural and lifestyle factors play an important role as well.

Simmons (1945) was among the first to look at aging in a cross-cultural manner. He examined 109 cultural traits for elderly in 71 societies using the Human Relations Area Files. His study provided the basis to begin to explore differences in how elderly individuals live, and it was an important study for pointing out the range of variability that exists in such areas as health care and the elderly, the role of the elderly in economic production, the distribution of wealth with regard to the elderly, and the organization of the family and the community as it affects the elderly. Sokolovsky (1983: 8) early on advocated for cross-cultural studies of aging to gain "an understanding of aging divorced from the narrow boundary of a single cultural perspective." Although there are relatively fewer studies documenting aging in traditional societies, there is a growing literature that begins to address the distribution of elderly within communities, the degree of economic participation of the elderly, various living arrangements, and the effect of chronic health problems on family and community functioning (Rubenstein et al. 2014).

Historical and demographic information on the proportion of elderly in traditional Native American communities is difficult to find. Dukepoo (1978) compiled a general account of growing old in a variety of Native American groups, but these amount to little more than a few life histories recorded for some elderly and unfortunately do not provide much insight into what the normal expectation was for living past the 50s in ancient times. For living Pueblo Indians in New Mexico, Rogers and Gallion (1978) report a variety of sociocultural and health problems plaguing those who do not have access to resources and who live in conditions of poverty. Munsell (1972) describes various sociocultural functions of elderly Pima Indians. Those and other reports in the literature on aging in Native American societies speak more to the problems encountered *after* contact and colonization than to the role of elderly in traditional societies. Life expectancy, health problems, and social roles taken up by the elderly are not discussed in explicit terms; therefore,

FIGURE 6.1 An elderly woman mixing clay for ceramic production in the Puebloan world. "The potter mixing clay" circa 1921 by Edward S. Curtis. Originally published in *The North American Indian*, Suppl. v. 12, plate 419. Digital version downloaded via the Library of Congress, www.loc.gov/pictures/item/2002711599/.

there is little in the way of precedents on which to base an analysis of prehistoric elderly Native Americans.

In the detailed ethnographic accounts presented by Eggan (1950) and Dozier (1970) for the Pueblo Indians who were studied by anthropologists more than most groups in the U.S., the elderly are presented as integral parts of the kinship and clan systems (Figure 6.1). For example, Dozier (1970: 137) states that "the oldest woman of this household is the head of the clan." Individuals can occupy preeminent positions within the clan based on seniority. There are also accounts of the elderly performing a variety of ritual ceremonies and passing down to the children information concerning origin myths and religious stories. However, in neither of these accounts of Pueblo culture is there explicit information regarding health and lifestyle of elderly.

In a sense, this lack of ethnographic specificity about this age category may be interpreted as suggesting that to be old in traditional Native American societies simply was on a continuum with the roles and duties of adults in general. The term *situated aging* has been used in anthropology to suggest that aging is a dynamic and socially embedded process that is shaped by specific cultural contexts and not necessarily by developmental or chronological age (Perkinson and Solimeo 2013).

Background and some things to consider

In traditional societies, the label of "elder" is culturally determined, and it does not correspond directly to chronological or biological age. Individuals labeled as elderly may in fact be only 45 years old in some cultures and 85 in others. In small-scale subsistence-based communities, approximately 10% of any given community is composed of elderly individuals (Sokolovsky 1983). Approximately 1% to 4% of "Third World" populations are made up of individuals aged 65 and older. For example, 2.6% of the population in Honduras and 2.7% in Ethiopia are over the age of 65.

For ancient populations, an estimation of the number of elderly is extremely difficult. Techniques for the assignment of age to skeletal remains are problematic for individuals over the age of 50. For most skeletal series, an unbounded category of "50+" is utilized for all older adults (Lovejoy et al. 1985; White et al. 2011). It is likely, however, that individuals much older than 50 existed, but techniques for the accurate assessment of chronological skeletal age do not presently exist. A new study by Buk and colleagues (2012) confirmed, using almost 1,000 pelves from different populations of known age and sex, that accurate age assessments are possible within three major age categories. These include adults younger than 30, adults aged between 30 and 60, and adults who are older than 60. Specificity within those categories decreases in reliability. Boddington and colleagues (1987) also had demonstrated that in older adults, there was an increasingly poor correlation between the traits on the pelvis used to age individuals and their actual chronological age. Bioarchaeologists have referred to this age category and life-history stage as the "invisible elderly," and new methods are being devised to facilitate providing ages for individuals that previously would have simply been placed in the 50+ age category (Cave and Oxenham 2014).

Vignettes

California coast

By all indications, the health of the inhabitants of the Channel Islands as well as the California coast declined leading up to AD 1300 (Walker and Thornton 2002: 519). There is evidence of infectious disease and an increase in the exposure to a range of pathogens in part due to the increase in large and densely settled communities. In the Channel Islands there was an intensification of marine resources, and in the coastal and interior regions there was an intensification of acorn processing as a means to producing food in an increasingly marginalized environment due to climate changes. Walker and Hollimon (1989) demonstrated that everyone had to work harder, but males, in particular, showed increasing amounts of arthritis and wear and tear on their bones. Although there are no studies focused exclusively on the elderly portion of the skeletal collections from these areas and periods, it can be assumed that the changes to the skeletons reported for this region in Chapter 5 had an effect on mortality in the older age categories.

Osteoarthritis rates were calculated for individuals over the age of 40 years and compared with individuals aged between 30 and 40 years and those under 30 years (Walker and Hollimon 1989: 179). The 30 individuals over the age of 40 years had the most osteoarthritic changes at the joint surfaces and these arthritic changes increased over time by comparing individuals from the earliest periods (3500–1170 BC) with the later ones (AD 400–1500), demonstrating the increasing patterns of work that came with settled and larger communities.

Signs of anemia in the older portion of the adults (aged 45+) showed that there were likely nutritional inadequacies that affected their overall health (Walker 1986: 348). For males over the age of 45, there was an overall frequency of 40.8% compared with the frequency for elderly females, which was 35.7%. Studies of elderly today find that about 10% of elderly populations over the age of 65 are anemic, and many of the studies show that a greater percentage of males develop anemia later in life than do age-matched females (Pang and Schrier 2012: 133). Some of the effects of anemia on older adults are that they are more prone to being tired, and there is a progressive decline in work performance, impaired cognition, and a susceptibility to falling (Price et al. 2011: 159).

There was also an increase in violence and warfare during this time. The Channel Islands and the California coast have been intensively analyzed in terms of the environmental instability that was experienced over time by the inhabitants and the general problems that it produced, particularly during AD 1200 (Jones et al. 1999). Evidence of nonlethal violence in the form of cranial depression fractures were found on 11.8% (18 individuals) of individuals aged as old adults (50+ years) from the Channel Islands and the coast of Southern California (Walker 1989: 317).

Because these cranial depression fractures were all similar in size and shape (and similar to those on younger and middle-aged adults discussed in Chapter 5) it has been suggested that they were made during a "culturally regulated pattern of violence, perhaps involving a specialized weapon" (Walker 1989: 319). These may have been the result of interpersonal conflict and competition over scarce resources. That elderly males and females were involved in this suggests that it may have been the leaders of the group who partook in this activity, and it is likely that it involved spectators.

Given some of these trends for increasing osteoarthritis, anemia, and potential for violent interactions, growing old on the California Coast presented the elderly with challenges that may have increased their probability of dying. The skeletal collections from this region are like many others that have failed to produce a significant percentage of individuals over the age of 50, so that researchers simply pool the data and consider everyone over 40 or 45 to be in the elderly category. It is difficult to tease out how the oldest people in that category were doing.

Pueblo Southwest

Because of the long-term excavation strategy on Black Mesa, a series of in-depth studies were undertaken on the portion of the population deemed to be 50 or older in years of age at the time of death. The following is taken largely from Martin and colleagues (1991: 214–220) and from Edwards (2005). For these ancient Americans, 18% of the total skeletal population are in the "50+" age category ($n = 32$). Compared with other skeletal populations from the Southwest, this is relatively high. Approximately 1% of the Dolores ancestral Pueblo skeletal remains (Stodder 1987) and 6.4% of the Grasshopper Pueblo (Berry 1985) remains are over the age of 50. For Chaco Canyon, approximately 2% of the collection is over 50 (Akins 1986), and for Pecos Pueblo, Ruff (1981) estimates that about 13% of the individuals are over 50.

The qualitative aspects of growing old on Black Mesa may forever elude us, but the skeletons of the older Black Mesa individuals provide a dimension to the understanding of aging that is not addressed in the bioarchaeological literature. The 12 males and 20 females are likely between the ages of 50 and 70 based on comparing and seriating individuals within this older age category although the lack of standards make this somewhat speculative. At least half of the 32 individuals could be placed in the 60–70 age category. Based on an assessment of morphological changes in the auricular surface of the pelvis, dental loss, degenerative joint disease and osteoarthritis, and the amount of bone loss (osteoporosis), there is little doubt that some of the Black Mesa elderly we well beyond 50 years of age.

Males who survive into old age are typically fairly robust and muscular individuals who show signs of a vigorous lifestyle. Although males suffered from an assortment of arthritic aches and dental problems, they are, as a group, not as infirm as one might expect. Older males in general showed signs of slight to moderate vertebral degeneration (osteophytes) that may have resulted in complaints about their aching backs. However, bioarchaeological data do not permit directly associating bony changes with pain. There sometimes can be pain in the absence of bony changes, and bony changes also can appear in the face of clinically inactive disease (Jurmain 1999). Although there was some osteoporotic bone thinning, based on densitometry and X-ray analysis, the loss was not clinically significant. Degenerative joint disease was variable across individuals, but at least two elderly males were somewhat crippled and partially immobilized because of severe cases of arthritis (Figure 6.2). There are a few cases of healed fractures in the elderly males. The most consistent trend, however, was in tooth loss. Most of the males exhibited significant dental loss and attrition on the few remaining teeth. Several individuals also suffered from advanced abscesses. Although the nutritional implication of tooth loss is difficult to assess, it can contribute to differential patterns of consumption that may affect dietary adequacy (Russell et al. 2013).

For elderly females, degenerative joint disease was not particularly pronounced, but there were several cases of vertebral osteophytosis with at least two of the females demonstrating what must have been debilitating cases of osteoporotic bone loss, along with bones that were very thin and fragile. Several females showed signs of bone thinning that approach clinical significance in terms of increased potential

FIGURE 6.2 Severe osteoarthritic lipping on the neck vertebrae. Photo by Debra L. Martin, no prior publication.

for fractures (based on the densitometry and X-ray analysis of long bones). Bone loss is not caused by any single disorder, but rather, it is the end result of a long, causal chain of events that includes diet, hormonal status, lifestyle, and general health.

Females, like males, also suffered from dental loss and in some cases, were completely edentulous (Figure 6.3). The dentition of both males and females showed heavy wear (Figure 6.4). New findings showing that females even today seem to lose their teeth at a significantly higher rate than males suggest that there might be both biological and cultural factors that underlie this disparity (Russell et al. 2013). Elderly females outnumber males in this relatively representative skeletal population (20 females to 12 males). If the normative role of women as reproducers is called into question (i.e., if not every woman spends her life in childbearing activities), then those women living to older ages may not have all directly engaged in reproduction (Martin and Horowitz 1984).

Reducing these observations to stereotypic notions of the frail elderly (women live longer but are fragile; males die younger, and those that survive are still strong) may seem inviting, but caution must be exercised in the interpretation of the data for the Black Mesa elderly. The observations on sexual dimorphism in adult males and females (discussed in Chapter 5) suggest that both males and females were robust and worked equally hard at tasks that require muscular strength. Second,

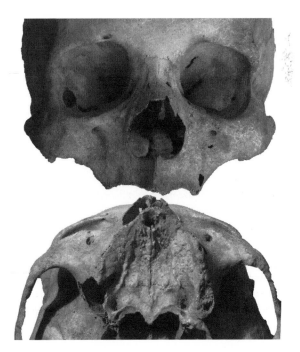

FIGURE 6.3 An elderly edentulous individual from Black Mesa, anterior view (top), palatal view (bottom). Photo by the authors, no prior publication.

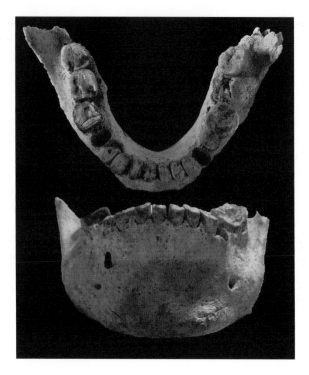

FIGURE 6.4 An example of heavy tooth wear, occlusal view (top), anterior view (bottom). Photo by Anna J. Osterholtz.

more reproductive-aged women died during those years than did age-matched males because of the increased risk to health and life during pregnancy and birthing. The reproductive history of women reaching old age cannot be deduced at this time, but it is possible that some of them were childless. Within the group of elderly females, there is extreme variability – with some very robust individuals and some potentially immobile, infirm individuals.

More interesting than the male–female differences perhaps are the possibilities that elderly individuals required some kinds of social support. That 18% of the population made it to the age of 50 and older suggests that a support system was in place that could help buffer those individuals who might have moved more slowly with their arthritic backs and thinning bones. Although some anthropologists have documented the "darker side of aging," that is, when communities practice nonsupport or institute death-hastening activities (Maxwell et al. 1984), neither the ethnographic literature on Pueblo culture nor the skeletal evidence suggests that elderly were not fully integrated into Pueblo society during the AD 900–1100 period.

To be old on Black Mesa was not notably different from being old in other parts of ancient America. The problems of bodily wear and tear most certainly affected the quality of life to a degree experienced by the many individuals approaching

70 years of age. The complete loss of teeth in the absence of modern dentistry may have significantly reduced the range of edible foods, but the problem could be overcome by altering the cooking strategies and the size of the foodstuff.

Mississippian/Lower Illinois River Valley

At Dickson Mounds, intense agricultural activities combined with fairly densely settled communities put the population at risk for infections, anemia, and trauma as discussed previously. While there were large skeletal populations analyzed, the research consistently lumped all of the adults together in one age category that included all 15- to 65-year-olds. Therefore, it is difficult to tease out the experience of the elderly in these settings (Goodman et al. 1984). Osteoarthritis rates for females jumped from 41% in the foraging groups to 67% in the agricultural groups and for males it went from 38% to 76% (Goodman et al. 1984: 295). While these data do not tell us how bad osteoarthritis might have been for the oldest adults, it does suggest that for all adults osteoarthritis rates increase significantly with agricultural lifestyles. It would be worthwhile to go back and reexamine the data, teasing out the older adults from the younger adults to see how each group within adulthood was affected by the intensification of an agricultural way of life.

Georgia Bight

For a sample of 142 individuals from one of the islands in the George Bight dating from about AD 1150 to 1450, only 4 individuals were aged 45+ years, and so no meaningful study of those individuals is likely to capture what aging was like (Larsen et al. 1990). A larger sample of 23 individuals over the age of 45 represented the earlier preagricultural foraging period and from those it was shown through analysis of the demographic features of the populations that the most robust (and presumably healthy) were the foragers, with more possibilities for early death in the agricultural periods leading up to contact. Data on bone structure for the three temporally spaced groups showed that the nutritional level and general activity level declined when comparing the foragers to the agricultural groups. Long-distance travel in particular decreased for males who likely took on more of the agricultural tasks (Ruff and Larsen 1990: 119).

To sum up

As the reader can surmise, not much is known about the elderly in early indigenous populations. Cave and Oxenham (2014) go so far as to say that the challenges of not having proper methods to reliably assess ages over 50 have contributed to the notion that very few people lived into old age and that they represent a largely invisible cohort. The Black Mesa data suggest that, in fact, some Native American ancestral groups did have individuals who lived into their 60s and possibly even their 70s. This is extraordinary to contemplate because it is difficult to imagine life without antibiotics and vaccinations. It is even more difficult to imagine a non–Western approach to aging and health because even in ethnographic works the elderly are understudied.

That there were completely edentulous, arthritis-ridden elderly living in the small hamlets on Black Mesa in AD 1000 is useful to know. It widens how life in ancient America can be imagined as it played out across the life span and suggests that there must have been significant understandings of local plants with pharmacological properties, and of a system of self-care and community support that helped individuals over the hurdles of the kinds of accidents and communicable disease that were likely ever present.

References

Akins NJ. 1986. A Biocultural Approach to Human Burials from Chaco Canyon, New Mexico, Reports of the Chaco Center, No. 9. Santa Fe, NM: National Park Service.

Berry DR. 1985. Dental Pathology of Grasshopper Pueblo, Arizona. In: Merbs CF, and Miller RJ, editors. Health and Disease in the Prehistoric Southwest. Tempe: Anthropological Research Papers, No. 34, Arizona State University. p 253–274.

Boddington A, Garland AN, and Janaway RC, editors. 1987. Death, Decay, and Reconstruction: Approaches to Archaeology and Forensic Science. Manchester: Manchester University Press.

Buk Z, Kordic P, Bruzek J, Schmitt A, and Snorek M. 2012. The Age at Death Assessment in a Multi-Ethnic Sample of Pelvic Bones Using Nature-Inspired Data Mining Methods. Forensic Science International 220(1):294.e1–294.e9.

Cave C, and Oxenham M. 2014. Identification of the Archaeological 'Invisible Elderly': An Approach Illustrated with an Anglo-Saxon Example. International Journal of Osteoarchaeology. DOI: 10.1002/oa.2408.

Dozier EP. 1970. The Pueblo Indians of North America. New York: Holt, Rinehart and Winston.

Dukepoo F. 1978. The Elder American Indian. San Diego, CA: Companile Press.

Edwards JL. 2005. Growing Old on Black Mesa: A Biocultural Assessment of Bone Mineral Density Patterns. Amherst: University of Massachusetts.

Eggan F. 1950. Social Organization of the Western Pueblos. Chicago: University of Chicago Press.

Finch CE. 2012. Evolution of the Human Lifespan, Past, Present, and Future: Phases in the Evolution of Human Life Expectancy in Relation to the Inflammatory Load. Proceedings of the American Philosophical Society 156(1):9–44.

Goldsmith T. 2014. Introduction to Biological Aging Theory. Crownsville, MD: Azinet Press.

Goodman AH, Lallo JW, Armelagos GJ, and Rose JC. 1984. Health Changes at Dickson Mounds, Illinois (950–1300 AD). In Cohen MN, and Armelagos GJ, editors. Paleopathology at the Origins of Agriculture. New York: Academic Press. p 271–306.

Jones TL, Brown GM, Raab LM, McVickar J, Spaulding WG, Kennett DJ, York A, and Walker PL. 1999. Environmental Imperatives Reconsidered: Demographic Crises in Western North America during the Medieval Climatic Anomaly. Current Anthropology 40(2):137–170.

Jurmain R. 1999. Stories from the Skeleton: Behavioral Reconstruction in Osteoarchaeology. Amsterdam: Gordon and Breach.

Larsen CS, Choi I, Fresia AE, Hutchinson DL, Lee-Thorp JA, Moore KM, and Powell ML. 1990. The Archaeology of Mission Santa Catalina de Guale. 2, Biocultural Interpretations of a Population in Transition. Anthropological Papers of the American Museum of Natural History 68.

Lovejoy CO, Meindl RS, Mensforth RP, and Barton TJ. 1985. Multifactorial Determination of Skeletal Age at Death: A Method and Blind Tests of its Accuracy. American Journal of Physical Anthropology 68:1–14.

Martin DL, Goodman AH, Armelagos GJ, and Magennis AL. 1991. Black Mesa Anasazi Health: Reconstructing Life from Patterns of Death and Disease. Carbondale: Southern Illinois University Press.

Martin DL, and Horowitz S. 1984. An Anthropological Framework for Examining Reproduction and Sexuality. Women's Studies Quarterly 12(4):19–22.

Maxwell R, Silverman P, and Maxwell E. 1984. The Motive for Geronticide. In: Sokolovsky J, editor. Aging and the Aged in the Third World: Part 1. Williamsburg, VA: William and Mary College. p 67–84.

Munsell M. 1972. Functions of the Aged among Salt River Pima. In: Cowgill R, and Holmes D, editors. Aging and Modernization. New York: Appleton-Century-Crofts. p 127–132.

Pang WW, and Schrier SL. 2012. Anemia in the Elderly. Current Opinion in Hematology 19(3):133–140.

Perkinson MA, and Solimeo S. 2013. Aging in Cultural Context and as Narrative Process: Conceptual Foundations of the Anthropology of Aging as Reflected in the Works of Margaret Clark and Sharon Kaufman. The Gerentologist 54(1):101–107.

Price EA, Mehra R, Holmes TH, and Schrier SL. 2011. Anemia in Older Persons: Etiology and Evaluation. Blood Cells, Molecules, and Diseases 46(2):159–165.

Rogers C, and Gallion T. 1978. Characteristics of Elderly Pueblo Indians in New Mexico. Gerentologist 18:482–487.

Rubenstein RL, Girling L, de Medieros K, Brazda M, and Hannum S. 2015. Extending the Framework of Generativity Theory through Research: A Qualitative Study. The Gerentologist 55(4):548–559.

Ruff CB. 1981. Structural Changes in the Lower Limb Bones with Aging at Pecos Pueblo [PhD dissertation]. Philadelphia: University of Pennsylvania.

Ruff CB, and Larsen CS. 1990. Postcranial Biomechanical Adaptations to Subsistence Strategy Changes on the Georgia Coast. Anthropological Papers of the American Museum of Natural History 68(1990):94–120.

Russell SL, Gordon S, Lukacs JR, and Kaste LM. 2013. Sex/Gender Differences in Tooth Loss and Edentulism: Historical Perspectives, Biological Factors, and Sociologic Reasons. Dental Clinics of North America 57(2):317–337.

Simmons LW. 1945. The Role of the Aged in Primitive Society. New Haven, CT: Yale University Press.

Sokolovsky J. 1983. Growing Old in Different Societies: Cross-Cultural Perspectives. Belmont, CA: Wadsworth.

Stodder ALW. 1987. The Physical Anthropology and Mortuary Practice of the Dolores Anasazi: An Early Pueblo Population in Local and Regional Context. In: Petersen KL, and Orcutt JD, editors. Dolores Archaeological Program: Supporting Studies: Settlement and Environment. Denver, CO: Bureau of Reclamation, Engineering and Research Center. p 336–504.

Walker PL. 1986. Porotic Hyperostosis in a Marine-Dependent California Indian Population. American Journal of Physical Anthropology 69(3):345–354.

Walker PL. 1989. Cranial Injuries as Evidence of Violence in Prehistoric Southern California. American Journal of Physical Anthropology 80(3):313–323.

Walker PL, and Hollimon SE. 1989. Changes in Osteoarthritis Associated with Development of a Maritime Economy Among Southern California Indians. International Journal of Anthropology 4(3):171–183.

Walker PL, and Thornton R. 2002. Health, Nutrition, and Demographic Change in Native California. In: Steckel RH, and Rose JC, editors. The Backbone of History: Health and Nutrition in the Western Hemisphere. Cambridge: Cambridge University Press. p 506–523.

White TD, Black MT, and Folkens PA. 2011. Human Osteology. San Diego, CA: Academic Press.

7

LIFE HISTORIES AND THE ARC OF TIME

One may ask why it is important for anthropologists to document patterns of health and disease for ancient Americans, especially when understanding health today is a more immediate and compelling concern. Why not concentrate efforts on people living today because the need is so great? One reason has already been alluded to: often the ultimate cause of poor health and early death is not proximally located; rather, it is an "upstream" manifestation of a situation displaced temporally and/or spatially (McKinlay and McKinlay 1974). The methods used here help to extract information about the past that encompasses environmental, cultural, and biological factors. Not only can disease and poor health be located in time and space, but the interrelatedness of ecological, behavioral, and biological variables can also be examined.

On one level, so-called diseases of civilization, such as cancer, tuberculosis, arthritis, and osteoporosis, have been shown to exist in groups that predate "civilization" by hundreds of years, thus suggesting that factors other than those relating to industrialization can put people at risk. On another level, anthropologists have been able to document the remarkable and deadly persistence of undernutrition, common infections, anemia, and other preventable diseases over thousands of years in some geographic locations.

Finally, it has only been through the archaeological record that anthropologists and historians have come to understand how changes over time in environment, political and economic structure, subsistence and diet, and settlement patterns can and do have profound effects on population structure and rates of morbidity and mortality. Although archaeological reconstruction can infer many aspects of subsistence and diet, it is largely circumstantial evidence and only indirectly is suggestive of health status. Issues of disease and nutritional adequacy and the impact of diet on population health and longevity cannot be fully realized without the human biological evidence.

The past does not need us, but the future does

The documentation of disease patterns in the past must be ultimately channeled back into the discussion of human behavior and culture change. For example, the patterns of variability in health and disease by age group, sex, and period for the people living in the Georgia Bight region have revealed something about the capacity of humans living through and adapting to major changes in their lifestyles, subsistence activities, diet, and environments. It was shown that humans sometimes suffer through these changes, and other times they modify, adapt, and expand their cultural and behavioral repertoire of responses.

Skeletal analysis as anthropological inquiry takes advantage of health data to assess short- and long-term consequences of adaptation. We can never know all the factors that played into the success of these past populations in adapting to all of the changes they have lived through over a 500-year span. While focusing on some important and major contributing factors in the preceding chapters, information concerning the people who were the ancestors of today's Native Americans comes more into focus.

There are ways to think about the past that have relevance today. For example, Madsen has investigated the possible use by ancient inhabitants of the Pueblo Southwest of grasshoppers and crickets in their ancient diet. He suggests that insects as a food resource made a "great deal of economic sense" (1989: 25). In one test case, 1,452 Mormon crickets were collected in one hour from bushes, grass, and the ground surface in Dinosaur National Monument along the Colorado–Utah border. Madsen estimates this amount to equal more than two pounds of edible, high-quality protein collected in one hour. This could be translated to four quarter-pounders in one hour of work.

In summarizing the experiences based on human remains, we have made considerable effort not to overinterpret the data. There has been a concerted effort to challenge some traditional stereotypes about human behavior by presenting alternative hypotheses whenever possible. Bioarchaeology is reaching a critical mass now where practitioners are benefiting from building on certain kinds of studies so that data can be linked across time and space as appropriate. In this way it can grow, diversify, and expand into ever-new areas of inquiry.

Bioarchaeology has a unique role to play here in that we can talk about the lives of all people within a community. We are interested in how people interacted and in how those cultural interactions shaped biology for the better (e.g., cultural buffering against disease or malnutrition) or for the worse (e.g., structural violence or pregnancy food taboos). Without the rigorous analysis of the actual human bones and teeth, such information may be lost, and our understanding of the past would be incomplete.

The common denominator across these kinds of studies will be a fierce commitment to systematic and robust empirical data collection that crosses different domains of biology and culture (which includes environment), and uses that data to test hypotheses. Hypotheses that are constructed using theorized ideas about human behavior in particular situations will facilitate providing meaning to the interpretations. That is the raison d'être of all of anthropological work – to explain human behavior so that there can be more mutual and beneficial outcomes for people living today. It really should be the goal of every bioarchaeologist to make the world a better place for people today and for people in the future (Martin et al. 2013).

One way to think about how to link the past to the present is this way. A cultural historian, Rebecca Solnit, ruminated in a thoughtful essay about the long arc of human history and how seeing important shifts in human behavior or social processes can sometimes take many generations or even longer. It was a call for taking the long view in understanding the ebb and flow of human behavior, population growth and decline, catastrophies, and social change. It was also a call for working to ameliorate endemic social problems facing people today such as poverty, inequality, poor health and diet, rampant preventable diseases, climatic catastrophes, and social violence. Urgency in attending to these historically contingent, locally placed, and globally relevant problems was conveyed in this way: "the past doesn't need us. The past guides us; the future needs us" (Solnit 2013).

This is a good way to envision research outcomes in bioarchaeology in a broader context. While bioarchaeology focuses on reconstructing the past, equally important is to make the past a guide for preparing for and dealing with the future. The bioarchaeological approach to understanding the past can document long chronologies of human activities, such as suffering and loss of life, with lines of evidence coming from traces of human bodies; the places humans lived, thrived, and died; and the durable things they created. Indeed, bioarchaeological data comes from all over the world, represents hundreds of different periods and cultures, and provides information on not only human deaths but also on the lived experience within their cultural and physical environments. In this light, the collective bioarchaeological studies discussed in this volume are guides for how to think about the future.

Bioarchaeology is at its best when it provides scientifically sound interpretations of the past that illuminate crucial moments in human history. There is no lack of interest in the past as demonstrated by the number of television programs dedicated to the ancient world. Turning an interesting and exotic finding about the past into something compelling in the modern world is an area where the bioarchaeological approach is most useful. If bioarchaeology and the study of human remains cannot be demonstrated to have relevance to today and by extension, into the future, it will be increasing difficult to "sell" to the public, to students, and to granting agencies.

There is much that can be learned from the past that is relevant to the present and to the future, particularly when the findings shed light on aspects of modern life that are not well understood or events coming down the road for which it is not clear how humans will fare. Bioarchaeology focuses on human adaptation in diverse biosocial environments during times of extreme challenges. Most would agree that the future needs explication, but we can only estimate human behaviors based on past responses. The past is there to be a guide in the same way that hindsight does. Bioarchaeology is poised to play a larger role in using the past as a guide because it integrates biological and cultural aspects of human life, and this is a unique scientific contribution; no other discipline has this multifaceted approach reconstructing the past as humans lived it.

There are many motivations underlying the desire to know more about humans in the distant past. Using scientific methods and hypothesis testing to reveal behavioral patterns (or lack of patterning) across different groups can yield unique insights into the human condition. These insights range from documenting the origins and evolution of human diseases to providing knowledge about ancestral diets and patterns of violence. Taken together, bioarchaeological studies shine a light on a part of human evolutionary and social history that is generally not well understood.

Anemia, osteoarthritis, communicable infectious diseases, and others common ailments are as much a problem for people today as they were in the past. The bioarchaeological data from ancient skeletons anchor this problem within a much larger time span and provide cross-cultural perspectives. Having the complete skeleton, as bioarchaeologists do, to test for toxic levels would only be possible on cadavers by modern-day researchers, which are difficult to come by. Bioarchaeologists have whole assemblages that represent all ages and both sexes. The interconnected ways that bioarchaeological investigations provide additional insight for the ongoing debates about lead ingestion by children are important. They bring to the fore the ways that biology and culture interact, as well as examine what underlies human foibles in disease prevention. This type of research also provides longitudinal evidence for how lead exposure can affect populations (e.g., Nriagu 1983). The past in this example is crucial as a guide for viewing lead poisoning within a broader perspective.

If modern bioarchaeology is to mature with the times and to accommodate increasing numbers of interested undergraduate and graduate students, it will necessarily need to build on ways to further integrate diverse data sets in the service of engaging in questions of significance to a broad audience. There is ample evidence that this is the trajectory bioarchaeology is on. What could grease the wheels for an integrated and engaged bioarchaeology is the opportune use of social theory.

The various indicators of stress seen across the life history of the earliest Americans certainly have overlapping etiologies, but the pattern of these changes confirm that disease was ubiquitous, affected infants and children to a degree not seen in adults, and was more likely related to morbidity than to mortality. There are lessons to be learned from these enterprising and resilient groups of early Americans. Behavioral flexibility has been hailed as the hallmark of human evolution, the outstanding feature that marks the path of human existence for the last several million years. However, the historical fact of colonization and subjugation has typically left indigenous people with few behavioral or cultural options. Modern progress and development, as it has been played out in traditional societies worldwide, are based on the routinization, standardization, and homogenization of human potential and human behaviors. This is not what we see in their ancestors and in the ancient populations.

Without the skeletal remains, we could not have discovered the adaptations for flexibility and responsiveness to change that define ancient people's existence. From death, patterns of life have emerged that speak to some very basic concerns that plague human groups today. The ancestral indigenous people may be no longer living, but their culture history and adaptations will live on as we come to better understand their remarkable duration and vitality in diverse regions across the U.S.

Uniquely American history lessons from ancient health

In the 1940s through the 1960s, as Native Americans were beginning the long fight for improvement of life on the reservations and for social justice, bioarchaeologists were studying skeletal material, but their questions were not about the facts of racism, poverty, disease, and early death that the descendants of the people they were studying were subject to (Martin 1998). Reports from the medical journals demonstrated that American Indian infant mortality and adult morbidity were alarmingly high and disproportionate to the rates for the general U.S. population.

This information, widely available, was not looked at historically to understand the impact and effects of economic and racial oppression related to the placement on reservations. This was a missed opportunity for bioarchaeologists to have used their anthropological training to broaden the context and discussion of native health and biology to a broader audience.

By sidestepping issues of importance to native people today, scientific data generated by physical anthropologists have not proved useful to Native Americans, and in fact, the data have been used in ways that aid in the continued tyranny of native people today. For example, Deloria (1997: 6) argues that elite white scientists plied their trade at the expense of Indians. In one example, he writes, "[In the 1930s] the idea that human cranial capacity demonstrated the intelligence of the different races [was] a piously proclaimed scientific truth. Indians were hardly on their reservations before government employees began robbing graves at night to sever skulls from freshly buried bodies for eastern scientists to measure." These kinds of activities, where skulls are used for the "progress of anthropological study" are the ones that Native Americans most associate with archaeology and bioarchaeologists.

During the 1980s a handful of studies conducted on southwestern human remains were more focused on a wide variety of biological indicators of pathology. Some did break out of the confines of descriptive morphology to conduct biocultural analyses that looked at adaptation, demography, and subgroups at risk, but it was the case of too little, too late. Discussions with Native Americans strongly suggested that what they most associate with bioarchaeology today is what they might call grave robbing. Even as NAGPRA became a reality in 1990, the discourse of bioarchaeologists continued to emphasize their own goals and interests over that of native peoples.

For those of us who remain committed to bioarchaeology, there is hope. As one example, investigations into the endemic health problems today of the groups such as the Tohono O'odham have shown high rates of diabetes, hypertension, and obesity. A coordinated, multidisciplinary effort brought together a team composed of Native American, anthropological, bioarchaeological, and medical personnel. Research on past diet and health suggested strongly that changes in diet were a factor in the increase in diseases. Armed with this scientific information, groups have voluntarily and enthusiastically begun incorporating traditional foods into their diets with positive health results (Fazzino 2008).

Concerning health effects of environmental pollutants, Native Americans have borne the brunt of doses of radiation due to their proximity to major areas of nuclear testing such as the Nevada Test Site and Los Alamos (Stoffle et al. 2001). Levels of lead in U.S. Department of Housing & Urban Development housing may be causing high levels of lead in native children (Bashir 2002; Malcoe et al. 2002). Traditional subsistence activities have exposed native people to toxic waste in rivers and oceans. Armed with hard data from bone and teeth that demonstrate "before" and "after" levels of these toxic mineral and trace elements, the data will be useful to activists working for better monitoring. Native American groups have also been exposed to uranium tailings, leading to generations of decreased health (Pasternak 2010). This linking of political processes and biological effects demands a broadly historical perspective and a multidimensional approach (Brulle and Pellow 2006).

Bioarchaeology can be used to attend to problems in the world today. Bioarchaeology is poised to enter a new era of research that is nonreductionist and focused on problem solving. We predict that bioarchaeological research will open new opportunities for collaborative research with archaeologists and Native Americans, and it will integrate biology in important ways into analyses of rapid cultural changes, climate change, increasing violence, and shifting political realities, areas of interest to a wide range of people.

To sum up

Human remains represent ancient populations in time and space, but there are numerous imprecisions with the kind of scientific work that bioarchaeologists do. Errors are introduced at many different places from how people are buried to how they are excavated hundreds of years later. Yet providing contextual information facilitates looking at moments in time and space where humans were living and dying, and it is here that bioarchaeology provides nuanced snapshots of the living. A delicate balance must be struck in the fact that we are segmenting reality into parts and parcels of time and space, but we do not want to deflect attention away from the big picture. That is what we hope we provided, a bit of a look at the big picture anchored as it were in scientific data gleaned from the human remains. The idea of critical inquiry and research is what science is about, not in memorizing isolated pieces of data. We hope that students and those who are not familiar with bioarchaeology will continue to frame questions and seek answers that open a world of possibilities for how to understand the past and be able to make connections between people in the past and people today. Anthropology is critically positioned to rethink how we approach the study of all humans to better understand behavioral flexibility and cultural resilience in the face of enormous changes such as droughts, warfare, population collapse, and infant deaths, to name a few. Ultimately we hope that students will follow the evidence wherever it leads them and that they will question everything.

References

Bashir SA. 2002. Home Is Where the Harm Is: Inadequate Housing as a Public Health Crisis. American Journal of Public Health 92(5):733–738.

Brulle RJ, and Pellow DN. 2006. Environmental Justice: Human Health and Environmental Inequalities. Annual Review of Public Health 27(2006):103–124.

Deloria V, Jr. 1997. Red Earth, White Lies: Native Americans and the Myth of Scientific Fact. Golden, CO: Fulcrum Publishing.

Fazzino D. 2008. Continuity and Change in Tohono O'odham Food Systems: Implications for Dietary Interventions. Culture & Agriculture 30(1–2):38–46.

Madsen DB. 1989. Exploring the Fremont. Salt Lake City: Utah Museum of Natural History.

Malcoe LH, Lynch RA, Keger MC, and Skaggs VJ. 2002. Lead Sources, Behaviors, and Socioeconomic Factors in Relation to Blood Lead of Native American and White Children: A Community-Based Assessment of a Former Mining Area. Environmental Health Perspectives 110(Suppl. 2):221.

Martin D. 1998. Owning the Sins of the Past: Historical Trends in the Study of Southwestern Human Remains. In: Goodman AH, and Leatherman TL, editors. Building a New Biocultural Synthesis: Political-Economic Perspectives in Biological Anthropology. Ann Arbor: University of Michigan Press. p 171–190.

Martin DL, Harrod RP, and Pérez VR. 2013. Bioarchaeology: An Integrated Approach to Working with Human Remains. New York: Springer.

McKinlay JB, and McKinlay D. 1974. A Case for Refocusing Upstream: The Political Economy of Illness. In: American Heart Association, editor. Applying Behavioral Science to Cardiovascular Risk. Washington, DC: American Heart Association. p 7–17.

Nriagu JO. 1983. Saturnine Gout Among Roman Aristocrats: Did Lead Poisoning Contribute to the Fall of the Empire? New England Journal of Medicine 38(11):660–663.

Pasternak J. 2010. Yellow Dirt: An American Story of a Poisoned Land and a People Betrayed. New York: Simon and Schuster.

Solnit R. 2013. Acts of Hope: Challenging Empire on the World Stage. TomDispatch. www.tomdispatch.com/post/677/.

Stoffle R, Zedeño MN, and Halmo DB. 2001. American Indians and the Nevada Test Site: A Model of Research and Consultation. Available electronically at www.doe.gov.bridge.

INDEX

Note: Page numbers with *f* indicate figures; those with *t* indicate tables.